CHURCH: WHAT WAS GOD THINKING?

Bruce Isom

The *Ekklesia* Series: Book 1

Church: What Was God Thinking? **by Bruce Isom**
Published by: Word and Spirit and Life Ltd.
P.O. Box 259, Tai Po Post Office
Tai Po, New Territories, HONG KONG

Phone: + (852) 6541 7768
Website: www.WordAndSpiritAndLife.com
Email: info@WordAndSpiritAndLife.com

Copyright © 2011 Bruce Wayne Isom II

All graphics and illustrations Copyright © 2011 Stephanie Isom. Used by permission.

Church: What Was God Thinking? or parts thereof, including but not limited to the text and graphics, may not be reproduced in any form, stored in a retrieval system or transmitted in any form by any means -- electronic, mechanical, photocopy, recording, or otherwise -- without prior written permission of the publisher.

Short extracts may be used for review purposes.

ISBN-10: 988-99653-2-1
ISBN-13: 978-988-99653-2-7

Sources in the public domain:

Scripture quotations marked **KJV** are from the King James Version of the Bible

Scripture quotations marked **WEB** are from the World English Bible

Greek definitions marked **Strong's** are from the Strong's Exhaustive Concordance of the Bible, by Dr. James Strong

Greek definitions marked **Thayer's** are from the A Greek-English Lexicon of the New Testament, by Joseph Henry Thayer

Greek definitions marked **Vine's** are from the Vine's Expository Dictionary of New Testament Words, by W. E. Vine, M. A.

Disclaimer: Word and Spirit and Life Ltd and Bruce Isom carry no responsibility or liability for any unintended or undesirable results related to the practical application of principles in this book. The concepts presented are meant to be used in entirety, but even so, there are many variables in ministry. The results negative and positive are up to the reader and the Lord. We do believe that if used correctly, the principles put forth in this book will bring good fruit in the lives of believers, congregations, and the Body of Christ.

Individuals mentioned in this book do not necessarily share the author's views expressed in this book. These views are my own.

Dedication

To the Lord Jesus Christ who changed my life.

To all who have stood with me on this long road,
especially my family
and
all those faithful to speak the word in season.
Your obedience to the Lord
has helped make the difference
in bringing this book into reality.

As the Bible says:
"The Lord Yahweh has given me the tongue of those who are taught,
that I may know how to sustain with words him who is weary:
he wakens morning by morning,
he wakens my ear to hear as those who are taught."
Isaiah 50:4 (WEB)

Table of Contents

Dedication iii
Foreword .... - 1 -
Introduction .... - 5 -
Chapter 1: Author's Story .... - 9 -
Chapter 2: Introducing the *Ekklesia* .... - 15 -
    What is Church, *Ekklesia*? .... - 16 -
    The Kingdom of God .... - 16 -
Chapter 3: The Birth of the *Ekklesia* .... - 21 -
    Ekklesia's Birth in the Upper Room .... - 21 -
    What This Means for Today .... - 23 -
    Connecting with God .... - 24 -
    Keys to Removing Obstacles .... - 26 -
Chapter 4: The Focus of the Early Church .... - 29 -
    Ekklesia Perseverance and Devotion .... - 29 -
    Apostles' Teaching .... - 30 -
    Maturity and Spiritual Gifts .... - 30 -
    Fellowship .... - 31 -
    Breaking Bread .... - 32 -
    Being Heavenly Minded .... - 32 -
    Prayer .... - 33 -
    Moving in God's Power .... - 34 -
Chapter 5: Fruit of the Right Focus .... - 37 -
    Signs and Wonders .... - 37 -
    Awareness of the Spiritual World .... - 39 -
    Discerning Truth from Error .... - 40 -
    In Review .... - 42 -

Chapter 6: Devotion to God Through Fasting and Prayer .... - 43 -
   Spiritual Disciplines .... - 43 -
   Fasting and Prayer .... - 45 -
Chapter 7: A Prophetic Message for the Modern Church .... - 47 -
   What Does God Want His People to Know About Him? .... - 48 -
   What Does God Like in a Church? .... - 49 -
   What Does God Dislike in a Christian Community? .... - 50 -
   What Instructions Does God Give the Church? .... - 51 -
   What Will God Do About a Church that Fails to Listen? .... - 52 -
   What Promises Does He Give To The Overcomer? .... - 52 -
Chapter 8: Priesthood of the Believer .... - 55 -
   The Nicolaitans and the Clergy-Laity System .... - 55 -
   All Believers Are Important .... - 57 -
Chapter 9: Stages of Spiritual Maturity .... - 61 -
   Infancy .... - 62 -
   Childhood .... - 62 -
   Teenagers .... - 63 -
   Young Adults .... - 65 -
   Spiritual Parenthood .... - 66 -
   Spiritual Grandparenthood .... - 69 -
   How to Become a Mature Christian .... - 69 -
Chapter 10: One Body, One Spirit .... - 71 -
   Be Filled .... - 72 -
   Love, the Most Excellent Way .... - 75 -
Chapter 11: Love in Ministry .... - 77 -
   What is Love? .... - 78 -
   Growing in God's Love .... - 80 -
Chapter 12: Leadership in the *Ekklesia* .... - 83 -

Minister	- 83 -
What a Servant-Leader Is Not	- 84 -
How a Leader Should Serve	- 85 -
How Servant-Leaders Lead	- 86 -
The Follower's Responsibility	- 87 -
Chapter 13: Identifying Spiritual Gifts	- 91 -
Ministry Burnout	- 92 -
Ways to Identify Spiritual Gifts	- 94 -
A Word of Caution	- 97 -
Chapter 14: Leaders Equipping Believers in the Gifts	- 101 -
Growing into Maturity	- 101 -
The Leader's Responsibility Regarding His Gift	- 104 -
Contrast: The Traditional Church Model	- 106 -
The Equipping Process	- 109 -
Diagram 1: The Equipping Process	- 112 -
Diagram 2: Apostolic Impartation in the Equipping Process	- 113 -
Chapter 15: Introducing Biblical Elders	- 115 -
Special Ministries of the Elder	- 117 -
The Qualifications for an Elder	- 118 -
Recognizing and Selecting Elders	- 119 -
Tough Love	- 122 -
Chapter 16: The Elder's Function	- 125 -
The Elder Helps Prevent Inappropriate Control	- 125 -
Elders, Apostles, Controversy, and Important Decisions	- 127 -
Respect for Elders, Overseers, and Leaders	- 128 -
Chapter 17: Bishops or Overseers	- 131 -
Description of an Overseer	- 132 -
Chapter 18: The Full-Time Minister	- 135 -

Ministers That Do Everything .... - 135 -
Ministers That Follow Man-Made Traditions... - 137 -
What a Minister Should Be Doing.. - 138 -
A Minister's Authority .... - 139 -
God Is Going to Change the Church .... - 140 -

Chapter 19: Apostles in the Early Church .... - 143 -
Foundations.. - 143 -
Why the Church Needs Apostles .... - 144 -
What Apostles Looked Like in the Bible .... - 145 -
Apostles Can Have Certain Ministry Focuses .... - 152 -

Chapter 20: Apostles in the Modern Church .... - 155 -
Apostles Repair Spiritual Foundations .... - 158 -
Possible Apostolic Weaknesses.. - 164 -

Chapter 21: The Test of a True Apostle .... - 167 -
Recognizing a False Apostle .... - 168 -
The Holy Spirit's Help in Discerning a False Apostle............................. - 168 -
Discernment Versus Judgment .... - 169 -
Issues a False Apostle May Have.. - 170 -
Contrast: True, Mature Apostles.. - 171 -
Apostolic Head Pastor Pushing for Everyone to be the Same .... - 172 -
True Apostles Lead Believers to Depend on Christ................................ - 173 -

Chapter 22: The Role of Prophets in the Church .... - 177 -
The Prophet's Function in the Body of Christ.. - 177 -
Combinations of Gifts.. - 180 -
Diagram 3: The Pastor-Prophet Combination .... - 181 -

Chapter 23: Old Testament and New Testament Prophets .... - 183 -
Old Testament Prophets .... - 183 -
The Old Testament Standard for Prophets .... - 185 -

The School of Prophets ....- 187 -
Chapter 24: Issues and Weaknesses of Prophets ....- 191 -
   Factors That Can Influence Effective Use of the Prophetic Gift ....- 191 -
   The Holy Spirit Can Speak Through Anyone ....- 192 -
   Discerning The Difference Between a False and True Prophet ....- 192 -
   Spiritual Issues of Which Prophets Need to be Aware ....- 193 -
   Weaknesses of an Immature Prophet..- 195 -
The Prophetic ....- 201 -
Chapter 25: The Prophetic Gathering...- 203 -
   Prophetic Gatherings ....- 203 -
   A Large Prophetic Gathering..- 204 -
   Small Prophetic Gatherings..- 204 -
   Informal Prophetic Gatherings...- 204 -
   Hosting Prophetic Gatherings ....- 205 -
Chapter 26: Things to Understand Regarding Prophetic Ministry...........- 209 -
   Prophetic Words that Need to be Handled with Care ....- 209 -
   Confirming a Prophetic Word ....- 211 -
   What It Means if a Word Does Not Feel Right.................................- 212 -
   What To Do About Unfulfilled Prophecies ....- 213 -
   Prophecy Often Challenges Comfort Zones...- 214 -
   Dealing with Confusion over Prophetic Words ....- 216 -
Chapter 27: The Gift of Pastor ....- 221 -
   The Difference Between the Gift and Position of Pastor.....................- 222 -
   The Pastor's Ministry Role ....- 223 -
   Venues for the Pastoral Gift ....- 225 -
   The Pastor's Function in Ministry..- 226 -
Chapter 28: The Role of the Teacher in the Modern Church...................- 231 -
   Who Can Be a Teacher?..- 232 -

ix

Biblical Teaching .... - 234 -
Uses for the Gift of Teaching .... - 236 -
Chapter 29: Issues Related to the Teacher .... - 239 -
False Teaching .... - 239 -
Accountability .... - 241 -
Possible Weaknesses of Teachers .... - 244 -
Chapter 30: The Evangelist .... - 247 -
Biblical Ways to Share the Gospel .... - 250 -
Venues for the Gift of Evangelism .... - 252 -
Weaknesses of the Evangelist .... - 253 -
Chapter 31: Other Spiritual Gifts .... - 257 -
Manifestational Gifts .... - 257 -
Words of Wisdom and Knowledge .... - 258 -
The Gift of Faith .... - 259 -
Gifts of Healing .... - 260 -
The Gift of Miracles .... - 261 -
The Gift of Discernment .... - 263 -
The Gift of Tongues .... - 267 -
Function Gifts .... - 271 -
Faith Gifts .... - 273 -
The Body is Diverse .... - 275 -
Chapter 32: Prophecy, Tongues, and Songs in the Spirit .... - 277 -
The Benefits of Praying in Tongues .... - 282 -
Prophecy Versus Tongues in the Gathering .... - 283 -
Tongues Are a Sign for Unbelievers .... - 284 -
How Prophecy and Tongues Can Be Used in the Assembly .... - 285 -
Issues That Interrupt Prophetic Flow .... - 288 -
Psalms, Hymns, and Spiritual Songs .... - 291 -

Chapter 33: A Picture of the Gifts Working In Body Life ....- 295 -

    Church Planting in Apostolic Teams ....- 295 -

    The Apostolic Evangelistic Team ....- 296 -

    An Apostolic Evangelistic Team in Action ....- 297 -

    The Apostolic Equipping Team ....- 298 -

    Judgment Versus Discernment ....- 302 -

    What a Gathering with all the Gifts Could Be Like ....- 303 -

Chapter 34: Putting It All Together ....- 307 -

Acknowledgments

To my wife, Mary, who spent many hours with me discussing and envisioning what Biblical Church should look like, as well as being a part of our ministry and editing teams.

To my two younger daughters, Stephanie and María, who spent many hours being a part of our ministry, prophetic, and editing teams.

To my son, Jon, I am so proud of who you have become.

To my family, who helped me realize that even though God was using me to write a book, it did not mean that it would be perfect and not need editing.

To Dick and Laura for giving me a glimpse of how the New Testament Church should function.

Thank you to the couple that prophesied over me that started me on my journey of writing this book.

Thank you to those that had prophetic words that helped me keep working on this book, including the person who warned me that I need to be patient during the process and the one who shared the prophetic word that our family has access to the library of Heaven.

Thank you to the many friends that supported me during the process of writing this book even though there were those who at times wondered if there was ever going to be a book.

Thank you to the many others that have supported me in my journey.

Thank you to all that have helped me learn about what Church should be like.

Foreword

Change is coming. We can smell it in the wind, see it on the tense faces of people on the street, hear it on the news. It's in the headlines of almost every country in the world. People are afraid. Do we as a church have any answers for them? Real answers. Answers that are written into our lives and that aren't just coming out of our mouths.

It is a time when evil roars, people are consumed by anything that promises happiness and the world is in agony. Purpose is dead in their hearts and hopelessness is killing them, their families, their children. They need hope like they have never seen it before -- shining like a beacon, burning like a wildfire, blazing like the sun -- through us, out of us, pouring like a mighty fountain from our lives.

The trouble is I don't feel mighty. I feel weak, afraid, deaf and blind, sinful and wretched -- and I am the church. I am a body part of Christ. Am I truly connected to the source? Am I plugged in to the power source that IS the Author of all Creation? Am I living in Christ like Paul? Or Peter? Walking in the power of God like Elijah? Or Moses? Why not? If God can do it and the Bible says it -- then why don't I believe it? Why do I deny His Power? Why do I think it was meant for all the ages of yesterday and not for now? Shouldn't the words of Jesus, "Because they did not believe" strike me to the core? Do I want to continue my life in unbelief, working hard to follow God without really following?

I'm tired of boot-strap Christianity. I've tried to pull myself up; I've yanked with all my might to lift myself out of the muck and the mire. I've read the Bible, prayed and listened to the best pep-talk sermons in the world but I still can't seem to get myself out of the mess I'm in. In the end, what will I have gained? What will my life have accomplished if it was "for" Him but without Him? What eternal value is there in that? Paul said, "Yes most certainly, and I count all things to be loss for the excellency of the knowledge of Christ Jesus, my LORD, for whom I suffered the loss of all things, and count them nothing but refuse, that I may gain Christ and be found in him, not having a

Church: What Was God Thinking?

righteousness of my own, that which is of the law, but that which is through faith in Christ, the righteousness which is from God by faith;" (Philippians 3:8, 9 WEB)

I want Him. I long to know Him and don't want to wait until Heaven to be in His Presence. I'm desperate to push in as close to Him as He will let me this side of Heaven ... and nothing or no one can tell me otherwise. And if that means experiencing Him in ways that not everyone understands, so be it. I crave to be so full of God's Presence and Love and Life that I walk into the grocery market and the people I pass in the aisle can feel Him -- and desire Him -- and revival happens right there. I dream of being on a plane with a captive audience and have my neighbor beg to have what I have (if not the whole plane). I long to make the world around me hunger for Him, feel Him, but it's not going to happen the way I am now. Something is missing.

The trouble is -- I need a doctor, a spiritual doctor ... godly mentors, guidance -- but the church is sick. It's meant to be a place of healing but I'm going to church and everyone around me is fighting and vying for their own agenda and afraid to take a stand in front of their brothers and sisters. And I can see it in their eyes, they're feeling pretty powerless too. The other problem is this: change is hard. People don't like it -- Christ-followers or not. The longer something is done a certain way, the less we want to accept anything different. If it has been a certain way for generations, whether there is a good reason for it or not, we are less likely to accept change -- the tradition BECOMES the Gospel, our gospel. For example, we dress up on Sundays. Why? Because we're supposed to, right? Well yeah, what would the Pastor think if I showed up in my work clothes? Well, that's the Pastor and, yes, he deserves my full respect. God has put him in authority over me. Who is in authority over him though? Well, the LORD. And what does He have to say about nice clothes? Well, the Bible is my solid source for that and it says ... hmm, let's see ... not to worry about what I should wear ... and umm, He's looking at my heart ... and in the Bible, James pointedly says not to treat someone who comes to Church dressed in nice clothes better than the one in old dirty clothes. Hmm,

Foreword

does God care what I wear to church on Sunday or is He concerned instead with the fact that I'm judging others because of what they're wearing? And what about how I've been unwilling to forgive the person sitting two rows ahead and to the left of me?

So what else about Church is not how the Bible says God wants it to be? Even more important is -- how did He design it to be?

Church: What Was God Thinking? starts at the foundation and puts together brick by brick the picture the Bible reveals of God's thinking on the church.

Bruce Isom speaks from his heart about his journey with the LORD and the Body of Christ over the past thirty-seven years. He shares His search for building the LORD's Body the way God planned and the way it needs to be -- a safe, whole and healing place for a world in upheaval.

After reading his book I am no longer satisfied. I must have more. I yearn for what God intended -- and still intends -- for His Body to look like. Not OUR body, HIS Body. The question is: Are we willing to give it back to Him?

My prayer and my hope is that you will open your heart as you read this book and let God address your preconceived notions of Church and allow Him to build a new perspective of His Church in you -- One that is built on the solid foundation of His Word and not on the shifting sands of human tradition. One that can find its source in the bedrock of Biblical truth and its power in the LORD; and carry the Body of Christ in His Glory and Love and Power through the last days as a lighthouse and a lifeboat for the world.

LORD, please make me and your whole Body of Christ into what You created us to be so that we can fulfill Your destiny for us to the fullest and nothing less. Amen.

Hungry for all God wants,
Gretchen Geyer

Introduction

The content of this book is an expression of things that I have been passionate about for decades. Years ago a prophet told me that God was going to give me a message that will go farther and farther. I did not know what to do about that word, so I just waited to see what God would do.

I have never considered myself to be a writer. This manuscript began several years ago when I received prophetic ministry from a couple that is well-known in certain circles to be strong in the prophetic. They did not know me or my history, but they basically said that God has given me a unique perspective and wants to use me to release a message for the Church. I knew this to be true and began seeking the Lord about what to do about it.

While I was praying about what to do, I felt like God said to write a book, but I began arguing with Him saying, "Lord, you have got the wrong guy." Finally I shared this with my family. I thought they would tell me that I was not hearing God. Instead, they gave me the exact opposite reaction. They were excited that the Lord would have me write a book, even though they knew it would take a miracle for it to ever happen.

I have always disliked writing. Before I began writing this book, it would take me over an hour to write an email that was only two or three sentences long. In fact, I rarely ever wrote anyone. Because of this, I set up voice recognition software to begin dictating this book into my computer. Eventually this felt somewhat clumsy, so I began typing instead. Since the message was burning in my heart, I wrote most of it in a matter of weeks. In fact, not all of what I have written fits in this book and I hope to release a second book fairly soon that continues sharing on the topic of Church. My family was amazed at how quickly this happened.

I have learned so much through the development of this manuscript. I originally thought that if God told me to write something, despite my lack of practice, that it would be perfect. When my editing

Church: What Was God Thinking?

team began looking at it, I was shocked. I have now realized this is much like people's growth in their spiritual gifts. Anointing and perfection are two different things. I am now very grateful that the Lord has given me a team that has some gifts that I do not. At the same time, I have been working to improve my writing skills. I am so thankful for this experience.

In this book, I have chosen a unique standard for capitalization. Many words which have to do with God and the Bible will be capitalized. "Church" is capitalized when it refers to the universal Body of Christ, not capitalized when it refers to local church gatherings.

Please consider: Because so much of what I am going to share will be new to many, there are a few things the reader should keep in mind.

Matthew 15:3 (WEB) He answered them, "Why do you also disobey the commandment of God because of your tradition?

People tend to get so stuck in tradition that they forget about what God wants. Jesus rebuked the leaders of His day for doing this. Although I have studied some church history and find it useful, especially in explaining how the Church has become what it is today, I feel that Scripture is the best place to look in order to find what God intended the Church to be.

I understand that there are many different viewpoints on this matter. However, I hope that anyone who reads this will be willing to search it out in the Bible, trying to be careful not to make judgments based on tradition and preconceived ideas. I also realize that I am not perfect. I hope my reader can look past things they disagree with or feel are wrong and keep an open heart to this message.

In this book, the Scripture references cited are primarily from the World English Bible and King James Version simply because they are in public domain. However, in the last thirty-seven years, I have also studied from the Revised Standard Version, New American Standard Version, New International Version, and the Amplified Bible. From my studies and my understanding, these translations all agree on the

Introduction

subject matter of this book. There are a few things that only the Amplified Bible contains, but Strong's, and Thayer's Greek and Hebrew dictionaries and lexicons also support what I wrote. I would like to encourage my readers to use the Bible translation they are most comfortable using with this book, so they can search things out in the full Scriptural context.

    Keeping these things in mind, let us move forward!

Chapter 1: Author's Story

In this book, I have many insights to share about the Church and what God created it to be. First, it would be helpful for the reader to know a little about me: who I am, where I have been, and how I gained the insights that I plan to share. Each person's journey with Christ is unique and influences his perspective in many ways. In this chapter, I want to tell a little about my journey.

I grew up in a broken family. During my early childhood, my parents did not get along due to their various issues. However, one of my neighbors, a lovely elderly lady, reached out to me and even took me to church with her. It was there that I first prayed to become a Christian.

After my parents divorced, I went to live with my mother and grandparents. My home situation improved, but we were not close. My grandparents also went to church and I went with them. Unfortunately for me, our church was not strong. The pastor had the gift of evangelism, and tried to evangelize from the pulpit. It seems he did not realize that, except for possibly some of the youth, most of the congregation was already saved. I went forward in an altar call and was baptized. Later however, I became extremely bored with church. Although I loved music, this church was mostly made up of old ladies that were not able to sing on key. Besides this, the pastor continued to

Church: What Was God Thinking?

only teach the Gospel message, crying every Sunday because there was not anyone coming forward to make a decision for Christ. As a result, when I left home, I knew little about the Bible. What I knew of Jesus I learned mostly from watching movies.

I had lost my interest in God. After all, if He was anything like what I saw in my grandparent's church, it seemed that other things were far more interesting. So I found a group of friends with similar interests and moved farther away from God. During this time, a mutual friend introduced me to Mary, who later became my wife. She needed music for synchronized swimming and came over to my house to borrow a record album. Although she had a boyfriend at the time, we became friends. She would even ask me questions about dating problems. I never told her that I did not know much about dating. I gave her the best counsel I could give. Although I really liked her, I tried my best to not let it influence my advice. In the end, she broke up with her boyfriend. After that, we would sometimes go out for coffee together and we developed a strong friendship.

Sometime later, I started having sleeping problems. I had insomnia for about a year. I tried sleeping medicine but felt more tired after using medicine than when I did not sleep. One of the rare occasions that I did sleep, I had a vivid dream that a demon was pointing down a road leading to hell and was telling me that I had to go there. I awakened, petrified.

During the nights I was not able to sleep, God began opening my eyes to the battle between good and evil. I read "Lord of the Rings" and felt that a war between light and darkness was truly happening in the earth. Since I wanted to know more, I began reading the Bible that my church gave me when I graduated from high school. This was the beginning of change for me.

In addition to insomnia, I also had a bicycle accident. Although it seemed I only had surface wounds, they just would not heal. Besides this, I liked Mary, but we were just good friends. One night, I read in the Bible about physical healing, so I prayed that God would heal me. I also asked God to let me sleep, and that He would bring Mary and me

Chapter 1: Author's Story

together because I liked her but we were just good friends. That night, I slept the best that I had slept in over a year, and my hands were healed within less than a week. It was amazing!

I was not a man of faith and I am not sure that I expected anything to happen when I prayed. God had answered my prayer for physical healing; now He decided to answer my prayer about Mary. Within a few days God began working in our relationship. One morning when I saw Mary, she grabbed my hand and said, "I love you," and then just kept walking. It happened so quickly that I thought she was just being friendly. Soon after that, she asked for a ride to school, and as she was getting out of the car, she did it again. Part of me thought she was just being nice, another part of me began wondering what was happening, and if she really did mean it.

Not long after this, Mary came to see me because she was upset about a friend of ours who was in trouble. We ended up spending most of the night talking. By morning, we decided we loved each other. God had answered all three of my requests.

After this, God began speaking to me. He said, "Look at what I have done for you. Aren't you going to follow Me?" I kept thinking I was hearing things and must be going crazy. Besides, I would think about the church I attended as a teenager. In addition, the one time I mentioned Christianity to Mary, she said she did not want anything to do with "that religious stuff." I told God I was not interested in religion. I did not mind receiving His gifts; I just did not want to commit to Him.

Sometime later, Mary's parents came to visit her and began encouraging us to get married. This continued for about four months. I kept thinking, "Why not?" In any case, I knew that I wanted to spend the rest of my life with her. So, I asked her if she would marry me. She said, "No" the first two times I asked because she was not ready to get married. The third time she finally said, "Yes!!!" We had a small, simple wedding.

For our honeymoon we went camping and ended up driving several days to visit my dad. Although we barely had enough money for our trip, we knew that we would have work when we returned. I had not spoken to my dad since I left when I was ten. I had not even sent him my picture. For some reason, right after getting married I wanted to see him.

We found him at the same house. I remembered where he lived, but as we pulled up, he was just moving the last things from his home. He was moving to the new house he had just built. I walked up to the house and asked to see him. He did not recognize me. I told him I was his son and he embraced me and cried. This was healing for both of us.

After returning home, we went to work detasseling seed corn. A month later, we had a break and decided to go camping in the mountains. A few days later, we went to visit a close friend. Mary wanted her to be the bridesmaid at our wedding, but this friend was unable to come.

When we arrived, we were surprised to learn that she had become a Christian. She lived in a street mission. She was fasting and praying that week for a list of friends, including us. We were invited to the evening meeting and, not wanting to be rude, we accepted the invitation. At the same time, I was nervous about it because of what God had already been doing in my life.

The meeting was quite relaxed. They asked if I knew anything about Jesus. So, I told them what I thought I understood. I did not know much, and what I thought I knew was not accurate. At the end of the meeting, they asked me to pray with them. As they prayed, alternating between tongues and English, the power of the Holy Spirit came on both of us. It was fascinating, but frightening too. As the meeting finished, I tried to wake Mary, thinking that she had gone to sleep, only to discover that she was crying. I did not know why. Some time later she shared with me that they were good tears because God touched her heart. Since I just wanted to leave, we drove back to the campground.

That night I slept in the car, but when I awoke in the middle of the night, Mary was gone. I found her in the shower house because she had not slept. We both agreed that we had experienced something

Chapter 1: Author's Story

unusual, but we decided we did not want to rush into anything. We needed to know first if Jesus was real. The result was that we decided to read the Bible together.

When I was a teenager, I thought the Bible was boring, especially when my grandfather told me that miracles no longer happen. When Mary and I started reading the Bible, my viewpoint changed. Because of what we experienced at our friend's Bible study, I knew God's power was for today. Scripture became so real that the words seemed to jump off the pages, reading it became fun. Because of this, we just wanted to read more and more of God's Word!

During our Bible reading time, God continued to speak to me, saying that following Jesus did not have to be like my church as a teenager. However, I was still nervous about becoming a Christian because I was afraid of what church would be like.

After a few months like this, we were ready to talk about what we wanted to do. One day, one of us asked the other what we thought about becoming a believer. After a short discussion, we both decided to follow Jesus. This has been the best decision that we have ever made.

The next step was to find a church. There were so many denominations. To make things more confusing, between both of our families over the last few generations, different ones had belonged to at least six different denominations. We wanted to choose the "right church," so we began studying the Bible to see what Church should be like. We also searched for a church that followed the pattern we saw in Scripture.

In the end, we found a church we liked. It was not identical to what we saw in the Bible, but it was the closest we could find. There were many other people like us, so we felt comfortable. This was the beginning of our journey in God.

That was in 1974. Thirty-seven years later and we are still deeply in love with Jesus and each other. Unfortunately, our first church no longer exists. However, Biblical Church has remained our passion. I have continued to search the Scriptures over the years, and have even been involved in several church plants. Twenty-six years ago, in 1985, I received my call to become a missionary. I have spent over seventeen years in Hong Kong. The first eleven years I worked with local churches and ministries, and then I moved into church planting and related support ministries. It has never been boring, and God has taught me so much!

In the rest of this book, I would like to share some of the insights that God has given me.

Chapter 2: Introducing the *Ekklesia*

Acts 17:10-11 (WEB) The brothers immediately sent Paul and Silas away by night to Beroea [Berea]. When they arrived, they went into the Jewish synagogue. (11) Now these were more noble than those in Thessalonica, in that they received the word with all readiness of the mind, examining the Scriptures daily to see whether these things were so.

In the previous chapter, I described my journey of becoming a Christian and my deep desire to attend a church that was like the Church in the book of Acts. Since my wife and I did not get saved through a local church, but through a friend who lived about eight hundred miles from where we lived, we had to choose a congregation to attend. This was the beginning of a lifelong study of what the Bible says about Church. In the last thirty-some years, we have been part of several good churches. Each one imparted good things into our lives but still lacked some key elements. In this chapter, I want to look at the history, basic definition, and the purpose of Church.

The Greek word for "church" is ἐκκλησία *ekklēsia.*
Thayer's definition: G1577 (pronounced: *e-klay-see'-ah*)
1) a gathering of citizens called out from their homes into
   some public place, an assembly; the assembly of the Israelites ...
 In a Christian sense:
  a) an assembly of Christians gathered for worship ...
  b) a company of Christians ...

    c) those who anywhere, in a city, village, constitute such a company and are united into one body
    d) the whole body of Christians scattered throughout the earth
    e) the assembly of faithful Christians already dead and received into heaven

1 Peter 2:5 (WEB) You also, as living stones, are built up as a spiritual house, to be a holy priesthood, to offer up spiritual sacrifices, acceptable to God through Jesus Christ.

What is Church, *Ekklesia*?

In the New Testament's original language, Greek, the word for Church is *Ekklesia* (pronounced *e-klay-see'-ah*). This word is not referring to a church building or a program. It is referring to the Body of Christ made of individuals worldwide. *Ekklesia* is not a structural building but living stones, individual believers, who are being built together into a spiritual house, which is the Church, the Body of Christ (1 Peter 2:5). In other words, all believers are the Church. My goal in writing this book is to share what Scripture says about the *Ekklesia*.

The purpose of this book is to see what the Bible says about Church and to see the Church reach its full potential. My heart in sharing is not to bring condemnation or judgment on anyone. Please read this with an open heart, checking it all out with Scripture. It is my prayer that you will see and take to heart what God wants to say so that, in Christ Jesus, you too can grow into the fullness of His high calling (Philippians 3:12-14).

How many people go to church and feel that something is missing? How many have vision from God burning in their hearts but it seems that there is no way to express that vision in the local church? If you you identify with these feelings, this book has some answers for you.

The Kingdom of God

It is important to first talk about the Kingdom of God. The Kingdom of God is Heaven coming down into the midst of the

Chapter 2: Introducing the Ekklesia

Church. The Kingdom of God is expressed through the Holy Spirit moving through believers as they follow His leading using His spiritual gifts. Moving in the gifts of the Holy Spirit is entering into what is in God's heart to build up the Body of Christ and then in this way, bringing that part of the Kingdom of God down to earth. Using His gifts and walking in obedience to His leading, Church becomes a spiritual symphony with God being the conductor.

When Jesus walked on the earth two thousand years ago, He spoke often about the Kingdom of God. In addition, after He rose from the dead, He continued to talk to His disciples about this subject. The following Scriptures are examples of what Jesus said about the Kingdom of God.

Luke 9:2 (WEB) He sent them forth to preach the Kingdom of God, and to heal the sick.

Luke 9:60 (WEB) But Jesus said to him, "Leave the dead to bury their own dead, but you go and announce the Kingdom of God."

Matthew 12:28 (WEB) But if I by the Spirit of God cast out demons, then the Kingdom of God has come upon you.

Luke 13:20-21 (WEB) Again he said, "To what shall I compare the Kingdom of God? (21) It is like yeast, which a woman took and hid in three measures of flour, until it was all leavened."

Acts 1:3 (WEB) To these he also showed himself alive after he suffered, by many proofs, appearing to them over a period of forty days, and speaking about God's Kingdom.

This is what the normal Christian walk is to be like. Proclaiming the Kingdom of God, healing the sick, obeying God in everything even if it means leaving behind what many people feel is important.

The Kingdom of God was made to be like yeast that spreads itself uncontrollably throughout the dough. Yeast is a wonderful picture of multiplication because, if given the right environment, it will reproduce faster than many living things on earth. Every yeast cell has the capability of multiplying. After a baker dissolves yeast with warm water

Church: What Was God Thinking?

and sugar, he then mixes this with flour and oil to become dough. It then feeds on the sugar and flour, multiplying itself until its spread becomes unstoppable. Soon there is yeast in the whole batch of dough. If this mixture is placed in a small bowl and then forgotten for a few hours, it will become a big mess because, as the dough expands, if left alone, it will run all over the place. This is an important key to growing the Church. Christians are not supposed to be like yeast that sits in the sealed package in the refrigerator. How often are formulas and gimmicks used to try to make churches grow? How does the result compare with the extreme church growth in the book of Acts? Is the quantity or quality at all like the Church in the New Testament? In the present day, people stand in awe if a church grows to one thousand to ten thousand people! This is a small thing compared to New Testament levels of church growth.

At present, there are churches using New Testament principles that are growing very quickly. Some of these churches are growing at a rate of ten thousand or more people a year. Iris Ministries in Mozambique is a group that has over ten thousand churches in their network. Most of these have been planted in the last nine years.[1] Obviously, most churches are not achieving the same results.

So what is the secret? It is not a secret at all. Do it God's way. The Bible gives keys that have been overlooked for many years.

John 5:19 (WEB) Jesus therefore answered them, "Most certainly, I tell you, the Son can do nothing of himself, but what he sees the Father doing. For whatever things he does, these the Son also does likewise.

Mark 1:16-18 (WEB) Passing along by the sea of Galilee, he saw Simon and Andrew the brother of Simon casting a net into the sea, for they were fishermen. (17) Jesus said to them, "Come after me, and I will make you into fishers for men." (18) Immediately they left their nets, and followed him.

When Christians follow God's way as outlined in the Bible, there will be massive church growth. People will want to give up everything

---

[1] www.irismin.org/p/background.php -- Accessed 01 August 2011

Chapter 2: Introducing the Ekklesia

and follow Jesus, just as they did two thousand years ago. If God's Church worldwide follows the leading of the Holy Spirit, they should not be surprised to see the same growth that is seen in the book of Acts as it becomes more normal. People will be filled with excitement about gathering together and being part of the Church. When Christians do Church God's way, they will have great excitement about being the *Ekklesia* and will want to do the works of Christ. So what is Church all about? In the next chapter, I will begin describing this by taking a look at the beginnings of the Church as recorded in the book of Acts.

Chapter 3: The Birth of the *Ekklesia*

To know what Church is meant to be, it is best to look at the book of Acts and other examples in the letters of the New Testament. It is also essential to know how the Holy Spirit works and how to experience Him. Church now may not look exactly the same as it did then, but it should have the same building blocks as the early Church.

Ekklesia's Birth in the Upper Room

Acts 2:4 (KJV) And they were all filled with the Holy Ghost, and began to speak with other tongues, as the Spirit gave them utterance.

Act 2:13-15 (WEB) Others, mocking, said, "They are filled with new wine." (14) But Peter, standing up with the eleven, lifted up his voice, and spoke out to them, "You men of Judea, and all you who dwell at Jerusalem, let this be known to you, and listen to my words. (15) For these aren't drunken, as you suppose, seeing it is only the third hour of the day.

Acts 1:8 (WEB) But you will receive power when the Holy Spirit has come upon you. You will be witnesses to me in Jerusalem, in all Judea and Samaria, and to the uttermost parts of the earth."

Luke 3:16 (WEB) John answered them all, "I indeed baptize you with water, but he comes who is mightier than I, the latchet of whose sandals I am not worthy to loosen. He will baptize you in the Holy Spirit and fire,

Church: What Was God Thinking?

When the *Ekklesia* was birthed through the Upper Room Prayer Meeting, several things happened. Acts 2:13-15 says that, as Jesus foretold, the Holy Spirit's power came upon those gathered in prayer, giving gifts and supernatural abilities to them. The Upper Room believers spoke in tongues for the first time and it looked like they were drunk. This experience of the Holy Spirit's power was referred to by John the Baptist as baptism in the Holy Spirit (Luke 3:16). This was the first group baptism of the Holy Spirit in human history, and it was dramatic. It even drew a crowd.

The onlookers likely did not know that this was a manifestation of being filled with the Holy Spirit but they could not help noticing that something unusual was happening. Peter informed the gathering crowds that Jesus' followers could not be drunk because it was too early in the day, and then he proceeded to share the Gospel. This event changed the course of the whole Church and touched many of those around. In fact three thousand people came to the Lord that day!

John 20:22 (WEB) When he had said this, he breathed on them, and said to them, "Receive the Holy Spirit!

Acts 10:44-48 (WEB) While Peter was still speaking these words, the Holy Spirit fell on all those who heard the word. (45) They of the circumcision who believed were amazed, as many as came with Peter, because the gift of the Holy Spirit was also poured out on the Gentiles. (46) For they heard them speaking in other languages and magnifying God. Then Peter answered, (47) "Can any man forbid the water, that these who have received the Holy Spirit as well as we should not be baptized?" (48) He commanded them to be baptized in the name of Jesus Christ. Then they asked him to stay some days.

John 14:16 (WEB) I will pray to the Father, and he will give you another Counselor, that he may be with you forever,

Romans 8:26-27 (WEB) In the same way, the Spirit also helps our weaknesses, for we don't know how to pray as we ought. But the Spirit himself makes intercession for us with groanings which can't be uttered. (27) He who searches the hearts knows what is on the Spirit's mind, because he makes intercession for the saints according to God.

Chapter 3: The Birth of the *Ekklesia*

Romans 8:13 (WEB) For if you live after the flesh, you must die; but if by the Spirit you put to death the deeds of the body, you will live.

What is the filling of the Holy Spirit? I have heard many people say different things about what this means. According to the Bible, being filled with the Holy Spirit is meant to be an ongoing experience, beginning at salvation (1 Corinthians 12:3; John 20:22), increasing through the baptism in the Holy Spirit confirming salvation (Acts 10:44-48; Acts 18:24 - 19:6), and continuing throughout the Christian life (John 14:16-17). It is an infilling of the power of God, giving each believer a direct connection with God (Romans 8:26-27), and the power necessary to live for Him (Romans 8:12-17).

Ephesians 5:18 (KJV) And be not drunk with wine, wherein is excess; but be filled with the Spirit;

The Greek word for "filled" is πληρόω *pleroō*.
Strong's definition G4137 (pronounced: *play-ro'-o*)
From G4134; to make replete, to cram, level up (a hollow), or (figuratively) to imbue, diffuse, influence, satisfy, complete, fill up, fulfill, to be or make full, to perfect or supply.

What This Means for Today

Some people believe that when a Christian first trusts in Jesus, he receives all the Holy Spirit that he is ever going to be given. In contrast, Scripture is clear that the infilling of the Holy Spirit must be a continual part of the Christian life. Scripture does teach that no one can say, "Jesus is Lord," or believe in Him except by the Holy Spirit, (1 Corinthians 12:3). Rather, Ephesians 5:18 commands believers not to be drunk with wine, but to be filled with the Holy Spirit. The Greek word for filled is *pleroo* (pronounced: *play-ro-o*), meaning to be replete with or in other words, to be bursting with the Holy Spirit. Why would Paul command the Ephesian believers to be filled with the Holy Spirit if, as Christians, they already received all they could upon believing in Jesus? Since Paul commands Christians to be filled with the Holy Spirit, I believe that believers do have a choice about whether or not they continue to be filled with the Holy Spirit on a day-to-day basis. Despite it being a personal decision, it is something each Christian must do. Scripture is clear that this is not just an option; it is also God's command.

Connecting with God

John 7:38 (WEB) He who believes in me, as the Scripture has said, from within him will flow rivers of living water."

When Jesus said that living waters would flow out of a person's innermost being, He was talking about the Holy Spirit. Being filled with the Holy Spirit is about having a deep relationship with the Triune God. By increasing the amount of quality time spent in God's presence and continuing each day to go deeper and deeper in relationship with Him, believers will see a proportionate increase in God's life flowing in and through them. When a person comes to the place that he can enter into God's presence and experience Him, I call this "connecting with God." Christians should not seek experiences as their primary goal, but if someone is seeking to be in God's presence, the experiences will come. Therefore, Christians will feel God more strongly and frequently when they spend quality time with Him.

Ezekiel 47:3-5 (WEB) When the man went forth eastward with the line in his hand, he measured one thousand cubits, and he caused me to pass through the waters, waters that were to the ankles. (4) Again he measured one thousand, and caused me to pass through the waters, waters that were to the knees. Again he measured one thousand, and caused me to pass through the waters, waters that were to the waist. (5) Afterward he measured one thousand; and it was a river that I could not pass through; for the waters were risen, waters to swim in, a river that could not be passed through.

Connecting with God might bring small experiences at first, but as a believer continues the effects become more powerful. Ezekiel 47 talks about the River that comes out of the Temple. As the man led Ezekiel farther into the water it became deeper, until it was too deep

Chapter 3: The Birth of the *Ekklesia*

for him to walk through it. This describes the progress of a person's relationship with God as he connects with Him. It is as if he starts out with a stream of God's power in him. As he continues that stream deepens, widens and becomes a river. The next thing he knows, it is deep, powerful, and intense, like Niagara Falls. Most people begin with just a little trickle. It is God's heart for Christians to grow in Him. God wants His love, power, and life to flow from their innermost being.

Matthew 15:8-9 (WEB) 'These people draw near to me with their mouth, and honor me with their lips; but their heart is far from me. (9) And in vain do they worship me, teaching as doctrine rules made by men.'"

A person can do all of the right things and still not really connect with God. The heart has to be in the right place. If anyone makes a formula out of having to do different religious works, that person will not automatically have a relationship with God. The religious leaders during Jesus' life on earth spent a lot of time doing so-called "spiritual" things that did not bring them close to God. Even though they did so much, Jesus said that their hearts were far from Him. Someone can go to church on Sunday, attend a small group or midweek meeting, every prayer meeting and church function, and still feel nothing for God. Each person's heart has to be in the right place to connect with Him.

2 Corinthians 3:18 (WEB) But we all, with unveiled face beholding as in a mirror the glory of the Lord, are transformed into the same image from glory to glory, even as from the Lord, the Spirit.

Amazing things happen when people spend time with God. In His presence, it is like they become pieces of burning coal and the Lord begins to blow on them and the fire of God within them burns hotter. Some call this being filled with the Holy Spirit, anointing, or moving in more authority. Whatever it is called, the truth of the matter is that as Christians spend time connecting with God, something happens.

John 15:7-10 (WEB) If you remain in me, and my words remain in you, you will ask whatever you desire, and it will be done for you. (8) "In

this is my Father glorified, that you bear much fruit; and so you will be my disciples. (9) Even as the Father has loved me, I also have loved you. Remain in my love. (10) If you keep my commandments, you will remain in my love; even as I have kept my Father's commandments, and remain in his love.

Mark 13:11 (WEB) When they lead you away and deliver you up, don't be anxious beforehand, or premeditate what you will say, but say whatever will be given you in that hour. For it is not you who speak, but the Holy Spirit.

As believers connect with God and obey Him, they will move more powerfully in the gifts the Lord has given them because He increases His anointing on them. Scripture is clear that God's anointing affects many parts of His children's lives, even the things they say. Jesus said that there would be times that they would not know what to say, but the Holy Spirit would give them the right words when they need them (Mark 13:11). When the Holy Spirit's gifts are operating in a Christians' life, they will touch the lives of many others.

Acts 5:32 (WEB) We are His witnesses of these things; and so also is the Holy Spirit, whom God has given to those who obey him."

Keys to Removing Obstacles

I want to give you, the reader, some tips for building your relationship with God. Obedience and repentance are main keys for being filled with the Holy Spirit. The sin of unbelief is a huge hindrance and many need to repent of this. In addition, many people do not get filled with the Holy Spirit because they do not feel worthy. In reality, without the cross, no one is worthy. That is why God gives salvation as a free gift. With the Lord's help, believers need to deal with these blocks, because if their hearts are not in the right place then the pure flow of the Holy Spirit will be blocked or limited in their lives.

Acts 2:38 (WEB) Peter said to them, "Repent, and be baptized, every one of you, in the name of Jesus Christ for the forgiveness of sins, and you will receive the gift of the Holy Spirit

Chapter 3: The Birth of the *Ekklesia*

Repentance does not simply mean saying, "I'm sorry." It means deciding, with God's help, to make a wholehearted effort to turn from sin and try to live for God in every area of one's life. When someone wants to live for the Lord, He will give that person His Holy Spirit. Although this will not make a person perfect, he will gain a strong desire to live for God and this desire will express itself in the way he lives. So the filling of the Holy Spirit leads to repentance and then empowers the believer to change.

Part of the work of the Holy Spirit is to convict people of sin (John 16:8-9). This might sound circular, since repentance is necessary for experiencing God's power. However, when a person wants to turn away from sin, it takes the Holy Spirit to give the grace to walk away from that sin. After this, that individual needs to keep being filled with the Holy Spirit to become fully free (Romans 8:12-17). Then the Holy Spirit will continue showing him other sins or weaknesses in his life and the cycle continues (John 8:31-36).

Romans 8:13 (WEB) For if you live after the flesh, you must die; but if by the Spirit you put to death the deeds of the body, you will live.

When God changes someone's life, it is like the children of Israel taking over the land the Lord promised to give them, because they had to fight to take and keep it. God deals with things a little at a time. As each person allows Him to take up residence in his or her heart, then change comes step by step as they follow His leading.

Psalms 16:11 (WEB) You will show me the path of life. In your presence is fullness of joy. In your right hand there are pleasures forevermore.

Since salvation is a free gift, the reader might wonder why people need to get rid of sin in their lives. Sin and its effects are like rotten garbage in a person's life. God wants Christians to get rid of this waste because it influences their thinking and what they do. Simply put, the Holy Spirit does not want to live in a house full of trash. He intends His children to become pure temples of His glory where they experience fullness of joy living in His presence.

Church: What Was God Thinking?

In summary, the Church is the community of believers worldwide and throughout history. This community was birthed in a prayer meeting where the Holy Spirit filled and empowered each believer, causing an explosion of power and bringing in more disciples. God created the Body of Christ to function in a certain way, and as the Church returns to that, Christians will experience more of what God intended. The first step is learning to connect with God in a way that allows the power of the Holy Spirit to flow individually and corporately. Since there is so much more to it than that, I will talk about this more in later chapters.

Chapter 4: The Focus of the Early Church

The Church was born out of a prayer meeting. However, it grew because of the devotion of its members, disciples of Christ. Let us take a look at those basic pillars of Christian community and life.

In Bible times, a disciple was an individual who wanted to be like the one that he followed. An Old Testament example is Elisha and Elijah. The apprentice went everywhere his mentor went so that his life would become like his teacher.

Acts 1:14 (WEB) All these with one accord continued steadfastly in prayer and supplication, along with the women, and Mary the mother of Jesus, and with his brothers.

Acts 2:42 (WEB) They continued steadfastly in the apostle's teaching and fellowship, in the breaking of bread, and prayer.

The Greek word for "to continue steadfastly or devotedly" is
  προσκαρτερέω *proskartereō*.
Strong's definition G4342 (pronounced: *pros-kar-ter-eh'-o*)
To be earnest towards, that is, to persevere, be constantly diligent, or to attend assiduously (diligently) all the exercises in a place, or to adhere closely to a person as a servant: - to attend and give oneself continually, to wait on continually

Ekklesia Perseverance and Devotion

The Greek word for "continued steadfastly" means having complete devotion and seriousness towards something. So the Church

Breaking Bread

Acts 2:46 (WEB) Day by day, continuing steadfastly with one accord in the temple, and breaking bread at home, they took their food with gladness and singleness of heart,

The third thing they devoted themselves to was breaking bread. The breaking of bread was not only a reference to communion, but also to the early Church's regular practice of eating a meal together. When believers eat together, it is often a relaxed time. They are more likely to share what is in their heart, discuss God's Word and minister to one another. Even many traditional churches have fellowship halls where from time to time they eat a fellowship meal. This practice began in the book of Acts and continues in many churches today.

When my family has gatherings in our home, we often begin with a simple meal. Each person brings part of the meal. This is a good time for all to share about their week and about what they have been reading in the Bible and learning in their walk with God. At times this gives us direction on what we need to do during our meeting, especially when someone brings up a significant subject or an important question. We try to keep the discussion centered on what the Bible says about the particular topic. Sometimes we pray for one person or encourage another. Other times someone new comes and we explain the format of our gatherings. This time of eating together provides opportunity for all these things.

Being Heavenly Minded

Colossians 3:1-2 (WEB) If then you were raised together with Christ, seek the things that are above, where Christ is, seated on the right hand of God. (2) Set your mind on the things that are above, not on the things that are on the earth.

Chapter 4: The Focus of the Early Church

Before I move on to the fourth and final devotion of the early Church listed in Acts 2:42, I want to address a concern that I have heard expressed in some Christian circles, regarding spending extended time in prayer.

Christians are to set their minds on things above, not on earthly things. Many individuals and churches have believed a mix of heavenly and earthly things and the result is some strange ways of thinking. I have heard many say that some people are "so heavenly minded they are no earthly good." This is a lie from the master of lies himself.

The trouble with this statement is that being heavenly minded is not a problem. God created everyone to be heavenly minded and this can result in a lot of good. All believers need to be heavenly minded to bring the Kingdom of God down to earth. If a person is "no earthly good," he is probably not truly heavenly minded.

When followers of Christ are truly heavenly minded, they discover God's intentions for their lives. This allows them to be used by God in ways that would otherwise be impossible. God created people to be instruments of the Holy Spirit. If they are not heavenly minded, this opens a door for satan to manipulate them for his purposes.

It is a problem when people are deceived into thinking that they are heavenly minded when they are not. The greater risk is to be too earthly minded. Keeping that in mind, let's move on to look at the fourth devotion of the early Church.

Prayer

Acts 2:42 says the fourth thing they devoted themselves to was prayer. When the Holy Spirit came, it was while they were in constant prayer, connecting with God. I have attended meetings where the

speakers were people who maintained a consistent prayer life of four to five hours a day. These people carry an amazing anointing.

If people were committed to spending extended time communicating with God, I believe that they would carry a similar ability to impact others. Even one hour of dialogue with God a day makes a difference in how much anointing believers have. It is vital for believers to be devoted to prayer so that they will be connected to God and walk in His power.

I discovered that connecting with God is vital for healthy Christian life. The reason I use the term "connecting with God" is that at one time I used to be part of a ministry that helped recovering drug addicts. When we worked with them we would pray for many hours at a time. After working with this ministry for some time, I realized that I had become mechanical about it, rather than my prayer coming from the heart. I realized that I needed to focus on Christ while praying. This caused me to experience more of Jesus and His power. I believe it is essential to spend quality time with God.

Prayer is necessary to keep Christians' hearts in the right place where God can change their lives. I have found that when I pray with my focus on God that He works on my heart to help me get rid of the things that are in the way of my relationship with Him. When I do this, He lets me know what I need to change in my life and gives me the power to do so.

Moving in God's Power

John 15:5 (WEB) I am the vine. You are the branches. He who remains in me, and I in him, the same bears much fruit, for apart from me you can do nothing.

If Christians connect with God by being devoted to prayer each day, they would see more of God's power working in their lives. In order to become all God created them to be, believers must connect with Him. He is the power source (John 15). He is the vine, we are the branches. A branch that does not have a healthy connection to the vine

Chapter 4: The Focus of the Early Church

will be limited in its fruitfulness. In contrast, a person fully connected with God will make a lasting impact on this world. This is part of the "greater works" that Jesus talked about in John 14:11-12. Those that connect with God will experience increased power on a higher level than in the time of Christ, and they will bring that to others as well.

Spending quality time with God will help believers see more miracles. Sometimes Christians pray for a person who is ill and give up because a five-minute prayer did not bring full manifestation of healing. This is not what God intends.

John G. Lake[2] was a man who lived in Spokane, Washington in the early 1900s. He prayed with people for hours every day until they recovered. Sometimes it would take weeks for healing to manifest, but in the end, the sick received their miracles. Many Christians would see similar results if they would devote more of their lives to prayer and connecting with God.

Prayer can be compared to making Chinese soup. In Hong Kong, they make some of the best soup in the world. In Cantonese cooking, there are two main types, one boils for several hours while the other only cooks for about half an hour. Everyone prefers the three-hour soup. When my ministry team prays with Hong Kong people, we tell them that building a relationship with God is similar to their favorite soup. It is God's heart that believers be transformed, becoming more like Jesus. It is a fact that the more time people spend with Him the more they will see the fragrance of Christ manifest through their lives and experience His refreshing and power working in and through them (2 Corinthians 3:18).

There is a wonderful book, Practicing the Presence of God. It was written centuries ago by a humble believer named Brother Lawrence.

---

[2] For more information about John G. Lake and his ministry, you can read John G. Lake: *The Complete Collection of His Life Teachings* compiled by Roberts Liardon, Tulsa: Albury Publishing. ISBN 1-67778-075-2
-- Or visit the John G. Lake ministry website at www.jglm.org

Church: What Was God Thinking?

He learned to use every moment, no matter what he was doing, in the presence of God communicating with Him in prayer.[3]

In the world today, certain work situations make spending time in prayer difficult. If Christians would be creative and take opportunities to pray during everyday activities like commuting to and from work, taking a shower, or washing the dishes, they would discover that they had more time to be with God. Quality time in the presence of God is powerful, changing lives. 2 Corinthians 3, especially verse 3:18, speaks of how God uses this to transform His children to become more and more like Him, so that His life shines through them.

God desires His people to commit to consistent two-way communication with Him. People often want a "fast food" answer to prayer. It seems that so many people think that giving God a few minutes a day is adequate. This is contrary to the examples in the Bible. For example, Daniel prayed three times a day, and long enough to get caught doing it (Daniel 6:10-11). Also, Paul commanded New Testament believers to pray continually (1 Thessalonians 5:16-18). I believe that in New Testament times, a person who only prayed for half an hour a day would have been considered a backslider! God likes to do a deeper work in people's hearts as they pray and connect with Him.

Each believer should seek to be more like Jesus, making it his or her goal to live wholeheartedly for Him. Their aim should be to spend hours a day connecting with Him and enjoying Him. Even an hour each day of quality prayer time will make a big difference in their experience of His anointing. Any Christian who does this will see spiritual gifts blossom in his life. Often, when a person connects to God in prayer, he will discover gifts he did not know he had. In the following chapter I will talk more about the fruit of having the appropriate focus.

---

[3] Brother Lawrence's book, *Practicing the Presence of God* is available free online at www.practicegodspresence.com/brotherlawrence/index.html -- Accessed 04 August 2011

Chapter 5: Fruit of the Right Focus

There are several issues I want to discuss regarding the fruit of devotion to apostolic teaching, breaking of bread, fellowship, and prayer. Specifically, the early Church had certain supernatural experiences that are not common today. Let us take a look at a few of them.

Signs and Wonders

Mark 16:15-20 (WEB) He said to them, "Go into all the world, and preach the Good News to the whole creation. (16) He who believes and is baptized will be saved; but he who disbelieves will be condemned. (17) These signs will accompany those who believe: in my name they will cast out demons; they will speak with new languages [tongues]; (18) they will take up serpents; and if they drink any deadly thing, it will in no way hurt them; they will lay hands on the sick, and they will recover." (19) So then the Lord, after he had spoken to them, was received up into heaven, and sat down at the right hand of God. (20) They went out, and preached everywhere, the Lord working with them, and confirming the word by the signs that followed. Amen.

Acts 2:43 (WEB) Fear came on every soul, and many wonders and signs were done through the apostles.

Church: What Was God Thinking?

John 14:12 (WEB) Most certainly I tell you, he who believes in me, the works that I do, he will do also; and he will do greater works than these, because I am going to my Father.

If Christians are devoted to what the Bible says they should be, then they will also experience these same signs and wonders. They will lay hands on people and they will be healed. They will cast out demons, multiply food, and raise the dead. This was a normal part of Biblical Christianity and also what Jesus commanded in the Great Commission in Mark 16. Therefore, believers have every reason to be committed to God in the same ways as those in the early Church as recorded in the book of Acts.

I have heard people ask "Why don't we see miracles like what happened in the Bible?" One reason is the amount of time spent on things that do not produce spiritual growth.

Ephesians 2:4-10 (WEB) (4) But God, being rich in mercy, for his great love with which he loved us, (5) even when we were dead through our trespasses, made us alive together with Christ (by grace you have been saved), (6) and raised us up with him, and made us to sit with him in the heavenly places in Christ Jesus, (7) that in the ages to come he might show the exceeding riches of his grace in kindness toward us in Christ Jesus; (8) for by grace you have been saved through faith, and that not of yourselves; it is the gift of God, (9) not of works, that no one would boast. (10) For we are his workmanship, created in Christ Jesus for good works, which God prepared before that we would walk in them.

God is sending out an awesome call for those who want to live one hundred percent for Him. He is saying to come up to Heaven to bring the Kingdom of God down to earth (Ephesians 2:4-10). Are you willing to answer that call? If you are, do not let anyone, anything, or any event in your life talk you out of it. Regardless of the cost or the difficulty, persist in following Jesus. This spiritual adventure is of far greater eternal value than anything that this world could ever offer! Whatever the cost, even if it means dying for the Lord, it is definitely worth it!

Chapter 5: Fruit of the Right Focus

Awareness of the Spiritual World

Acts 27:23 (WEB) For there stood by me this night an angel, belonging to the God whose I am and whom I serve,

Acts 8:26 (WEB) But an angel of the Lord spoke to Philip, saying, "Arise, and go toward the south to the way that goes down from Jerusalem to Gaza. This is a desert road."

Another fruit of focusing on God is angelic visitation. From reading the New Testament, it is apparent that this type of encounter was common among early believers. There are at least ninety-nine verses in the New Testament that mention angels. Paul, Philip, and many others saw and spoke with them. This powerful experience still happens among many today who seek God wholeheartedly.

In the years that I have been a missionary in Hong Kong, I have discovered that people can tune out the realm of the supernatural. Before they become Christians, people here see all kinds of spirits and demons. After believing in Jesus, they are often told that the spirit realm does not exist. Before long, these individuals no longer see angels or demons. This shows that people can shut down on the spiritual world.

John 16:13-14 (WEB) However when he, the Spirit of truth, has come, he will guide you into all truth, for he will not speak from himself; but whatever he hears, he will speak. He will declare to you things that are coming. (14) He will glorify me, for he will take from what is mine, and will declare it to you.

It is God's heart that His people learn to discern what is of Him and what is not. Many adults are frightened of seeing into the supernatural realm and, as a result, have tuned out the spiritual world, angels included. Some of these people are concerned that they will be deceived by satan and end up in error. If believers keep their focus on Jesus, obey Him, spend time connecting with Him and becoming students of the Bible, then the Holy Spirit will help them discern truth from falsehood.

Church: What Was God Thinking?

Sometimes God shows people what He is doing through the appearance of angels. In the summer of 2005, my ministry team attended a church conference about healing. One of the speakers had the gift of seeing angels. When he saw them blowing on a person, he knew God was going to release healing. This allowed him to be aware of what God was doing and invite others to participate by agreeing in prayer for that person to be healed. In sharing this, I do not mean that angels have to be involved in the healing process. God can do anything He wants in whatever way He wants.

In order to experience the Holy Spirit, God's people need to learn about Him first. One of the best ways to learn is through ministries that move in the gifts of the Holy Spirit, including the gifts of healing, miracles, and the prophetic. Of course, such a ministry must have a strong Biblical foundation and each member should be focused on developing strong Scriptural understanding. They have much to teach about God's work.

Discerning Truth from Error

1 John 4:4 (WEB) You are of God, little children, and have overcome them; because greater is he who is in you than he who is in the world.

God wants His people to experience Him. He is the Lord of all creation, material and immaterial. Likewise, humanity has been created to be both physical and spiritual. Jesus promised to lead His children into all truth. At the same time He made people to experience Him and His creation. Many Christians are frightened of the spiritual world because they are afraid of being deceived and as a result live mostly in their fleshly minds. Living by fear rather than by faith results in living in the flesh rather than living by the Spirit (Romans 8:1-4). Those who are teachable and maintain focus on Jesus might make a few mistakes, but the Spirit of God is greater than he that is in the world (1 John 4:4).

I want to emphasize that openness to Godly experiences does not mean throwing out discernment. However, believers must make sure that they use Biblical discernment and not wrong judgments. Many are

Chapter 5: Fruit of the Right Focus

so frightened of anything spiritual that they reject all of it. Such people would do better to seek training from others with experience. Christians need to learn to identify what is from God and what is not. All believers should desire to have everything that God wants to give them.

There are people who are frightened by the power of God. Some of these people claim that the supernatural gifts of the Holy Spirit stopped functioning after the twelve apostles died.[4] If people are afraid of Godly experiences, they will miss out on much of what God has for them in the Kingdom.

Matthew 28:20 (WEB) teaching them to observe all things that I commanded you. Behold, I am with you always, even to the end of the age." Amen.

God has not stopped working among His people. Jesus promised to be with them until the end of the age (Matthew 28:20). Even in the Old Testament, the work of the Holy Spirit can be seen. Before the New Covenant, there were prophets and some received healing miracles. Scripture is clear that God never changes (Hebrews 13:8; James 1:17).

2 Timothy 3:1-5 (WEB) But know this, that in the last days, grievous times will come. (2) For men will be lovers of self, ... (5) holding a form of godliness, but having denied its power. Turn away from these, also.

Christians should want to avoid being counted among those who deny God's power. Paul even said to keep away from such people.

---

[4] Part of this interpretation of Scripture depends on 1 Corinthians 13:10:
- There are people who argue that the "perfect" referred to in 1 Corinthians 13:10 is the Bible. They conclude that the gifts of the Holy Spirit were only for the early Church. (The complete canon of Scripture was accepted in the west in the fourth century A.D.)
- However, since Jesus is the one and only perfect one (Hebrews 4:15, 9:28), and He will return in all His glory at His Second Coming (Matthew 25:31; John 14:2-3; Hebrews 10:35-37), then when He returns this verse will be fulfilled. Therefore, the gifts of the Holy Spirit continue to be available for believers.

Sadly, their unbelief can affect others so that they will not move in the power of God to the extent that He desires.

Compromising the work of the Holy Spirit for the sake of "unity" is a poison. Trying to be in unity with those who deny His power through toning down the work of the Holy Spirit is compromise. It must not be attempted because this is choosing a form of spiritual death and grieves the Holy Spirit (Ephesians 4:30). It can also become an excuse to limit God's work in believer's gatherings. When a church or leader chooses so-called "unity" instead of submitting to the Holy Spirit, they are saying that conforming to lower standards is more important than obeying God. After all, the Holy Spirit is the third member of the Trinity. They should be standing up for God, the most important person in Christian's lives. Instead they choose to compromise, and so make an idol out of unity.

In Review

The early Church was committed to four things: the Apostle's teaching, Fellowship [*koinonia*: participation], Breaking of Bread, and Prayer. Such devotion released the power of God in their community. They experienced God in many ways, including angelic activity and signs and wonders. This is God's pattern for Church. This is what He intended each of us to be dedicated to as the Body of Christ. We will be amazed at what He releases among us when we, as Christians, are devoted to Him in these same ways.

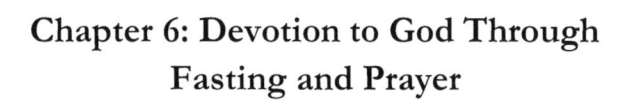

Chapter 6: Devotion to God Through Fasting and Prayer

Spiritual Disciplines

Colossians 3:1-3 (KJV) If ye then be risen with Christ, seek those things which are above, where Christ sitteth on the right hand of God. (2) Set your affection on things above, not on things on the earth. (3) For ye are dead, and your life is hid with Christ in God.

One spiritual discipline largely neglected in the Church today is the practice of fasting and prayer. In this chapter, I would like to share about the importance and benefits of fasting.

Although Paul in Colossians 3:1-3 tells people to set their affections on things above not on things of earth, many find it hard to focus on Jesus. It is common for believers to be passive in their walk with the Lord, being more concerned about materialistic issues than having a deep relationship with Jesus. Too often, Christians allow these concerns to block them from setting their hearts on God.

In various places around the world, when the workday ends, people return home exhausted and needing to take care of their other responsibilities. It seems that this leaves them so tired that all they can do is sit back, play games or watch TV. In the end, there is little energy left except for sleeping. These individuals depend on their weekly church service to survive in God. Without quality time with the Lord, this lifestyle drains the spiritual life out of people.

Regardless, God wants quality relationships with His people. This involves taking specific action. Believers must passionately protect time with the Lord. They should limit or even remove those things in their lives that distract from God. In addition, they need to communicate with Him beyond a daily quiet time.

Acts 6:4 (KJV) But we will give ourselves continually to prayer, and to the ministry of the word.

The early Church was extremely different. They were devoted to prayer. In contrast, many modern Christians are addicted to TV, computers, houses, cars, and materialism. Believers today have so many distractions!

I would like to challenge you to abstain from all distractions for three months. Instead, spend that time praying, studying the Bible, fasting, and gathering with other believers to experience what the Church is supposed to be.

What would the gathering look like? Believers could follow the Scriptural command to confess sins to one another, and pray for each other (James 5:16). Rather than doing this for a few minutes, what if individuals immersed each other in prayer for several hours? During this time, those who speak in tongues could soak others in the Spirit, praying and singing over them. Also, people can both anoint each other with oil and prophesy over one another. In addition, they can sing worship songs that come to mind, especially if it has to do with what is being prayed. These are just a few elements in the 1 Corinthians 14 style New Testament gathering.

Children can be included in meetings too. Sometimes parents do not believe this. However, as long as they are not disruptive, having children in church services is exciting! They are able to enter into the spiritual realm easily. Children quickly learn how to hear God,

Chapter 6: Devotion to God Through Fasting and Prayer

prophesy, lead out in song, and even teach from Scripture. They have much to contribute.

Of course sometimes, such as during confession of sin, it is best to have people take turns caring for the children. Other times even the men and women must meet separately to share struggles or confess sins more freely.

When people cannot attend gatherings, they can practice this with their families. If people do not have this option, then they can spend extended time alone with God, praying in tongues, and waiting on the Lord. If God puts something on their heart, then they can speak, sing, or pray into that. In this way, believers can move deeper in their relationship with God.

Long-term communion with God causes a deep impact on the individual believer and on the Christian community. If people try this, even just for three months, they will see a big difference in their hearts. They discover that in a healthy way they become "addicted to" Jesus and begin moving in the Holy Spirit's anointing. Why stop there? This is only the beginning and it will only get better.

Fasting and Prayer

Matthew 4:2 (KJV) And when he had fasted forty days and forty nights, he was afterward an hungered.

Fasting is an important part of the Christian walk. Jesus set the example by beginning his ministry with an extended fast. Likewise many that move powerfully in the anointing incorporate this in their lifestyle. In addition, Christians that do this are sensitive to the spirit realm. As long as people are physically able, it can be an amazing experience. This practice sharpens believers' sensitivity to the Holy Spirit and Godly spiritual things. These are all good reasons to fast.

Acts 10:30 (WEB) Cornelius said, "Four days ago, I was fasting until this hour, and at the ninth hour, I prayed in my house, and behold, a man stood before me in bright clothing,

Church: What Was God Thinking?

Acts 13:2 (WEB) As they served the Lord and fasted, the Holy Spirit said, "Separate Barnabas and Saul for me, for the work to which I have called them."

Acts 14:23 (WEB) When they had appointed elders for them in every assembly, and had prayed with fasting, they commended them to the Lord, on whom they had believed.

Amazing things happened in the Bible when people fasted. In Acts 10, Cornelius was fasting and praying when he saw an angel. As a result, his entire household came to faith in Jesus and was baptized both in water and in the Holy Spirit. In Acts 13:2, when the believers fasted God gave them a word that Barnabas and Saul should be sent out as missionaries. In Acts 14, there was also fasting and prayer when they appointed elders in leadership. This practice is vital to the Christian life.

Apostles and elders should pray that the Lord will reveal who the leaders should be. If leaders are picked just because they seem capable, then wrong people may become leaders. Moreover, the Lord created time, so He also sees and understands the end from even before the beginning. He knows who the leaders are in God's Kingdom. Besides, He also knows who can handle leadership and who cannot. He is aware that some cannot handle it. Many have weaknesses that do not show up until they experience the stress of being in leadership.

Fasting and prayer helps the apostles and leaders to be more aware of what those weaknesses are so these issues can be dealt with appropriately. Thus, the purpose of this is not to stop people from moving into leadership but to make sure that they are ready and to help them on the way.

In summary, a regular practice of fasting is not only Biblical, but also beneficial to believers, helping them maintain an undivided focus on God. Besides this, it helps in hearing the Lord's voice specifically in the area of making decisions. These are just a few of the many blessings that come from fasting and prayer. I pray that more Christians will discover this in days to come.

Chapter 7: A Prophetic Message for the Modern Church

To become the people God has called His children to be, it is necessary to understand His thoughts about Church. Few places express it as well as Revelation 2-3, commonly known as the "Letters to the Seven Churches."

There are many ideas about the Seven Churches of Revelation. Some view them as historical and literal, speaking of the churches in the specified cities in Asia Minor at the end of the first century. They think that during the first century after Christ, they were in the spiritual situations mentioned by Christ in His Revelation to John. Another historical view is symbolic, that these churches represent different parts of the church age. A final perspective is an end-time view, that they represent different types of churches throughout history and at the end of the age.

Instead of getting lost in the different interpretations, I prefer to focus on the fact that these letters give a clear glimpse of how God views the Church and His heart for His people. Through this perspective, I can move beyond the various theological arguments and the emotion associated with the Seven Letters and focus instead on God's heart for the Church.

The Seven Churches are seven groups of people. Often individuals of a congregation or churches in a geographical area have similar attributes as members of the group grow closer to each other. Generally, individuals will be commended or judged along with the assembly they attend. The overcomers are the exception, because they manage to stay unpolluted in spite of the atmosphere of their churches.

In a future book I plan to share more in depth on the seven churches, but I will summarize here.

Each of the Seven Letters follows a set format. Every letter starts with a revelation of Christ and proceeds to share the situation of the church, both its strengths and weaknesses. Jesus continues with a warning, a charge, or instruction to the church. Then He repeats a message in each letter, "Let him who has ears to hear, hear what the Spirit says to the churches." He concludes with a promise to those who overcome.

So what do these letters say about what God wants for the Church and how He intends it to be? First, God desires His Church to know Him. Second, Christ wants His Church to have the characteristics He values. Third, He desires that His people set aside anything that would pollute their worship of Him, whether individually or corporately. Fourth, God hopes His children will listen to Him and treasure understanding Him. Finally, Jesus promises those who value what He values and persevere regardless of opposition that He will reward their faithfulness. Let us take a brief look at the messages presented in these letters.

What Does God Want His People to Know About Him?

The following are truths about who God is, and how He relates to His people as revealed in the Letters to the Seven Churches: He is the beginning and the end. He rules all creation. There is no one like Him: He is the one true God.

He has ultimate authority over the Church, over the spiritual realm, and over the opportunities given to His people. He died for them and conquered death. He is the passionate God who zealously loves His children and is jealous for their affection.

He truly is the God who will take action on behalf of His people. He provides opportunities for His children that cannot be opposed. He

Chapter 7: A Prophetic Message for the Modern Church

searches hearts and minds and He will repay each person according to their deeds. Finally, He rebukes and disciplines those He loves. Because of who He is and what He has done for all He has created, He has the right to judge. When He speaks of the things He sees and knows, He tells the truth. He does not distort, or exaggerate, nor does He betray Himself or His children.

God's people must grab hold of the truth that the God of all creation who loves them and died for them is the only one who has authority to judge, and that His words to the churches are motivated by love. The feel of these letters then changes from that of messages from an angry God. Rather, they are loving communication from One who has the right to say something. In fact, He must speak up because of His burning, jealous passionate love for all He has created. Understanding who God is helps each believer to relate to Him in a less fearful, yet reverent way. Revelation of Christ is key to being a passionate community of believers who are fully committed to God.

What Does God Like in a Church?

First, the strength, reputation, or financial status of a church is of little importance to God. The letters to Smyrna and Sardis make this clear. Rather, God values relationship, love, faith, and spiritual riches. The things His children do also matter to Him: he commends churches for serving Him, working hard, and doing good deeds. Even so, according to the letter to Thyatira, other churches' actions or situations do not set the standard, but rather the growth and improvement of an individual Christian community.

From these letters, it is apparent that Christ values churches whose members persevere, endure hardship, and do not tire of living Godly lives. In addition to all these things, faithfulness to God and His Word are vital. He commends churches for staying true to Him in suffering and even martyrdom. Those that face internal weakness and external pressure are commended by Him for not denying His name.

Church: What Was God Thinking?

The last three characteristics mentioned in the letters regarding what God likes in a church are perhaps the least politically correct. Christ makes it clear that He values a church that does not compromise. Those that have no toleration for wickedness, false teachers, false prophets, or false apostles receive praise from Him. Likewise, He encourages those that have been able to remain untainted in the midst of less than ideal situations.

Understanding what God values is a part of what it takes to give believers and Christian communities appropriate focus in their lives and ministries. Perhaps equally important is to know what God dislikes among His people.

What Does God Dislike in a Christian Community?

The first type of issue I wish to discuss that is mentioned in the Seven Letters is regarding the things that churches accept. Tolerance is perhaps not so valued by God as it is by many in the modern world. He rebuked several churches for tolerating idolatry, occult activity, sexual immorality, overbearing leaders and false teachers. Christ warned those who held to false teaching, Nicolaitan practices, and impure lifestyles that they would not get away with it.

Perhaps the greatest issue talked about in the Seven Letters is how much God cares about His relationship with His people. This passage of Scripture gives a glimpse of the depth of those feelings. His heart is broken over those who do things for Him but no longer have passionate love for Him. In the letters, His sadness over those who no longer have enthusiasm for Him, or who instead only maintain casual interest in Him is obvious. Some continue in good deeds, but others no longer even continue doing things for Him. It is shocking that in His own Church, He could be left on the outside, knocking on the door asking to be let back in, but the letter to Laodicea shows that this does happen. The result of all of these things is the spiritual sickness suffered by the churches in Sardis and Laodicea. Of Sardis, Christ said they had a reputation of being alive, but were actually spiritually dead.

Chapter 7: A Prophetic Message for the Modern Church

In the same way, Laodicea was in a desperate situation and yet unaware of it. They thought they were rich, but in fact were spiritually destitute.

In order to become all that God created her to be, the modern church must be aware of these things. Moving on, the letters provide instructions to churches that believers today should follow to return to their destiny as the Bride of Christ.

What Instructions Does God Give the Church?

Christ does not rebuke every church mentioned in chapters two and three of Revelation. However, He leaves instructions to all of them. For those facing hardship, He encourages them to not be afraid of future suffering. To the uncompromising in Thyatira, He exhorts them to hold on to what they have until He returns. Similarly, the believers in Philadelphia are instructed to hold on so no one will "take their crown."

For those churches God does rebuke, He also gives a fair amount of instructions. These are essential! They are Christ's prescription to cure various spiritual conditions. In the letters, God instructs believers to wake up, humble themselves, and realize their true situation. He asks them to strengthen themselves in any good characteristic they still have, no matter how weak, so they do not lose that too. When they become aware of their need, they must go to Christ for it. The three things mentioned are spiritual riches, righteousness to cover shame, and healing anointing to restore spiritual sight.

Then Christ encourages believers to remember their past love for Him, what they received from Him, and what they heard. After remembering, they are to repent, return to their early passion for Him, and obey what they have been taught. Finally, and most importantly, each believer and community must open themselves to God's presence, letting Him back in their personal lives and their gatherings. After all, what is the point of a Christian community where Christ is not present?

Let us take a look at what the consequences are for rejecting or following Christ's instructions in the letters.

Church: What Was God Thinking?

What Will God Do About a Church that Fails to Listen?

Believers who understand the consequences of leaving God's protection should want to follow Him always. The cost of disobeying is too great. According to the instructions to the Seven Churches, any church that does not take action regarding their situation will lose their position as a church and will also lose the experiential presence of God. In the words of the letter to Laodicea, they will be "spit out of His mouth." Secondly, they invite the judgment and opposition of God Himself. Lastly, Christ's return will be a surprise to them; they will be completely unprepared for His coming.

After looking at the negative consequences, how about looking at the amazing reward for doing things God's way? Although the promises in the letters are relatively symbolic, believers should keep in mind that as the Creator of the Universe, He can and will give fantastic rewards to those of His children who choose to remain true to Him. In my next book, I will go into more detail about the meaning of the rewards promised to the overcomer. For now, here is an overview.

What Promises Does He Give To The Overcomer?

One type of reward of obeying Christ is for this life. There are several promises given to different churches. The first is a pledge to feast with Him. This is talking about enjoying the presence of God as individuals and as a Christian community. It also refers to being satisfied in one's heart and life through intimacy with God. The second promise, given to the Philadelphian church, is an open door that no one can shut. The third is that even enemies of the church that do not fear God will acknowledge Christ's love for these believers. The final one is a promise many assume will happen automatically for any believer. However, Scripture is clear this promise is for the faithful church, Philadelphia. This reward is protection from the season of difficulty that will be experienced on a global scale.

Chapter 7: A Prophetic Message for the Modern Church

The second type of promise is regarding salvation. God ensures the overcomer that he will not be affected by the "second death," the lake of fire. In addition, their names will never be removed from the Book of Life, and Jesus will acknowledge them before His Father and the angels.

The third type of reward has to do with believers' eternal relationship with Christ. They will receive a crown of life and white garments. These could be literal or symbolic.

Revelation 22:16 (WEB) I, Jesus, have sent my angel to testify these things to you for the assemblies. I am the root and the offspring of David; the Bright and Morning Star."

Perhaps the harder promises to understand are about receiving a new name. The promises related to this include: having Christ's name, God the Father's name, and the name of the New Jerusalem written on them. This has to do with intimacy and ownership. Ownership means that the overcomers have God's seal of His Holy Spirit on them and they belong to Jesus. On a similar note, the hidden manna is defined in John 6:30-35 as referring to Christ, He is also the bright and morning star (Revelation 22:16). Essentially Jesus promises to give of Himself to the victorious Christian.

In Matthew 28, Jesus made a promise to believers to be with them always, even to the end of the age. This is extended in Revelation 2-3. First the overcomer is told he will walk with Christ forever. This speaks of intimacy restored to the level of the Garden of Eden, where God walked with Adam and Eve in the cool of the day. Furthermore, victorious Christians are told that they will be made into pillars in the temple of God and that they will never leave it. Again, this speaks of eternity in the indescribable bliss of God's presence.

The last two promises given to the overcoming Christian are about relationship with God and authority. Believers are presently seated with Christ in heavenly places (Ephesians 2:4-10). This reward will make that position permanent, as Christians receive the right to sit with Him

Church: What Was God Thinking?

on His throne. Finally, God will give them authority over the nations, along with Jesus, to reign with Him.

In summary, the Letters to the Seven Churches give an amazing glimpse into God's heart for the Church and for each and every one of His people. They are messages from a loving Father to His children, in hopes of seeing their relationship with Him become all that it should be. This chapter summarized all seven of the Letters that are found in chapters two and three of the last book in the Bible, Revelation. In my next book, I will discuss them individually with more detailed explanation.

Chapter 8: Priesthood of the Believer

Revelation 1:6 (WEB) and he made us to be a Kingdom, priests to his God and Father; to him be the glory and the dominion forever and ever. Amen.

According to Revelation 1:6, all Christians are priests, having been made a kingdom of priests to God with Jesus as our High Priest (Hebrews 3:1). This is not merely for a few; God has ordained all believers to be His priests (1 Peter 2:9). Many people know this truth in principle, but few understand the full implication in regard to the function of the Church.

The Nicolaitans and the Clergy-Laity System

Church: What Was God Thinking?

Revelation 2:6 (WEB) But this you have, that you hate the works of the Nicolaitans, which I also hate.

The Greek word for "Nicolaitans" is Νικολαΐτης *Nikolaitēs*.
Strong's definition G3531 (pronounced: *nik-ol-ah-ee′-tace*)
From G3532; a Nicolaite, that is, adherent of Nicolaus: - Nicolaitane.

Νικόλαος *Nikolaos*
Strong's definition G3532 (pronounced: *nik-ol′-ah-os*)
From G3534 and G2992; victorious over the people; Nicolaus, a heretic:

νῖκος *nikos*
Strong's definition G3534 (pronounced: *nee′-kos*)
From G3529; a conquest that is, triumph - victory.

λαός *laos*
Strong's definition G2992 (pronounced: *lah-os′*)
People (in general)

    Who are the Nicolaitans? This is a great question, because in Revelation 2:6, God mentions their deeds as something He cannot accept. Christians should pay attention anytime God says He hates something. But what does this mean? Just looking at the passage it seems a little puzzling. However, upon examining it more closely, it is not that hard to understand. Aside from the historical aspect, much can be learned about the Nicolaitans from simply looking at the word. This word is made up of two basic Greek words "*Nikē*" meaning victory or to conquer, and "*Laos*" meaning people or laity. So Nicolaitan means "those who conquer the laity" or "those who conquer the people."

    The sin of the Nicolaitans is not allowing God's children to function in their God-given roles as priests (1 Peter 2:5, 9; Revelation 1:6). Such leaders set themselves above those they claim to serve, feeling that they are the gifted ones and everyone else is too immature or lacking ability to function in their God-given gifts. Even if this is true, these leaders often have little interest in raising other's maturity levels or equipping them to serve. In other words, they want power and control.

Chapter 8: Priesthood of the Believer

In essence, the Nicolaitans say to their people, "You must come to me to be fulfilled in God." Jesus hates this. Many times leaders do not realize that this is what they are doing. Part of the reason for this is that the Nicolaitan leadership style has been handed down through centuries of traditions regarding church leadership.

God hates it when most of His priests are not permitted to become the gifted people that He created them to be. It is imperative that the Church have Biblical New Testament leadership. God created each believer to connect with Him and to be empowered to use their God-given spiritual gifts in ministry.

God did not introduce the clergy-laity system to the church. What I mean is that He did not intend there to be a small number of believers in leadership positions that would take the place of God's people fulfilling their function in the Body of Christ. Leaders are to be fathers, not dictators.

All Believers Are Important

Besides this, believers do not have to go through someone else to communicate with God. Christ's death and resurrection allows each person direct access to God's throne (Hebrews 10:19-22; Hebrews 4:15-16). This is not just for a few that somehow have become "good enough" to connect with God. He intended that the more mature would train the other priests (Ephesians 4:11-16). In this way, leaders step into their appropriate role as older brothers and sisters in the Lord that help and guide others in the Christian life. I am not saying that people no longer need to obey those in authority over them. What I am saying is that leaders have a great responsibility to guide others into the freedom of Christ. The laity have just as much of a right and responsibility to serve God as those already in leadership roles.

As a leader, I know that if I do not prepare others to enter their destinies and God-given roles in the Kingdom, I will face God's judgment. Because of this, I feel it is tragic when leaders do not know what gifts their people have. I have been to many churches full of gifted individuals who simply attend meetings and do little! After a church gathering, they might feel encouraged. They may even feel inspired, but God created them for so much more! The Body of Christ is missing out by not doing Church the Biblical way.

1 Peter 2:5 (WEB) You also, as living stones, are built up as a spiritual house, to be a holy priesthood, to offer up spiritual sacrifices, acceptable to God through Jesus Christ.

Many places in Scripture describe God's intention for the Church. 1 Peter 2, says that Christians are being formed into a spiritual priesthood, and should offer spiritual sacrifices to God. 1 Corinthians 12-14 talks about what these sacrifices are and how to offer them to God. Although other places in Scripture describe the purpose of the Church, these chapters express the heart of Church, concentrating on what believers' gatherings should be like. A look at these passages is helpful in understanding Christians' responsibilities as priests.

1 Corinthians 12:1 (KJV) Now concerning spiritual gifts, brethren, I would not have you ignorant.

In 1 Corinthians 12:1 Paul begins by discussing spiritual gifts. He did not want the church to be ignorant about them because they are a central part of body life, meant to be used and not buried.

1 Corinthians 12:3 (WEB) Therefore I make known to you that no man speaking by God's Spirit says, "Jesus is accursed." No one can say, "Jesus is Lord," but by the Holy Spirit.

Many leaders fear allowing others to minister because they are concerned that what they do might not be the Lord's will. In fact, as long as individuals accept correction and remain teachable, they should be released to function in their gift as soon as possible. As the group moves in the gifts and power of the Holy Spirit, the Lord often gives discernment regarding what people are doing.

For example: if someone comes into a church and begins dominating the meetings every week, I do not believe this is of the

Chapter 8: Priesthood of the Believer

Spirit of God. Such people must be stopped, gently, firmly, and quickly. If they start to do things that are harmful to others in the congregation this is not through the Spirit of the Lord. The gifts of the Holy Spirit are meant to build up the Body of Christ.

The role of apostles and elders is essential as people use the gifts of the Holy Spirit. The leaders especially need to discern what is going on in the gatherings. This does not mean that apostles and elders must say something about every prophecy. In one of my previous church plants, during the meetings, when everyone agreed, sometimes no one would say anything; they would just allow what was happening to continue. Other times, when the leaders did say something, it was to confirm the direction the group was taking, or the prophecy that was spoken. Leadership is there to help protect the use of the gifts and the free work of the Holy Spirit in the assembly.

1 Corinthians 12:4-6 (WEB) Now there are various kinds of gifts, but the same Spirit. (5) There are various kinds of service, and the same Lord. (6) There are various kinds of workings, but the same God, who works all things in all.

In summary, the priesthood of the believer covers more than the widely accepted understanding of it -- that each person can approach God privately as an individual. They also have an important role in the church gathering, helping each other connect with God through the use of various spiritual gifts. Without this, Church is missing a huge part of its primary function and purpose.

Chapter 9: Stages of Spiritual Maturity

1 John 2:13-14 (WEB) I write to you, fathers, because you know him who is from the beginning. I write to you, young men, because you have overcome the evil one. I write to you, little children, because you know the Father. (14) I have written to you, fathers, because you know him who is from the beginning. I have written to you, young men, because you are strong, and the word of God remains in you, and you have overcome the evil one.

Just like the natural stages in human development, there are stages to spiritual growth. The stages of development in natural life provide a good analogy to the process of maturity among believers. Leaders need to understand this so they can guide people and help them grow. This is essential for both leaders and followers. People have different measures of maturity levels. In this chapter, I want to share with you my perspective on the matter.

Hebrews 5:12-14 (WEB) For although by this time you should be teachers, you again need to have someone teach you the rudiments of the first principles of the oracles of God. You have come to need milk, and not solid food. (13) For everyone who lives on milk is not experienced in the word of righteousness, for he is a baby. (14) But solid food is for those who are full grown, who by reason of use have their senses exercised to discern good and evil.

Infancy

In the natural, there are different stages each person must go through to mature. First, everyone begins in the baby stage, needing mom and dad to do almost everything for them. In some ways, this is similar to a new believer, experiencing a fresh beginning. As Paul said in Hebrews 5, spiritual infants need to be fed milk which means that they must familiarize themselves with God's Word and discover how to apply it to their lives. For infants, everything is new, and there is so much to learn. In general, they require pastoral help and nurture to help them grow, learn how to pray, and answer Bible questions that others ask them. This is the beginning of a believer's spiritual development.

Childhood

Next comes childhood. Spiritual children do some things for themselves but there are still many things to learn. In the natural at this stage, parents begin to feel relieved that their children are less dependent on them. They feel joy in watching them mature. This should be the same in the Kingdom of God. Pastors should feel excited about young believers moving into their God-given gifts and ministries.

Young believers make many mistakes at this stage, but this is simply a part of the maturing process. Healthy parents want their children to grow, so they encourage them to learn from their experiences. This is a necessary part of growing up. Leaders have to give people space to learn from their mistakes.

The childhood stage is a time for healing, training, and nourishment. In the natural, since young children catch childhood illnesses easily, they require extra care and healthy nourishment. In the same way, spiritual children need God's healing in their lives. It is the role of those with a pastoral gift to assist Christians in this phase so they can receive healing from past sins and wounds. They also help

Chapter 9: Stages of Spiritual Maturity

these believers receive sustenance from the Word of God. During this stage, Christians begin learning to pray and to study the Bible independently. It is a good time for believers to begin picking up their cross and to carry it every day (Mark 8:34-38). This is an important step for moving on to maturity.

It is of grave importance that everyone be grounded in Scripture as the foundation for their lives. Believers must understand Biblical truth. Each Christian needs to read their Bible regularly and study it as much as possible (Acts 17:11; 2 Timothy 2:15; 2 Timothy 3:16-17). In these last days, believers' understanding, heart knowledge, and practical application of Scripture will help make the difference in their spiritual survival (2 Timothy 3).

Teenagers

After childhood, believers move on to the teenage stage. Spiritual teenagers are mature in some ways and immature in others. This is possibly the hardest phase for parents. Teenagers want to be adults and are able to think like adults at times, but in some ways still think and act like children. In the natural, many parents hold their teenagers back out of fear of what they might do or that they may get hurt. In some cultures, the teenager must wait until leaving home to become responsible and mature, because when they leave they have freedom to make mistakes and learn from them without their parents' constant supervision and interference.

Many in the Body of Christ never get as far as the teenage stage. Instead they become stagnant and resign themselves to mere attendance in a modern traditional church. Some become dissatisfied and complain behind the leader's back. On the other hand, they may become passive spectators because they do not feel they have a choice. Many church leaders do not take them any further because they do not know how. If they have not already done so, apostles, prophets, and elders should help these believers discover their own vision and calling, preparing them to walk in it (Ephesians 4:11-12). Spiritual teenagers should be encouraged to take steps to move into their ministries and spiritual gifts so they can mature in their walk with God. In this stage, a suitable measure of independence along with appropriate oversight aids in spiritual growth. This helps them develop into healthy spiritual adults.

In one of my previous churches, I witnessed a clear example of the benefits of releasing individuals in the teenage stage. There was a group of teenagers among the youth who were considered troublemakers by the leaders. I believe they were not only teenagers in the natural, but in the spirit as well. After high school graduation, one of these young men switched to another congregation for practical ministry training. His new church made him a youth leader, equipped him and gave him opportunities to minister. He changed dramatically as a result, growing in his life and ministry.

There are a lot of semi-mature believers sitting in pews just waiting to find out who they are in the Body of Christ. They have grown as much as possible in their church environment, but they are limited in how much more they can mature as Christians until they are given the freedom to become the person God called them to be, ministering to others. Often they just need to be released to grow in their God-given vision and calling.

In my family, my wife and I believed our teenage children should be given as much freedom as we could appropriately give them while they were still in our home and we still had input into their life decisions. We were by no means perfect, but God's grace has made a huge difference in our relationships. When we became parents, we were very young in the Lord. We did receive some wise counsel and excellent training on how to raise our children Biblically with firm, yet loving discipline and healthy boundaries. They knew there were consequences to their actions. By the time our children were in their mid-teens, since they had earned our trust, we gave them a great deal of freedom. For example, when they were out with their friends and had a change of plans, all they had to do was call us and confirm with us that they were safe and if their change of plans was acceptable. Even

Chapter 9: Stages of Spiritual Maturity

though our kids were not perfect, they earned our trust through their choices.

As a father, I had to learn not to be overbearing. I recognized that by this time my children needed to have a degree of freedom in making decisions. For many years, my wife and I had been equipping and preparing them for this transition to independence. I would give them advice when they asked for it, but I would also gently and lovingly share with them things I felt that they needed to know. As a result, our communication was strong and they felt free to ask for our input.

We also trusted God to watch over our children. My wife and I often prayed that if there were hidden things that should be addressed, God would bring those things to light, and He did. God was faithful to reveal problems so that we could proactively deal with them.

Similarly, each believer must go through the spiritual teenage stage in order to develop a healthy sense of independence, learn how to work well with others, and how to function as mature adults. Everyone has a choice of how they will go through their teenage phase. This stage could last a long time for some and a short time for others.

Young Adults

When a person becomes an adult, they should already know how to live with others and be able to do most things independently. Those few in the modern traditional church who reach spiritual adulthood are often encouraged to teach Sunday School or, if they want to minister, to attend seminary. Many times, they will be placed in ministry in the church, but this ministry will not necessarily coincide with their personal vision. This is a huge mistake and a waste of the mature believer's gifts and potential. This may be one reason that many believers lack motivation in the basic disciplines of the Christian life. Leaders must trust that as they equip their people, God will provide the manpower required for the various ministries of the church.

Spiritual adults have unique characteristics. Before I list them, I feel it is necessary to clarify that this has nothing to do with age. Rather, this is a description of spiritual maturity. They are able to start ministries or churches. They move in the power of the Holy Spirit and humbly live by the Bible's standard. Since they delight in following Christ, they do not require as much correction, although when they do need it they take it well. As Christians become mature, they want to know when they are making mistakes.

This is different from teenagers who, in general, dislike correction and pretend they are perfect. A mature Christian no longer feels the need to pretend. They recognize that even though a strong relationship with God and training in Scripture helps prevent mistakes, that before Heaven no one is perfect and mistakes will happen. They know they must remain accountable to others. In summary, spiritual adults are faithful, transparent, and reliable.

Spiritual Parenthood

The next maturity level is parenthood. Here are some characteristics that will be helpful in recognizing spiritual parents. One difference between adults and parents is how much they can give and how much they will lay down their lives for the people God has put into their care. A young adult might babysit but will not usually love and care for children as much as the parents. As believers grow, they become able to nurture others, imparting blessing into their lives.

Less mature Christians may have already discipled others to some extent, but to some degree their lives are still centered about their own needs. As a person becomes a parent they learn how to appropriately take care of the spiritual needs of the people they are discipling and how to take care of their own needs at the same time. From the time they reach adulthood and become parents, they help younger believers develop their own gifts. Note that a spiritual parent will still go to their own spiritual parents for help with ministry problems. In this stage of maturity, believers move into the mantle of their ministry gifting with increasing maturity and focus.

Chapter 9: Stages of Spiritual Maturity

So how can spiritual parents be recognized? They not only desire to impact their world, they have the ability to do it. Believers who are less mature often feel drawn to them because of their maturity as Christians, learn from their example, and receive help in their maturing process as well. These are some defining characteristics of spiritual parents.

If a church's leaders are not yet spiritual adults, this could cause serious problems. It is essential that leaders have grown into adulthood themselves, and as a result, trust their people to minister. Leaders who have not yet reached this stage are sometimes inclined towards being controlling, preventing everyone else from becoming adults. True maturity means setting aside personal importance or demands for service (Luke 22:25-27).

I want to clarify that everyone should have people in their lives that they minister to, and others that care for them. Leaders do need to feel valued by others. Furthermore, in order to be healthy, young believers must learn to care for others according to their ability. Ministers should teach this. It is God's will that churches develop in such a way that everyone in the congregation ministers to one another and also to their leadership.

Spiritual parents should find their community and support from others in the same stage of maturity. People in the same time of life get along well and love to spend time with each other, accepting one another. I want to give an example of this from the natural world. When my children were younger, my wife and I learned much about rearing children from other parents. We also enjoyed spending time together sharing with them, because we were in the same stage in our lives. This is a sign of healthy parents.

1 Corinthians 4:15 (KJV) For though ye have ten thousand instructors in Christ, yet have ye not many fathers: for in Christ Jesus I have begotten you through the gospel.

God wants all His children to mature into spiritual adulthood. When Paul said in 1 Corinthians 4:15, that there were not many fathers,

Church: What Was God Thinking?

I do not believe he meant that this was or should be normal. God is a good Father, He does not want His people to be stunted in their spiritual growth.

Philippians 2:19-22 (KJV) But I trust in the Lord Jesus to send Timotheus shortly unto you, that I also may be of good comfort, when I know your state. (20) For I have no man likeminded, who will naturally care for your state. (21) For all seek their own, not the things which are Jesus Christ's. (22) But ye know the proof of him, that, as a son with the father, he hath served with me in the gospel.

In the Kingdom, unlike the natural world, a mother or father in Christ can be young (1 Timothy 4:12-16). Timothy was a young man, and yet Scripture describes him as a mature Christian. So much so, in fact, that Paul commended him, saying that he was unlike other believers because he laid his life down for others. Age has little to do with spiritual parenting, rather it is about living a life of sacrifice.

The Church can learn much from spiritual parents. Some fathers and mothers in Christ are changing the world. God is raising up people in this generation who can move strongly in the power of the Holy Spirit, bringing the New Testament back to life, and affecting the whole world. God wants Christians to learn from such people, applying the things they teach. It is essential that every believer has spiritual parents who can teach them not only how to use their gifts but also how to begin in ministry.

Some fathers and mothers in Christ work in the background. They do not stand up in front of a big church every Sunday. It is possible that the only people who know them are those they have helped by ministering to them in the background. On the other hand, their spiritual children may become visible in the church, depending on their gifts. Regardless, those in the parenting stage do not have to become famous.

Chapter 9: Stages of Spiritual Maturity

Spiritual Grandparenthood

The final level of maturity is the grandparent. Paul was in this category, and Timothy might have been as well. All believers should hope to reach this stage. Spiritual grandparents have raised spiritual children to maturity, and their children are now spiritual parents themselves. Such people have so much that they can teach and impart to the Body of Christ. They have great depth in their relationship with God and much experience. Besides this, they are an incredible encouragement to most everyone they meet.

Spiritual grandparents have much wisdom to share with those less mature than themselves. They have gone through different struggles and experienced so many victories over temptation, sin, trials, and challenges. They have overcome and are now living in their destinies. God has used them in so many ways, such as divine healing, casting out demons, and signs and wonders.

Their lives are full of adventures with God. As a result, they can encourage those younger in the Lord through their great stories and the many lessons they have learned about the Kingdom of God. These insights are essential to the young believer's spiritual growth. May the world be filled with Christians who reach this maturity level!

How to Become a Mature Christian

James 1:22 (WEB) But be doers of the word, and not only hearers, deluding your own selves.

So what can be done to reach maturity? Often Christians want to grow up in a short time. They may not want to pay the price necessary to arrive at maturity. Growing in God is a process and only He knows how long it will take. Of course, there are some things that those who want to mature more quickly can do. For example, they can devote themselves to prayer, fasting, Bible study, and obedience to God and His Word.

Church: What Was God Thinking?

Many in the Church are "hearers" of the Word but not "doers" of the Word. It is so strange to me that these same people wonder why their lives bear little similarity to believers from New Testament times. People must realize spiritual maturity does not just happen and it cannot be imparted, they have to take action to reach it.

In summary, the stages of spiritual maturity parallel the natural realm. A believer begins in spiritual infancy, passes through childhood, becomes a teenager, and then an adult. The adult can mature to become a spiritual parent and eventually a grandparent. Each of these stages are significant and cannot be skipped, but diligent pursuit of God can speed the maturing process.

Chapter 10: One Body, One Spirit

In this chapter, I would like to discuss more about the purpose and function of the Church. 1 Corinthians gives Christians specific instructions regarding the gathering of believers. This will be helpful in discovering God's purpose for Church.

Some people have told me that the Corinthian church is a bad example to use in this type of discussion because the believers in Corinth had so many issues with sin. Actually, I appreciate this church. If they had not made so many mistakes Paul would not have needed to write this letter. Without 1 Corinthians, believers would have much less information regarding God's intention for His Church. So, without further delay, let us see what the Apostle Paul had to say.

1 Corinthians 12:12-13 (WEB) For as the body is one, and has many members, and all the members of the body, being many, are one body; so also is Christ. (13) For in one Spirit we were all baptized into one body, whether Jews or Greeks, whether bond or free; and were all given to drink into one Spirit.

In 1 Corinthians 12, Paul begins by describing the Church as a human body. He states that just as each part of our physical body is essential, so each person has an important role in the assembly. The

Church: What Was God Thinking?

His children to become spiritual "couch potatoes." Instead, it is His plan that when Christians gather, they should *all* use the gifts that God has given them. Every one of these gifts is important. God intends all believers to actively function in His Body.

1 Corinthians 12:18-24 (WEB) But now God has set the members, each one of them, in the body, just as he desired. (19) If they were all one member, where would the body be? (20) But now they are many members, but one body. (21) The eye can't tell the hand, "I have no need for you," or again the head to the feet, "I have no need for you." (22) No, much rather, those members of the body which seem to be weaker are necessary. (23) Those parts of the body which we think to be less honorable, on those we bestow more abundant honor; and our unpresentable parts have more abundant propriety; (24) whereas our presentable parts have no such need. But God composed the body together, giving more abundant honor to the inferior part,

Each individual is essential. Even people who consider themselves insignificant are indispensable in the Kingdom of God. No one is without a significant role in God's family. This is God's intention for His Church.

In the traditional church today, however, those with a seminary degree are often considered most important. Somehow people have come to consider intellectual intelligence and a degree as necessary to ensure their leadership has a special relationship with God. That is ridiculous! Four years of school do not, in itself, give anyone a relationship with God. It does not even guarantee that someone has the gift of teaching, let alone a pastoral gift. One of the biggest problems with the Church today is that many leaders are moving outside of their gifting. This is like a foot trying to be a hand, or a hand trying to be a mouth. It does not work well.

For example, some evangelists try to be the main minister in a congregation and for some reason they try to make everybody else be evangelists too. When some teachers are in charge, they try to make everyone students that simply sit and acquire intellectual knowledge. Paul said that Church is not intended to be a venue for only one gift. It is not one big ear that only listens to teaching, one big foot that only

Chapter 10: One Body, One Spirit

goes out to preach the Gospel or one big mouth that only prophesies. It is the Body of Christ, and it is not meant to function without most of its parts.

1 Corinthians 12:25-26 (WEB) that there should be no division in the body, but that the members should have the same care for one another. (26) When one member suffers, all the members suffer with it. Or when one member is honored, all the members rejoice with it.

God has placed each member of the Body of Christ together to care for one another. Christians desperately need each other. In the same way, the gifts of all who love the Lord and are brought into church gatherings are essential for everyone to be encouraged and equipped in the way God intended. What the Body does not need is members that dominate, are unwilling to submit to God, or have an uncaring attitude towards sin.

Love, the Most Excellent Way

The following chapter, 1 Corinthians 13, talks about love. I believe that Paul put the love chapter in the middle of two sections about spiritual gifts because it is the heart of the Church. If the gifts are not used in love, they can destroy people.

I want to tell a story to illustrate this. One time I was repairing a roof. I had just eaten lunch and was sleepy. In order to do the job, I needed to remove the protective guard on the saw blade and when I accidentally hit the switch there was trouble. The saw did not know the difference between the roof and my fingers. I cut them badly enough that I had to go to the emergency room and get stitches. This is what the gifts can do without the protection and guidance of love.

The gifts of the Holy Spirit are like power tools, if they are handled correctly, much can be accomplished in a short time. On the other hand, spiritual tools used wrongly may send the one with the gift or those receiving ministry to the spiritual emergency room. This is why the Church needs leaders to facilitate and monitor the use of the

Church: What Was God Thinking?

gifts. In addition, if believers view each other as being in the learning process, then they can give each other love and grace. This helps minimize the damage caused by mistakes. Love covers a multitude of faults (1 Peter 4:8).

In summary, the Church is like a human body, or like an orchestra. Each member has a part and is important. When the Church is allowed to function properly, it is exciting and powerful. However, love is needed as a safeguard to ensure that everyone is blessed as a result.

Chapter 11: Love in Ministry

John 13:34-35 (WEB) A new commandment I give to you, that you love one another, just like I have loved you; that you also love one another. (35) By this everyone will know that you are my disciples, if you have love for one another."

Love is the essential ingredient for a healthy church. Power without love does not help anyone. In contrast, when the power of the Holy Spirit is mixed with Godly love towards others, the result is dynamic. In this chapter, I want to explore this concept further.

1 Corinthians 13:1 (WEB) If I speak with the languages [tongues] of men and of angels, but don't have love, I have become sounding brass, or a clanging cymbal.

Spiritual gifts without love are pointless. 1 Corinthians 13:1 is an analogy, comparing the use of tongues without love to a noisy gong or cymbal. The first time I saw a Chinese funeral, with crowds of people wailing while banging gongs and cymbals, gave me a clearer understanding of this Scripture. The funeral was so noisy! The combination was intense, chaotic, and unpleasant.

Similarly, when anyone uses spiritual gifts in an uncaring or unloving way, it can make others uncomfortable. It is not surprising that there are people who afterwards want nothing more to do with that particular gift. Of course, offense is not always a sign that a gift is not being used in love. Depending on theology, background, or wounding, people might be offended, even with love. At the same time, love helps minimize the potential problems that arise out of ministry.

1 Corinthians 13:2-3 (WEB) if I have the gift of prophecy, and know all mysteries and all knowledge; and if I have all faith, so as to remove mountains, but don't have love, I am nothing. (3) If I dole out all my goods to feed the poor, and if I give my body to be burned, but don't have love, it profits me nothing.

It is incredible to me that anyone could move in the gifts and power of God, doing wonderful things, and not have love. However, Scripture says it is possible. Sadly, people can move mountains, preach wonderful sermons, give amazing prophecies, and yet destroy people because of lack of love.

Romans 11:29 (WEB) For the gifts and the calling of God are irrevocable.

Believers who do not have love in their lives can still move in the gifts. This is because God does not take supernatural abilities away from His people (Romans 11:29). This promise demonstrates His faithfulness. It also shows that moving in the gifts and the power of the Holy Spirit is not an indicator of a deep relationship with God. Love, not power, is the sign of intimacy with God.

What is Love?

The Greek word for "love" is ἀγάπη *agapē*.
Strong's definition G26 (pronounced: *ag-ah'-pay*)
From G25; love, that is, affection or benevolence;
specifically (plural) a love feast: - (feast of) charity

Godly love goes far beyond warm fuzzy feelings for others. Love is both an action word and mankind's greatest need. It is also a free gift.

Chapter 11: Love in Ministry

In the New Testament, they called church meetings "love feasts." There is no question that love is vital to the Church.

Love is one of humanity's greatest needs. Most people are desperate for it. Wounding blocks out the ability to feel or receive love, causing some people to deny or subconsciously shut down their desire for it. The work of the Holy Spirit brings God's love to people's lives. Through the gathering of believers, He enables everyone to love and care for each other. Christian community is a central part of God's strategy to restore true love in this broken world.

1 John 4:8 (WEB) he who doesn't love doesn't know God, for God is love.

1 Corinthians 13:4-7 (WEB) Love is patient and is kind; love doesn't envy. Love doesn't brag, is not proud, (5) doesn't behave itself inappropriately, doesn't seek its own way, is not provoked, takes no account of evil; (6) doesn't rejoice in unrighteousness, but rejoices with the truth; (7) bears all things, believes all things, hopes all things, endures all things.

Lack of love is the fruit of a very serious problem. 1 Corinthians 13:1 says that if someone does not love, he is nothing. 1 John 4:8 says that anyone who does not love does not know God. In contrast, when the Holy Spirit is active in a person, love as described in 1 Corinthians 13:4-7 will become his lifestyle. *Agape* love is evidence of intimacy with God.

All mankind needs God's love. At the same time, in the world, the enemy has twisted the idea of love to something self-centered. People think they need to look out for "number one," and then they reap what they sow, resulting in everyone becoming increasingly selfish. In contrast, those who sow God's love, reap His love in return, providing the opportunity for more and more people to experience love.

Loving others unconditionally begins with the individual (1 John 3:1-3). People should love first and not worry about whether or not everyone else responds in kind. Besides this, they must understand that different people have different love needs. Each person should aim to get to know better the others in their gatherings in order to be able to love them in the way they can receive. For example, one of the ladies in my fellowship feels loved when others spend time in prayer with her. Another person likes to be hugged. I feel loved when people take time to talk with me. As each person considers others' needs and gives accordingly, the whole group can experience love.

1 Corinthians 13:8-10 (WEB) Love never fails. But where there are prophecies, they will be done away with. Where there are various languages [tongues], they will cease. Where there is knowledge, it will be done away with. (9) For we know in part, and we prophesy in part; (10) but when that which is complete has come, then that which is partial will be done away with.

Since God's love is infinite and eternal, each person should focus on strengthening their relationship with Him and being filled with His love. Anyone who thinks otherwise has been tricked by the enemy and needs healing. When Jesus returns and His people see Him face to face, they will no longer need the spiritual gifts (1 John 3:1-3). In contrast, God's love will always continue. So, since the gifts are temporary, but love is forever, love should be each person's highest aim.

Growing in God's Love

1 Corinthians 13:11 (WEB) When I was a child, I spoke as a child, I felt as a child, I thought as a child. Now that I have become a man, I have put away childish things.

Every believer must give up childish ways, grow up, and learn to love the way Jesus does. A child always wants things his own way, and may pout if things do not happen in the way he wants. In contrast, spiritual adults have learned how to care for themselves and others at the same time. They have figured out how to do this without neglecting their own needs or the needs of their family. As spiritual and natural children mature, adults then have more time to look after the church and to spend with people they want to love to Christ. Being able to love the way that God wants us to love is a sign of maturity.

Chapter 11: Love in Ministry

1 Corinthians 13:12 (WEB) For now we see in a mirror, dimly, but then face to face. Now I know in part, but then I will know fully, even as I was also fully known.

Scripture is clear that nobody knows everything God has for His children (1 Corinthians 2:9). During Bible times, the analogy of a mirror was easily understood. Mirrors were nothing like they are today, reflecting a fuzzy image, not a clear picture. This describes people's view of spiritual things. Believers only see a part of what God has for them. In this way, faith is directly connected with love.

In prophecy, God often tells only a little bit of the future He has prepared. Sometimes, He wants Christians to ask Him for more. There are other secrets God will wait to reveal until Heaven. Since the gifts are temporary, and at best what can be seen is only an incomplete picture, believers must cling to the things that are eternal (2 Corinthians 4:18).

1 Corinthians 13:13 (WEB) But now faith, hope, and love remain -- these three. The greatest of these is love.

In summary, love is most important. Unlike the gifts which are temporary, faith, hope, and love are eternal. They are gems that Christians can hold onto now and throughout eternity. The gifts of the Spirit are only power tools to be used while here on earth. The most important part of life is the love shown to God and others.

Chapter 12: Leadership in the *Ekklesia*

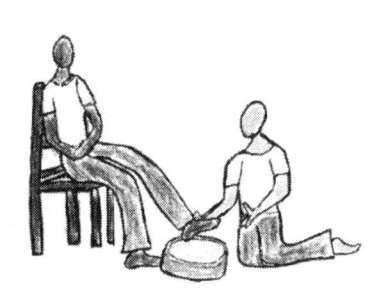

Matthew 20:25-28 (WEB) But Jesus summoned them, and said, "You know that the rulers of the nations lord it over them, and their great ones exercise authority over them. (26) It shall not be so among you, but whoever desires to become great among you shall be your servant. (27) Whoever desires to be first among you shall be your bondservant, (28) even as the Son of Man came not to be served, but to serve, and to give his life as a ransom for many."

Minister

The Greek word for "minister" is ὑπηρέτης *hupēretēs*.
Strong's definition G5257 (pronounced: *hoop-ay-ret'-ace*)
From G5259 and a derivative of *eresso* (to row); an under oarsman, that is, (genitive case) subordinate (assistant, sexton, constable): - minister, officer, servant.

When discussing Church, it is necessary to talk about leadership. In Matthew 20, Jesus Christ, who is our example, defines the type of leaders He wants in the Church.

The Bible says that Jesus is the Good Shepherd (John 10). Looking at His life, people can see what that is. Jesus laid down His life for His sheep. This is not only referring to the cross. He lived his life giving to others.

Although many do not understand how someone can be a leader and a servant at the same time, Jesus is our example of how to do this.

Church: What Was God Thinking?

When someone is called to be a minister, like Jesus, he must lay down his life for others. He should be committed to equipping and facilitating others to grow in the Lord and in their gifts, helping them develop intimacy with the Good Shepherd.

Ministers need to also be committed to helping set people free from bondage in their lives (Isaiah 61:1-4; Luke 4:18). They must have a heart to see others fulfill the vision that God has given them (Ephesians 2:10; 4:15-16).

What a Servant-Leader Is Not

When people hear about servant-leadership many times they hear the word "servant" but not the word "leader." At one time I was in a church that tried their best to incorporate the concept of servant-leadership, however, many thought the leaders should do whatever the people wanted. This is just as much in error as the other extreme where leadership does not try to equip and release their people.

Jesus said that He was a servant but I do not see the disciples trying to tell Him how to serve them. Jesus spent His life helping people by bringing the "Kingdom of God" to earth and training those that believed in Him to do the same. Then Jesus taught those that followed Him to do as He did, equipping people who, in turn, will train others (Matthew 28:18-20; 2 Timothy 2:2).

1 Corinthians 11:1 (WEB) Be imitators of me, even as I also am of Christ.

I want to make it clear that I am not talking about a church that has no leadership. Rather, God is calling his whole Church to return to Biblical Christianity. He is calling ministers to lead with His heart (1 Corinthians 11:1). This is not to condemn anyone because many have a calling and vision to follow God with their whole lives. My hope is that they will have a heart to see individual believers impact the Church so that it becomes like yeast that reproduces throughout the whole lump of dough, the world (Luke 13:20-21).

Chapter 12: Leadership in the *Ekklesia*

How a Leader Should Serve

1 Thessalonians 5:14 (WEB) We exhort you, brothers, admonish the disorderly, encourage the fainthearted, support the weak, be patient toward all.

Hebrews 10:24 (WEB) Let us consider how to provoke one another to love and good works,

Leaders are meant to be facilitators. However, they should not become like a god to others by dominating their lives, controlling them, or trying to dictate their destiny. Leaders must never try to usurp God's authority.

God's leadership style is so different. He is not controlling or domineering. Not only this, but He is the only One who truly knows and understands the destiny of everyone He's created, yet He allows people to choose whether they will follow Him and live out their calling.

There are times when a leader needs to help people deal with sin and weakness in their lives, and aid them in setting healthy boundaries (1 Thessalonians 5:14). When this is done appropriately and with a heart to help them grow, I view this to be entirely different from ungodly control. It is true that believers are commanded to stir each other up to love and good deeds (Hebrews 10:24), but this must be done without manipulation or control. The leader's main job is to equip and release others into their calling, to help them become everything they were created to be, so that they can fulfill their destiny.

One of the jobs of a servant-leader is to learn how to set the captives free and facilitate others in that same ministry. Most people are held back by their past. If a leader help believers get rid of their excess baggage, they will be much stronger disciples. Most Christians cannot enter into their destiny until they receive healing from God. Helping others in the healing process can be a difficult ministry, but for those gifted and called to serve in this way, it is very rewarding. There is no joy compared to watching God transform someone's life! I will discuss the leader's responsibility further in later chapters.

How Servant-Leaders Lead

Servant-leaders should receive input. However, their openness is not an excuse for anarchy. Godly leaders make decisions by listening to others, hearing from God, and sensing what is best. They think of individuals in their group, wanting to help each person to be the best they can be. The leader is in the position of facilitating, coordinating, and final decision-making all with loving authority.

Even if a leader is somewhat in the background, people still know that he is their leader. I have heard different pastors say, "If we are not telling others what to do, no one will know we are leaders." I believe the opposite is true. Leaders are called to be fathers or mothers in Christ to those they serve. A good father will be recognized as a leader by his spiritual children without advertising his position or overusing his authority.

I have also heard others say that if someone is not a take-charge type of leader, he will run out of work. In truth, for a servant-leader, this is just not possible. He might minister in a different way than before, but there will be plenty of work for all in the Kingdom until everyone on earth is saved, equipped in their spiritual gifts, and prepared to fulfill the calling God has for them. There will always be people that need equipping for ministry.

Many times leaders get in the way of others using their gifts, especially in some traditional modern churches. This creates an imbalance in the congregation. To compensate for the many who have little or no opportunity to use their gifts, the full-time minister often fills the vacuum, doing almost everything that needs to be done. He becomes the main visionary of the church. He teaches, counsels, handles administration and visitation. The worship leader picks all the songs. The evangelists are among the few allowed to use their gifts

Chapter 12: Leadership in the *Ekklesia*

because their ministry will help fill the pews. This is another reason for lack of spiritual maturity in the Church today.

The Follower's Responsibility

1 Corinthians 16:15-16 (WEB) Now I beg you, brothers (you know the house of Stephanas, that it is the first fruits of Achaia, and that they have set themselves to serve the saints), (16) that you also be in subjection to such, and to everyone who helps in the work and labors.

Hebrews 13:17 (WEB) Obey your leaders and submit to them, for they watch on behalf of your souls, as those who will give account, that they may do this with joy, and not with groaning, for that would be unprofitable for you.

In this chapter I talked about a leader's responsibility to the Church as a servant. However, followers do have responsibilities as well.

2 Timothy 2:2 (WEB) The things which you have heard from me among many witnesses, commit the same to faithful men, who will be able to teach others also.

Submission to authority is vital to the Church. I feel that I need to stress this. Regardless of personal issues, people must follow Scripture and submit to their leaders. Just because the leadership in a church is open to the model in this book, it does not mean that everyone can do whatever they want. Those in authority need to consider whether their people are obedient and faithful in using their gifts before they are released into ministry.

The follower's responsibility is not changed by the concept of servant-leadership. A believer chooses what congregation he wishes to attend and who he will follow. Regardless of any difference of opinion or belief, once leaders are chosen they must be obeyed. If, after getting to know his leaders, a person feels he can no longer submit to them and has tried to work the issue out without any result, it may be best for everyone if that person looks for a church and ministers that he can respect in the right way.

Before I go much further, I do need to clarify. People can have the right heart, and be in submission, and yet still appeal to those in authority. Sometimes something is important to a person and when the leader made a decision, they overlooked that for some reason. It is possible they did not think it through or see all sides of the issue. When a follower respectfully expresses disagreement he provides an opportunity for the leader to consider the matter in a different way. Regardless of whether or not the leader accepts it, however, the follower needs to honor the leader's decision.

Some might ask: what should a person do if he does not agree with his leaders? This will likely happen sometime. I have dealt with this issue in almost every church I have attended.

For so many years, I have longed to see a church like the one I talk about in this book. This is one of the biggest reasons I have not been in full agreement with those churches but that did not stop me from submitting to their leadership. So I did my best to avoid causing trouble. I did not want to disrupt other people's work.

After believing in Jesus for about twenty years, God finally released me to begin new churches. Since then, I have been part of several church planting teams and sometimes in leadership. God taught me so much in the process and told me to share what I have learned by writing this book.

A person may disagree with their leadership out of brokenness and need for healing in their lives. This can distort the way people perceive and process life and prevent them from trusting others, especially leaders. If anyone reading this book has a lot of hurt and they know it, they should seek a place where they can receive healing. For those attending a church with this type of ministry, they should treasure the opportunity to pursue wholeness.

Another reason people might find it difficult to be in agreement with their leaders is difference of vision. For those attending a church that expects the members to follow its vision, they should be on guard

Chapter 12: Leadership in the *Ekklesia*

against bad attitudes. Instead, they must pray for their leaders and their own hearts. It is possible that God will change the situation in the church, give them the grace they need to stay, or move them elsewhere.

It is true that no leadership is perfect. At the same time, those who know that they cannot submit to a leader should also be aware that, Scripturally, they are not locked in to attending a particular congregation. On the other hand, those who are continually moving from church to church must examine themselves just in case the problem is with them, not with their leaders.

In some situations God tells people to stay where they are, and I am not referring to that. However, if someone chooses a Christian community, regardless of the reason, then the Bible says they need to submit to their leaders, listen to them, and respect their authority.

I am not saying that followers must be passive. The saying, "Children must be seen, and not heard," does not apply to God's children. At appropriate times it might be good for members of a congregation to privately tell their leaders respectfully that they disagree with them and why. This could make a difference with the way things are done at their church.

For those full of vision, there may be a time when God releases such people to start a new work, become part of a church planting team, or follow their calling in other ways. Of course, they must seek the Lord to confirm that it is really His will before they do this. Those who do end up starting new churches should be prepared to learn many things. They will likely understand their leaders better as a result! For me it has been the best part of my life but also the most challenging.

2 Corinthians 2:9 (WEB) For to this end I also wrote, that I might know the proof of you, whether you are obedient in all things.

2 Corinthians 2:9 gives a unique perspective on authority in the Church. The word obedient here is an interesting word in the Greek. It means attentive listening that proves itself in obedience (*Strong's Exhaustive Concordance of the Bible*, definition G5255). This is like when a

parent has told his children to do something and they have not done it. As a result, he turns to them, and says, "Are you listening to me?" The proof of their listening is in whether or not they respond by doing what they are told.

People need to submit to their fathers and mothers in Christ, especially when a word of correction is spoken. It is also vital, however, that spiritual parents do not discipline others over things that are neither significant nor sinful.

In summary, a Biblical leader is meant to be a servant who prepares God's people to fulfill their destinies. Ministers are not given the position for personal gain. They are also not meant to take over the believer's role in Church or to control others. Instead they are to facilitate others to participate according to their spiritual gifts, helping each person reach their full potential.

I will discuss leadership's role in equipping further in the following chapter.

Chapter 13: Identifying Spiritual Gifts

Discovering spiritual gifts is the first step in the equipping process. Before discussing how to do this, I feel it is necessary to point out the reasons why this is so important. In previous chapters, I have mentioned that fellowship involves each person contributing to time spent together, through the use of the gifts for mutual encouragement. In addition, people that minister with their gifts tend to have greater fire for God and more opportunities to grow than those who do not. Doing this helps prevent burnout. Scripture is very clear that the use of spiritual gifts is an essential element of Biblical Church.

It is imperative that ministers educate others on the five-fold ministry and other spiritual gifts. This will help individuals and leaders understand each other. In order to have appropriate expectations, members of a congregation need to recognize their ministers' gifting. This will help believers identify their leaders' ministry focus and how they are called to equip.

Ministry Burnout

Before I talk about how a leader can help his people discover their spiritual gifts, I want to share more regarding the risk of burnout in ministry.

It is essential for people to know and understand what their ministry giftings and callings are. Those who desire spiritual gifts must be careful not to mistakenly think they have a particular gift; this can result in striving. I have seen some people who are strong in one particular area and yet they insist they are gifted in another.

One example is a person called to be an apostle who is trying to be a traditional pastor of a church instead of raising up a leadership team. Another is a prophet who thinks he is a pastor. If such a person is put in charge of a congregation, and begins trying to equip everyone he can run into problems because he does not have the necessary gift to manage the situation. He will soon discover that he does not have the anointing to be a pastor.

If this prophet persists in pastoral ministry, he could easily burn out trying to raise young Christians into maturity unless God gives him special grace to function pastorally. One reason for this is the prophetic personality tends to be very strong and straightforward. Many times young believers need someone who is gentle and nurturing to care for them and help them get moving in the right direction.

One way to provide balance is to have a leadership team working with the full-time minister. Each member of this team needs to have at least one of the five-fold ministry gifts. All of the equipping gifts should be represented in the group; each person needs to be able to freely function in their gifts. They must listen to each other and so help keep one another in balance.

Trying to move in another's gifting is like plugging a power tool into the wrong voltage. A person who does this might not be able to function properly. In contrast, when someone operates his own gift, he will have what it takes to use that gift. The anointing will be on him to do the work God has called him to do.

Chapter 13: Identifying Spiritual Gifts

When I moved back to Hong Kong from the U.S.A. in 1994, I brought a printer with me. The electric current in North America is different from Hong Kong. In the U.S. it is 110 volts, and in Hong Kong it is 220 volts. One time, I was helping with a computer club and was talking rather than paying attention to what I was doing. I plugged my printer into the Hong Kong current instead of the converter that I had bought and in two seconds it was completely ruined. The Lord showed me that the printer was like ministry. Many people try to operate in a ministry that is not their gifting. They may not burn out as quickly as my printer did, but it could happen sooner or later.

It must be recognized, however, that moving in gifts one does not have is not the only reason for burn out. There are other factors that cause problems, even when using the gifts God has given. Other possible contributing causes include not getting enough rest, not spending enough time with God, spiritual warfare (including a spirit of witchcraft coming against the person), unforgiveness, judging others, becoming arrogant or prideful, or even being disobedient to God.

Besides this, being forced to use gifts one does not have, or being put down for walking in one's gifting, even if it is used correctly, feeling pressured to limit use of a gift, or being harshly criticized for making mistakes, can be contributing factors. Timing is also an issue: getting ahead of God's plan is a cause of burnout. Understanding one's gift and calling and receiving ministry from others helps prevent or treat ministry burnout.

Another major cause of burnout that is common is that of carrying the emotion, anxiety, and responsibility for various ministry situations. Having an intercessory prayer team is helpful in dealing with this. In addition, ministers need a lifestyle of prayer that includes habitually and continually casting their cares on God (Philippians 4:4-8, 1 Peter 5:7).

People need to learn the truth that Christ's yoke is easy and His burden is light, as long as they maintain gentleness and humility (Matthew 11:28-30). They also need to follow Jesus' example by only doing what they see the Father doing instead of trying to fix every problem and responding to every need in sight (John 5:19-20).

Jackie Pullinger, a missionary in Hong Kong that my family has previously worked with, once said to me that if people are getting upset about what is happening in ministry, they need to change their perspective and look at the long-term picture, not the short-term results.

I have found that feelings of frustration, disappointment, and heartbreak happen in ministry. At the same time, God sees the seeds that have been planted, and He alone knows if, when, and how they will bear fruit. Different individuals will produce fruit in different types and amounts depending on the state of their own hearts (Matthew 13:18-30); people make their own choices. Holding to these truths is helpful in preventing being weighed down by difficult ministry situations and disappointing results.

Regular healing prayer sessions are essential for anyone involved in ministry, to help prevent burnout. I know of some churches that require their leaders to receive one full week of inner healing prayer every year. Although serving people can be rewarding, it can also be stressful and difficult. Those who are always pouring out their lives to others also must have time when they receive.

Now that I have looked at a few reasons why a leader should help his people discover their gifts, including the risk of burnout, I would like to give a few tips about how to do this. In addition, I wish to talk about certain methods that are commonly used, although less successful or accurate.

Ways to Identify Spiritual Gifts

A good leader takes responsibility to know his own gift and help his people discover their gifts. After this, the leader must train them in how to operate in spiritual gifts. This is the foundation for the rest of the equipping process. So how can he do this? Perhaps first I should mention one common, but relatively ineffective way to try to discover a person's gift.

Chapter 13: Identifying Spiritual Gifts

1 Corinthians 2:9-14 (WEB) But as it is written, "Things which an eye didn't see, and an ear didn't hear, which didn't enter into the heart of man, these God has prepared for those who love Him." (10) But to us, God revealed them through the Spirit. For the Spirit searches all things, yes, the deep things of God. (11) For who among men knows the things of a man, except the spirit of the man, which is in him? Even so, no one knows the things of God, except God's Spirit. (12) But we received, not the spirit of the world, but the Spirit which is from God, that we might know the things that were freely given to us by God. (13) Which things also we speak, not in words which man's wisdom teaches, but which the Holy Spirit teaches, comparing spiritual things with spiritual things. (14) Now the natural man doesn't receive the things of God's Spirit, for they are foolishness to him, and he can't know them, because they are spiritually discerned.

It is imperative for believers to not look to motivational gift surveys to discover their spiritual gifts. Sometimes people take these tests and end up trying to move in gifts that are not theirs. People should not use the natural mind to try to figure out their own or others' spiritual gifts.

Gifts are given by the Holy Spirit. At the same time, individuals do have natural abilities from God. When I talk about the gifts, however, I am not referring to these inborn talents. Rather, I mean spiritual gifts that a believer receives supernaturally, usually some time after accepting Jesus and being filled with the Spirit.

Sometimes these spiritual gifts show up in a person's life without outside prayer for impartation. Other times, they manifest when an apostle or a prophet calls them forth prophetically. I have taken motivational gift surveys and they did not accurately portray my spiritual gifting. Not only that, having taken them more than once, I got different results according to my circumstances. These tests are subjective and are dependent on natural human insight. Some of these surveys have said the opposite of what God, through prophets, had said to me. Because of this, I believe that people need to hear God for this area of their lives.

When Moses was called by God, he thought his personality was the very opposite of what God was asking him to be. Moses said that he was not even a good speaker because he felt clumsy when talking. Yet God sent him to a ruler and used Moses in a way that seemed contrary to his personality. He struggled with his calling because of a lack of self-confidence, however his humility was his chief qualification (Numbers 12:3). God knew who Moses truly was and He made His power perfect despite human weakness. At the right time, Moses' spiritual gift was clearly made manifest.

2 Peter 1:21 (WEB) For no prophecy ever came by the will of man: but holy men of God spoke, being moved by the Holy Spirit.

One way the leader can know his church member's gifts is by inviting people gifted in the prophetic to hear God for them. Every prophetic word must be tested.

One way leaders can confirm it is by looking at the individual, how the prophetic word fits with who God created them to be. This might seem abstract. To understand this, leaders should take time to know their people as well as their spiritual and ministry inclinations. This gives some clues as to whether a prophetic word fits, and if so, how it fits. Sometimes gifts are released in a person's life through prophecy, but will not manifest until the gift is activated by using it. Prophetic words can be confirmed in a variety of ways.

1 Corinthians 12:31 (WEB) But earnestly desire the best gifts. Moreover, I show a most excellent way to you.

Philippians 2:12-13 (WEB) So then, my beloved, even as you have always obeyed, not only in my presence, but now much more in my absence, work out your own salvation with fear and trembling. (13) For it is God who works in you both to will and to work, for his good pleasure.

Another way to identify an individual's gift is through that person's desires. Through commanding Christians to "earnestly desire" the higher gifts, 1 Corinthians 12:31 implies that as believers grow, they can move into these gifts. Paul would not have instructed believers to yearn for something they could not receive. Besides, God usually puts the

Chapter 13: Identifying Spiritual Gifts

longing in an individual's heart for the ministry to which that person is called. If someone wants a gift, it is often God's will to give them that gift when He feels the person is ready for it.

A Word of Caution

I do feel it is necessary to speak a word of caution. Receiving a prophetic word confirming a calling in that area does not imply that an individual has the ability and maturity to use the gift properly. Rather, this is an opportunity to begin growing. It is vital that each believer be trained in submission to their leadership in order to ensure they are learning to use their gift appropriately.

Some people think that they are called to one gift but are really called to another. A possible reason for this is that they want the higher gifts so much that they think they already have them. Prophetic confirmation through a mature prophet can help to identify one's true gifting and calling. For those that do not have access to someone like this, others who move in the prophetic in the local church can possibly do the same thing. However, at some point it is good for a mature prophet to confirm what those in the congregation have heard, just to make sure. Confirmation is essential.

Psalms 37:3-6 (WEB) Trust in Yahweh, and do good. Dwell in the land, and enjoy safe pasture. (4) Also delight yourself in Yahweh, and he will give you the desires of your heart. (5) Commit your way to Yahweh. Trust also in him, and he will do this: (6) he will make your righteousness go forth as the light, and your justice as the noon day sun.

Proverbs 3:5-6 (WEB) Trust in Yahweh with all your heart, and don't lean on your own understanding. (6) In all your ways acknowledge him, and he will make your paths straight.

Suggested Reading: 1 Corinthians 12:30-13:13

Church: What Was God Thinking?

The longing to move in the gifts must not take the place of believers' love for the Lord. It is possible to make an idol out of spiritual gifts. Each person should make sure that he is pursuing God, the Giver, and keeping their desires for the greater gifts in submission to Him. Every Christian needs to set aside striving and trust God's timing. When people are devoted to the Lord, as they continue growing in Him, the gifts and callings that He has on their lives will naturally begin to manifest. So, the priority should be to first seek God, and then desire spiritual gifts, rather than seeking God for the sake of spiritual gifts.

Sometimes prophets impart spiritual gifts to others. These might be gifts that an individual had already wanted, or it could be something they never considered. My spiritual gifting has been confirmed by prophets. I find it affirming to have someone who does not know me prophesy over me and verify that I am headed in the right direction. Although I appreciate this type of confirmation, there have been times that gifts were not activated in my life until a prophet spoke the prophetic words over me. I find this exciting and encouraging.

Romans 1:11 (WEB) For I long to see you, that I may impart to you some spiritual gift, to the end that you may be established;

In New Testament times, if the local church did not have a gift, the apostles imparted it to someone in the church as directed by the Holy Spirit. The apostles then trained the one that received this impartation until he was ready to equip others in the same gift and so multiply those that could participate in that particular ministry, each in their own unique way. This became an ongoing process of multiplication of spiritual gifts (2 Timothy 2:2).

Group confirmation is one way to identify a person's immediate gifts. If someone already has a gift, and uses it in a group, often those around that person will recognize his ability. It will be obvious to other believers.

1 Timothy 4:14 (WEB) Don't neglect the gift that is in you, which was given to you by prophecy, with the laying on of the hands of the elders.

Chapter 13: Identifying Spiritual Gifts

Some time ago, a man attended a gathering I hosted regularly. My ministry team and I felt that he had the gift of teaching. On a different day, a friend of mine came to a meeting and confirmed this man's gift. He felt like God said we should release him to minister.

Before this, when participating in discussions, he would usually respond with short answers. I asked him to teach and he started sharing on the Lord's Prayer. He spent two months on this subject and it was great. One of these times a pastor from another church visited our meeting. He was so touched by what this brother taught that he took notes. Releasing people into their callings is a blessing to the Body of Christ.

Ephesians 2:10 (WEB) For we are his workmanship, created in Christ Jesus for good works, which God prepared before that we would walk in them.

Finally, in identifying people's spiritual gifts, it is necessary to note that there is a big difference between a gift of the Spirit given to an individual and God's calling on that person's life. The calling of God is what God wants a person to accomplish in his life. The gifts are the power tools that help him fulfill that calling.

In summary, leaders today must listen to the Spirit and learn from Him what people are called to do in ministry and then take steps that are necessary to prepare them, releasing them as much as possible as they mature in their gifts. Scripturally, the local church bears the greatest responsibility in equipping.

Of course, if a church does not have anyone capable of training others, it is not wrong to bring someone from the outside or to go elsewhere for that. If there are people in the church who can equip others, however, they should be given space under the leader's authority to do that. The full-time minister needs to be diligent to deal with any issues that would prevent or hinder this. The health of the Church depends on leadership who are willing to make the effort to strengthen the Body in these ways.

Chapter 14: Leaders Equipping Believers in the Gifts

In order for believers to move on to maturity, people not only need help to recognize their spiritual gifts, they also need to be trained in those gifts. The leader has a key role in this process. In this chapter, I want to address various issues regarding equipping and describe what it should look like by using Scriptural examples.

Growing into Maturity

Hebrews 6:1-2 (WEB) Therefore leaving the teaching of the first principles of Christ, let us press on to perfection -- not laying again a foundation of repentance from dead works, of faith toward God, (2) of the teaching of baptisms, of laying on of hands, of resurrection of the dead, and of eternal judgment.

1 Corinthians 4:15-16 (KJV) For though ye have ten thousand instructors in Christ, yet have ye not many fathers: for in Christ Jesus I have begotten you through the gospel. (16) Wherefore I beseech you, be ye followers of me.

How does maturity happen when believers are not doing anything? Paul said there are not many fathers in Christ. This does not mean he wanted to keep it that way. So he said, "Be imitators of me." All believers are meant to grow up to become spiritual parents.

Church: What Was God Thinking?

One time a prophet visited my congregation and shared a vision that he had seen before about the Church in the U.S.A. being like a big fat baby with a large milk bottle. Sadly, I believe this is often true, but I pray that it will change for the better. When leadership does not allow believers to use the gifts and ministries that God has given them, these ministers are like parents commanding a baby not to learn how to walk. People need to be in a safe place where they can mature even if they make mistakes, just like a toddler learning to walk. They also must have leaders who will help and correct them gently and lovingly.

There is a word that describes what some churches are like today, codependent. This is a broad subject so it is hard to describe fully in a paragraph. However, I want to mention one form that is expressed in some modern churches. In these communities, the leadership limits their members' growth, resulting in a congregation full of dependent spiritual infants, fulfilling the leader's need to have others rely on them. This kind of church does not have very many mature people.

Spiritual parents in the Kingdom, like any healthy parents, should feel excited when their children grow and can do some things by themselves. They enjoy their children but also look forward to their next stages of development.

Leaders should be thrilled when believers begin using their gifts in ministry. Spiritual children may make a lot of mistakes, but this is a normal part of the maturing process. If parents stopped them from trying to walk out of need for them to stay in infancy or fear of them falling, they would be very sick parents.

In the Body of Christ, leaders that do not want their spiritual children to grow up need serious professional help. Ministers should be willing to let their people make mistakes as they mature and encourage them to learn from those mistakes. Good leaders learn how to facilitate and release their spiritual children to grow.

Proverbs 18:16 (WEB) A man's gift makes room for him, and brings him before great men.

Chapter 14: Leaders Equipping Believers in the Gifts

Until an individual is trained and gains experience using their gift, they will likely use the gift immaturely or not at all. Churches that equip their people provide an environment for those who are serious about growing in the Lord to walk in authority in their gifts. Proverbs 18:16 says that one's gifts bring him before great men. When a leader releases sincere believers, who knows what they will accomplish in their lifetime?

Ephesians 4:11-16 (WEB) He gave some to be apostles; and some, prophets; and some, evangelists; and some, shepherds [pastors] and teachers; (12) for the perfecting of the saints, to the work of serving, to the building up of the body of Christ; (13) until we all attain to the unity of the faith, and of the knowledge of the Son of God, to a full grown man, to the measure of the stature of the fullness of Christ; (14) that we may no longer be children, tossed back and forth and carried about with every wind of doctrine, by the trickery of men, in craftiness, after the wiles of error; (15) but speaking truth in love, we may grow up in all things into him, who is the head, Christ; (16) from whom all the body, being fitted and knit together through that which every joint supplies, according to the working in measure of each individual part, makes the body increase to the building up of itself in love.

Young believers should begin learning to use the gifts of the Holy Spirit. This may be something simple, such as tongues, helps, or even prophecy. Regardless, they can begin moving in the gifts any way that God chooses to use them.

When the Holy Spirit came at Pentecost, even young Christians prophesied and spoke in tongues and unbelievers received the interpretations (Acts 2:3-6, 14-21; 1 Corinthians 14:21-25). As people move into spiritual adulthood, they should grow into equipping gifts, referred to as the five-fold ministry. That is apostles, prophets, evangelists, pastors, and teachers. These gifts are not for building a large personal ministry or to make any one person look good, rather they are to be used for serving the Body of Christ. In this way, everyone in the Body has the opportunity to mature.

One of the biggest obstacles that a leader can face when he wants to equip and release his people is the mindset that the leader should do all the ministry and work. In a situation like this, leaders may only be able to start training a few people from the group. Hopefully body ministry will start to spread from those people to the rest of the church, because others recognize the change in those who have received coaching. If the leader has put time, hard work, and prayer into the situation and yet it does not change, he might consider passing his church to someone else and starting something new (Luke 5:37-39). This should only be done as a last resort.

The Leader's Responsibility Regarding His Gift

Read Ezekiel chapter 34.

It is also essential that people do not abuse their positions of authority. Believers need to avoid using their gifts to manipulate or control people. What I mean is that a leader must never make it awkward for individuals to make their own decisions according to God's leading by putting "spiritual" pressure on them to do what the leader wants them to do. This would not be acting in love. A leader's goal should not be to impress others with the gifts he has and how well he uses them but rather to nurture and strengthen the Body of Christ.

For example, say a leader named Jack needs someone to do children's ministry during his church meetings, but he could not find anyone to do it. So Jack looks at someone in his church and thinks to himself, "That person would be brilliant in children's ministry," but God had not spoken to him. If Jack says, "I feel that God has called you to work with children. By the way, we need you to work in children's church," he would be using his position in the church and what seems like a prophetic word to pressure the other person into obedience.

In this case, Jack might be pretending to prophesy or may even think that he heard God about the situation. Even if it was a genuine word from God, in using it this way, the problem is that Jack would be using the gifts of the Spirit to manipulate.

Chapter 14: Leaders Equipping Believers in the Gifts

Christians must be open to God as they examine their own hearts and motives. As in the previous example, Jack might think that he heard God. If God has not spoken to that person about helping with the children's ministry, Jack could be mistaken. Whether he heard from God or not, it is important to allow that person to hear from God for themselves. If the Lord is really speaking, as long as people are open to Him, He can and will confirm His word.

If that person does not feel called to work in children's ministry, it would be inappropriate for Jack or anyone else to insist that they heard God correctly. If Jack placed this person in children's ministry, he might burn out because this was not what God asked him to do, at least not yet. This could result in harm to the person by putting him in a situation that He did not intend. It may also affect others involved in this ministry, including the children. This is why it is so vital to always move in love, without manipulation or pressure.

On the other hand, it would be appropriate for Jack to simply ask a person if they want to help with children's ministry. The important thing is that Jack should not try to influence others to do what he wants them to do. The problem is when a person misuses spiritual gifts to manipulate people.

It is also a leader's responsibility to equip those God has entrusted to his care and help them grow in maturity, releasing them to use the gifts and walk in the calling God has given them. For those who have not yet received vision from God, he should teach them, helping them to learn how to pray, hear God about their destinies, identify their gifts, and grow in their callings.

When a leader allows others to use their gifts, it does not take away from his ability to use his own spiritual giftings. The pastor of the first church I attended gathered a group of thirty to forty men for Bible study one morning a week. Then, almost every other Sunday, he would let one or two of them preach. This group of men grew very quickly in the Lord. The pastor also taught in the church service regularly. This provided an opportunity for others to grow in using their own gifts.

Church: What Was God Thinking?

Leaders need to recognize that each person has received an anointing. The gifts of the Holy Spirit are part of the anointing that God gives all believers. If leaders do not create a place in the Body of Christ for all to use their gifts, then they quench the work of the Spirit in the Church and in people's lives. As a result, they are not even having Church.

(See 1 Corinthians 12-14, for an explanation of what Church [*Ekklesia*] is supposed to be like).

Contrast: The Traditional Church Model

Acts 4:13 (WEB) Now when they saw the boldness of Peter and John, and had perceived that they were unlearned and ignorant men, they marveled. They recognized that they had been with Jesus.

Leaders often stop people from growing in their gifts and calling because they have not been to seminary. I find this amazing, since Jesus' main apostles were uneducated. Many in the Church today ignore those without training, and yet Jesus chose such people to be leaders, taking three years to teach them as they followed Him and assisted in His ministry. It saddens me when leaders overlook people who have not been to an institutional Bible school or seminary. The practice of the early Church was very different.

Ephesians 4:11-12 (WEB) He gave some to be apostles; and some, prophets; and some, evangelists; and some, shepherds [pastors] and teachers; (12) for the perfecting of the saints, to the work of serving, to the building up of the body of Christ;

Acts 14:23 (WEB) When they had appointed elders for them in every assembly, and had prayed with fasting, they commended them to the Lord, on whom they had believed.

In reading the New Testament, one can clearly see that leadership was usually raised up locally to use their gifts. This training did not take place in a seminary; rather it was done as people worked together as a

Chapter 14: Leaders Equipping Believers in the Gifts

ministry team. Often the newly discipled leaders were then facilitated by the church to coach others in using the same gifts. In the case of a new work, an apostolic equipping team would train new believers. There will be more about the apostolic equipping team in a later chapter.

It would be wonderful if churches grew strong to the point where they no longer needed to look elsewhere for their primary equipping. Of course, different communities of believers have different strengths. We, as Christians, can learn much from one another. In situations where a congregation lacks individuals with a certain gift or knowledge on how to use that gift, there are several options to consider. Individuals can be brought in from other churches or selected church leaders and members can be sent elsewhere to receive training so that they can return to their local church and instruct others. In fact, I am not sure that seminary is the best place for training. As far as I know, seminary was not a word in the vocabulary of the early Church.

Seminary has become a sad substitute for Biblical equipping. One reason I believe this is that too often seminary graduates end up with less faith in Christ than they had before they began their schooling.

There are some reasons why this happens. Part of this is because of the intensity of academic study. Much time in seminary is spent in trying to understand the infinite God through a finite human mind. Traditionally, much of the curriculum focuses on intellectual understanding of God and ministry with little practical training or opportunities to gain experience. This can be draining on a person's relationship with God.

1 Corinthians 2:4 (WEB) My speech and my preaching were not in persuasive words of human wisdom, but in demonstration of the Spirit and of power,

Seminary is an academic experience. Often those who study there gain a lot of head knowledge, but still have not proved themselves to be leaders. Seminary is not all bad, but equipping needs to be done in such a way so that ministers are trained practically for ministry, not merely intellectually. The Gospel message in the Bible was demonstrated in power, not head knowledge (1 Corinthians 2:4).

Nearly every time I talk to pastors about their seminary training, they tell me that they do not use most of what they were taught. In day-to-day ministry, it is often not necessary to have the degree of theological knowledge gained in seminary. Those who have a heart for ministry must learn about practical things that help people in their everyday lives. At the same time, I do not think theology is wrong, I teach people basic Biblical theology during the equipping process. I do feel a college or seminary education is unnecessary for training in Scriptural truths or practical application of those truths in everyday life.

A number of years ago, I visited my daughter in Phoenix, Arizona. She was part of a ministry training school there called Master's Commission.[6] While they were there, the students spent an hour in prayer each day, about three hours daily in Bible study and the rest of their time in practical ministry. They had an outreach in the inner city where they brought many children to Jesus. The students seemed to really be in love with the Lord. This school makes disciples prepared for life and ministry.

Matthew 6:33 (WEB) But seek first God's Kingdom, and his righteousness; and all these things will be given to you as well.

As leaders train people, they need to be teaching and giving people the time to build a relationship with God. Leaders should want others to fall in love with Jesus and grow in their first love. Christians must aim to have a deep relationship with the Lord above all else. When love is the main focus, there will also be more anointing on the use of the gifts. God blesses those who seek Him first (Matthew 6:33).

---

[6] Master's Commission USA is now located in Lewisville Texas. Their webpage is masterscommissionusa.com -- Accessed 09 August 2011

Chapter 14: Leaders Equipping Believers in the Gifts

The Equipping Process

So what does Biblical equipping look like? I believe that understanding the process will make it easier to apply the concepts in this book.

An example of equipping was Elijah and Elisha. Elijah was told by God to anoint Elisha as a prophet (1 Kings 19:16, 19-21). Then Elisha learned from Elijah by being around him and watching his life. Scripture is not clear how long Elisha was an apprentice but he was not fully released until his mentor was gone. When Elijah was taken to Heaven, he passed his mantle to Elisha (2 Kings 2: 8-14). This action is a picture of Jesus' life.

When Jesus ascended to the Father, He passed His earthly mantles to others by giving all of His followers the Holy Spirit. As a result the Spirit gives Christians the gifts that Jesus had used on earth (Jesus had more than one mantle, or spiritual gift, to impart to others).

Luke 10:1 (WEB) Now after these things, the Lord also appointed seventy others, and sent them two by two ahead of him into every city and place, where he was about to come.

Another example of equipping and releasing was Jesus and His disciples. Twelve men learned from Jesus in a very close relationship. The disciples ministered at different times, but from the Scriptures, it seems that they mostly learned by spending time with Jesus and watching His life and helping in His ministry.

Close to the end of His ministry on earth Jesus sent out seventy men to demonstrate the Kingdom of God to Israel. These men were equipped to some degree or else they would not have been able to do the Works of God in power. This time Jesus did not go with them but sent them out to do what He had shown them. When they came back He taught them how to do the things that they could not do. When the time was right, God took Elijah to Heaven. Jesus also ascended to Heaven after the Resurrection, allowing them to use what they had learned.

Church: What Was God Thinking?

I am not saying that in order to release believers in ministry, a leader has to be taken up to Heaven in a cloud. Rather, the point is that there are several aspects involved in the process. It is, in some ways, similar to learning a new language.

When I began studying Cantonese in Hong Kong, I tried to learn it in a classroom. My daughters took a much more practical approach. They spent time listening to others speak, and then if they needed to they would ask those who knew English what words meant. They learned some basic vocabulary and started putting together simple sentences. They did attend classes to help them learn the tones and pronunciation.

After three months they left those classes and learned by practicing with each other and friends. At first, they could say little, but would observe. Later they were able to speak more, but still occasionally needed help from people who spoke English. After more time and hard work, they could express most anything they wanted to and some people even thought they had a parent that was Chinese.

Eventually, this second language almost became like a first language to them. There are some things they find easier to express in Cantonese than in English. Growth in the equipping process is similar to this.

The role of the equipper can be compared to a coach who is training a team in a particular sport. Because of this, I use words like coaching to describe the process. This is also to emphasize that the equipper is much more than just a teacher. Since the learning process should be practical as well as informative, I refer to the learner as an apprentice.

I do want to clarify, however, that I am not talking about the equipper becoming authoritative in a controlling way or neglecting the feelings of the individual. Rather, I want to describe the equipper's desire to recognize individuals' gifts and assist them to become the best that they can be in God, so that each member of the Church is able to contribute to the Body of Christ as a player would to a team.

Chapter 14: Leaders Equipping Believers in the Gifts

In the early stages of equipping, the apprentice receives teaching from the person coaching him. His trainer gives him basic knowledge of his gift including issues in using the gift, understanding of how it works, and simple guidelines. The apprentice also observes the mentor so he can see in real life what he is learning. This helps him to grasp some concepts that are more difficult to express.

In some cases, the mature believer might not even realize some of the factors involved in the use of that specific gift, but the learner can pick these up through observation. During this time, the apprentice also begins receiving healing ministry, specifically for issues that would affect him in ministry.

Once the apprentice has learned the basic concepts, it is time for him to begin using his gift. The mentor should be there to supervise. This gives opportunity to see what his apprentice's strengths and weaknesses are. The coach will also be able to see if he needs more training. Through time, practice, and loving guidance, the apprentice should grow in his anointing and skill while using his gift.

After the apprentice shows that he can be responsible and is able to apply what he has learned consistently, he is ready to exercise his gift with less supervision. The mentor must give him space to do so until the apprentice is ready to be fully released to minister. Please note that he will maintain accountability even as a mature leader. Eventually, after he gains experience, he will be ready to be a mentor himself, and the process will begin again with another individual of the same gift. In this way, the Kingdom of God can grow with all members of God's family reaching their potential.

In summary, when leaders recognize the gifts of their people, and choose to train them, this not only benefits themselves but the whole Body. To be effective, leadership must leave traditional ideas of what equipping looks like. Instead, they should embrace Biblical discipleship. The result will be mature believers taking their God-given roles in the Body of Christ.

Diagram 1: The Equipping Process

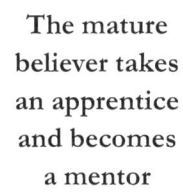

- The mature believer takes an apprentice and becomes a mentor
- The apprentice ministers with the mentor to learn from him
- The mentor allows the apprentice to function relatively independently but with oversight
- The apprentice is ready to minister without needing the mentor's direct input in most ministry situations

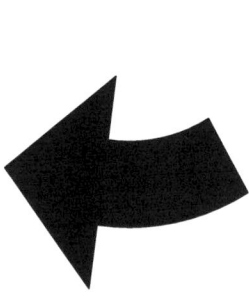

Chapter 14: Leaders Equipping Believers in the Gifts

Diagram 2: Apostolic Impartation in the Equipping Process

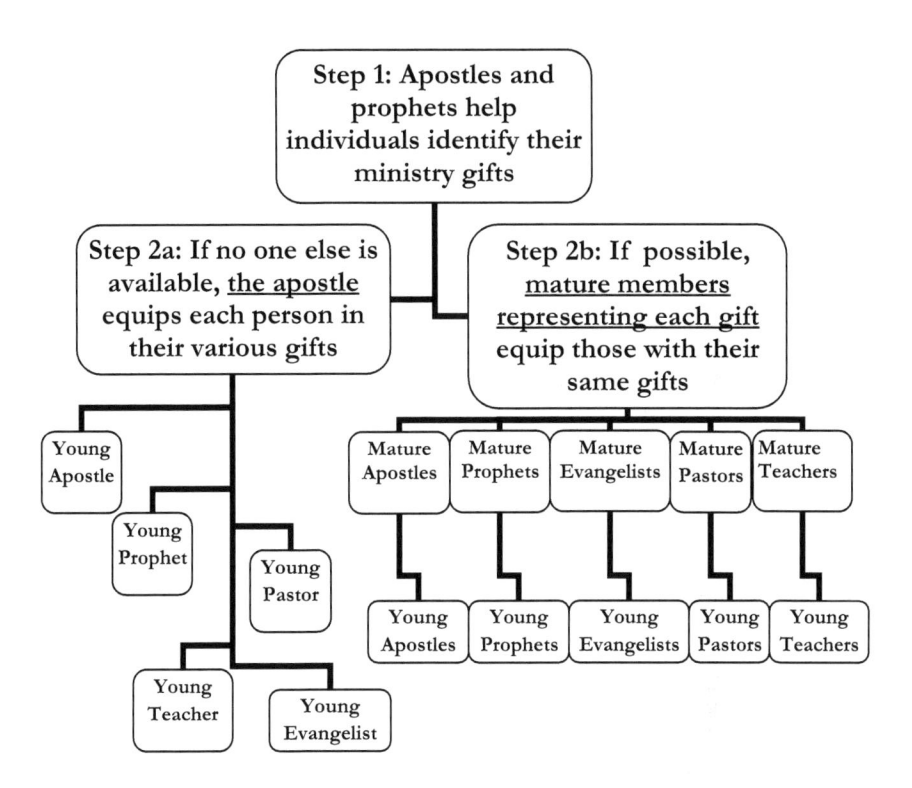

Step 1: Apostles and prophets help individuals identify their ministry gifts

Step 2a: If no one else is available, <u>the apostle</u> equips each person in their various gifts

- Young Apostle
- Young Prophet
- Young Pastor
- Young Teacher
- Young Evangelist

Step 2b: If possible, <u>mature members representing each gift</u> equip those with their same gifts

- Mature Apostles → Young Apostles
- Mature Prophets → Young Prophets
- Mature Evangelists → Young Evangelists
- Mature Pastors → Young Pastors
- Mature Teachers → Young Teachers

Chapter 15: Introducing Biblical Elders

Acts 20:17 (WEB) From Miletus he sent to Ephesus, and called to himself the elders of the assembly.

The Greek word for "elder" is πρεσβύτερος *presbuteros*.
Strong's definition G4245 (pronounced: (*pres-boo'-ter-os*)
Comparative of πρέσβυς *presbus* (elderly); older; as noun, a senior; specifically an Israelite Sanhedrist (also figuratively, member of the celestial council) or Christian "presbyter": - elder (-est), old.

An elder is a type of leader that bears partial responsibility in overseeing a group of believers. The elder's role is essential to the Church, bringing health and balance in Christian community, since they are mature believers called to protect and strengthen the Body of Christ. I would like to share more about their role and qualifications in this chapter.

1 Corinthians 4:15-16 (WEB) For though you have ten thousand tutors in Christ, yet not many fathers. For in Christ Jesus, I became your father through the Good News. (16) I beg you therefore, be imitators of me.

Church: What Was God Thinking?

Elders function as facilitators so that each person has an opportunity to grow in the Lord and in the unique gifts that God has given them. The position of elder is not merely an occupation or task to be accomplished. Elders love the flock of God and want them to become the best they can be in the Lord.

Elders are the type of people that everyone in the Church can look up to and want to imitate. At the same time, leaders should not desire others to become their clones. They want them to be who Jesus created them to be. All believers should want to grow in the Lord so that their lives will be good examples of what it means to follow Jesus.

Acts 20:17 (WEB) From Miletus he sent to Ephesus, and called to himself the elders of the assembly.

Acts 20:28 (WEB) Take heed, therefore, to yourselves, and to all the flock, in which the Holy Spirit has made you overseers, to shepherd the assembly of the Lord and God which he purchased with his own blood.

1 Peter 5:1-3 (WEB) I exhort the elders among you, as a fellow elder, and a witness of the sufferings of Christ, and who will also share in the glory that will be revealed. (2) Shepherd the flock of God which is among you, exercising the oversight, not under compulsion, but voluntarily, not for dishonest gain, but willingly; (3) neither as lording it over those entrusted to you, but making yourselves examples to the flock.

What does the Bible say about elders? In Acts 20:17, Paul met with the elders of Ephesus, and in verse 28 he calls them overseers. In 1 Peter 5, the apostle Peter gives some instructions for elders. Peter says that they must not be interested in personal benefits or people looking up to them, instead they should have a heart for the Church. Their leadership role is to make sure that gatherings are not out of order, no one takes over the meetings, and people are able to use their gifts. Finally, they should never be overbearing. This will enhance the health and strength of the Christian community.

Elders need to know when to be in the foreground and when to be in the background. Their oversight should not be controlling or

Chapter 15: Introducing Biblical Elders

overbearing. They must understand how to facilitate others in using their gifts.

When an elder is operating in his own gift, however, he does not have to be in the background. Furthermore, he should be more dominant when someone is out of order, teaching wrong theology, or teaching something inappropriate for the group. If the timing feels off, an elder must be careful that it is the Lord and not a matter of personal preference or a desire to control. Every church should have elders that can be sensitive to the needs of the group.

One example of when an elder should step in is when someone is presenting a teaching that his group is not yet mature enough to receive. In one of my previous church plants, we had a gathering for young believers. Sometimes visitors tried to teach theology that was not only too deep but also would have brought confusion caused by unnecessary cross-cultural and historical references. In this case, my team gently took action to stop this. There are other times when elders or a leadership team need to take action, this is just one example.

I believe it is best for elders not to all have the same ministry giftings. In fact, I feel that elders should come from all the different gifts. The Church needs elders that are from each of the ministry gifts: apostles, prophets, teachers, pastors, and evangelists. This is so the Church will not become partial towards one or a few giftings, to the neglect of other spiritual gifts. It also allows each person to bring different perspectives that are important to the healthy function of the Body of Christ.

Special Ministries of the Elder

James 5:14-16 (WEB) Is any among you sick? Let him call for the elders of the assembly, and let them pray over him, anointing him with oil in the name of the Lord, (15) and the prayer of faith will heal him who is sick, and the Lord will raise him up. If he has committed sins, he will be forgiven. (16) Confess your offenses to one another, and pray for one another, that you may be healed. The insistent prayer of a righteous person is powerfully effective.

Church: What Was God Thinking?

Elders walk in the power of the Holy Spirit and help others to experience this power. When people are sick and need healing they call for the elders to pray for them. James says that the prayer of faith brings healing. Even though, through the cross, all believers' sins are cleansed and covered by the atonement, some Christians find it difficult to accept God's forgiveness (1 John 1:9). Elders have special spiritual authority to release faith in believers' hearts to know that God forgives them.

God has granted every Christian spiritual authority, but elders are already moving in their authority to proclaim forgiveness of others' sins (John 20:23). Some people are more likely to believe an elder because of their spiritual maturity. Prayer for healing and proclaiming forgiveness of sin are both significant ministries that elders have to the Body of Christ (James 5:14-16).

1 Timothy 4:14 (WEB) Don't neglect the gift that is in you, which was given to you by prophecy, with the laying on of the hands of the elders.

In addition to moving in their own gifts with authority and maturity, elders also have the ability, together with apostles and prophets, to prophetically call out people's gifts. They can then equip those people in the power and gifts of the Holy Spirit.

The Qualifications for an Elder

Titus 1:5-6 (WEB) I left you in Crete for this reason, that you would set in order the things that were lacking, and appoint elders in every city, as I directed you; (6) if anyone is blameless, the husband of one wife, having children who believe, who are not accused of loose or unruly behavior.

God wants people in the Church that produce fruit of the Holy Spirit. Even if a person does not become an elder, God desires every Christian to have the characteristics of an elder. The qualifications for elders are high, yet these will become a part of believer's lives as they mature and grow in the Lord.

Chapter 15: Introducing Biblical Elders

There are many leaders of the modern-day Church that do not have these characteristics. One of the reasons for this could be that leaders are often busy and might not feel that they have much time to spend connecting with God. This results in immature leaders and under-developed people in their congregation. Excellence is important to God and He wants to give it to His children.

1 Peter 5:2-3 (WEB) Shepherd the flock of God which is among you, exercising the oversight, not under compulsion, but voluntarily, not for dishonest gain, but willingly; (3) neither as lording it over those entrusted to you, but making yourselves examples to the flock.

James 2:26 (WEB) For as the body apart from the spirit is dead, even so faith apart from works is dead.

God has called mature believers and especially elders to a high standard, becoming examples for the Church (1 Peter 5:1-3). However, Jesus asks everyone to aim for that same standard. Christian's lives are to be a practical expression of faith, His Word living in their hearts (Ephesians 2:8-10; James 2:26). It should be difficult to find many things wrong in an elder's life. This does not mean he is perfect, but he is open to God's work in his life.

Recognizing and Selecting Elders

Proverbs 18:16 (WEB) A man's gift makes room for him, and brings him before great men.

Most people feel that elders are reliable. In fact, potential elders can often be identified by the trust that people have for them (Proverbs 18:16). Healthy leadership, especially elders, often recognize when God is preparing someone to be an elder, if they know their people well. This can result in more mature leaders for the Church.

Potential elders still may need loving nurture and guidance. Some people gain other's respect as they mature, but are not ready to be recognized as elders. The authority believers receive from God is proportionate to their intimacy with Him (Matthew 25:14-29). As a result, they will have greater impact on others. At the same time, potential elders should be careful not to usurp authority, doing whatever they want.

Some might think they have matured enough to be elders, but have not yet. They need to trust caring leadership to release them when the time is right. The Holy Spirit's leading must be followed in appointing new elders.

1 John 3:8 (WEB) He who sins is of the devil, for the devil has been sinning from the beginning. To this end the Son of God was revealed, that he might destroy the works of the devil.

Choosing an elder should not be based on his or her past, rather it should be based on present maturity. Sometimes a person is good elder material and leaders hold him back because of his past even though the issues are already resolved.

1 John 3 says that Jesus came to do much more than merely forgive sins. He came to destroy the works of the devil. He came to bring the Kingdom of God down to earth. When leaders hold someone back who has proven himself to have overcome past sin or failure, it is like saying that God cannot change lives. On the other hand if someone has been a believer for years and still has not experienced God's transforming power, he does not yet know the Lord in the way he should.

Leaders must seek God about who to appoint as elders. If someone wants to be one and is confirmed as one by the Holy Spirit through the gift of prophecy, leaders should begin training him for that ministry.

Titus 1:6 (WEB) if anyone is blameless, the husband of one wife, having children who believe, who are not accused of loose or unruly behavior.

The Greek word for "child" or "children" is τέκνον *teknon*.
Strong's definition G5043 (pronounced: *tek'-non*)
From the base of G5098; a child (as produced): - child, daughter, son.

Chapter 15: Introducing Biblical Elders

The Greek word for "faithful" is πιστός *pistos*.
Strong's definition G4103 (pronounced: *pis-tos'*)
From G3982; objectively trustworthy; subjectively trustful: - believing, faithful, sure, true.

If someone's adult children do not believe, can he still be an elder? The Revised Standard Version (RSV) says that an elder's children must be believers; however the King James Version (KJV) simply states that they need to be trustworthy. This verse in the original language combines these two meanings. To clarify further, *teknon*, the Greek word for children means an underage child. I believe that when someone's children become independent adults, but are not following the Lord, and yet he has all the other qualifications, the person can function as an elder.

There are many reasons why second generation Christians choose not to follow God, depending on various situations. For example: sometimes people's lives are not transformed by God until after their children have grown. Although they might have a high level of maturity, their children still do not follow the Lord. Other times parents have been following the Lord for a long time, but their adult children choose to reject the Christian life. This is their personal choice and does not necessarily reflect on the parents. So even if someone's adult children choose not to follow God, I believe he can still be an elder.

However if someone has problems with his children who are not yet adults, this is a different matter. According to Scripture, this issue could prevent him from becoming an elder. Titus 1:6 in the RSV says, "Their children are not to be charged of being profligate or rebellious." The word "profligate" means to be wildly extravagant or wasteful. If children have no self-control, it may be a matter of the child's rebellion, but another possibility is that their parents let them do whatever they want.

When parents spoil their children it might be because they do not have self-control themselves or they did not learn how to discipline their children well. Sometimes this is the result of an inner healing issue for one or both of the parents. I have known some of the greatest people that are passive when it comes to dealing with their children. If such a person becomes an elder, there would be some risk of them being passive about problems that arise. They also may lack wisdom in helping others choose what is right. Their undisciplined lives could carry into leadership, resulting in many doing whatever they want, even when they are in error or in unrepentant sin. This would hurt the community.

In addition, there are unique stresses and challenges in being an elder. While children are still young and in the home, it is essential for their parents to give them the love and attention they need. Children grow up quickly and those busy years once gone are gone for good. God has entrusted children to the care of their parents and it is vital that parents be faithful in that trust. Sadly, too many children have been wrongly "sacrificed" for the sake of their parents' ministry.

Tough Love

Elders need to know how to appropriately use "tough love" both in ministry and in their private lives. "Tough love" is firm, loving discipline, often involving difficult choices for the individual's long-term good. It is also vital for them to not ignore their children for the sake of ministry. Children do reach a point in their lives when they have to become their own individuals and at that time it is possible that they stop listening to their parents. When elders have properly cared for and disciplined their children they should not be held back because of their children's unwise choices as adults. Their grown children are accountable to God for their own lives and choices.

Acts 14:23 (WEB) When they had appointed elders for them in every assembly, and had prayed with fasting, they commended them to the Lord, on whom they had believed.

In summary Scripture tells how to choose elders. They are supposed to be selected not only by having the qualifications of an

Chapter 15: Introducing Biblical Elders

elder, but also through prophetic confirmation by the Holy Spirit. They must not be chosen on the basis of a leader's personal feelings.

In Acts, the apostles and the rest of the Church fasted and prayed before selecting an elder. This practice is necessary to make sure that those deciding this are hearing from the Lord, thus preventing appointment by mistake. If a group of leaders feels that someone would make a good elder and the person desires this position but the Lord says, "No," this might mean that he is not ever supposed to become one. It could also mean that God wants to do some work in his life first. Regardless, elders must be selected according to the Holy Spirit's direction.

Chapter 16: The Elder's Function

The Elder Helps Prevent Inappropriate Control

Part of the function of elders and overseers is to supervise meetings to prevent domination by any individual. 1 Corinthians 12-14 describe how the church meeting is supposed to be. The gathering is a time for everyone to use their gifts under the Holy Spirit's direction. Oversight is necessary for the church to function properly.

Some people like to control a meeting by claiming that it is God. They cannot be talked out of doing their own thing, sometimes even declaring it to be God's will. This is contrary to the Spirit's character. Although He works through His people, He does not control any gathering through just one individual. Such people need to deal with their control issues before they would be ready to think about becoming elders.

I want to share something that has happened in different churches that have a team leadership structure without a clearly defined leader. I have seen ministries that began with the understanding that the leadership was going to operate as a team. However, after working together for awhile, one of the team members decides to become the head pastor without discussing it with anyone else. Members of the congregation begin calling him pastor. At the same time, he becomes increasingly controlling, dominating the work. He always seems to hear God on what should be done in the meetings and the future direction of the work. In doing this, he not only makes it so the leadership cannot function as a team, but also blocks group participation in meetings. In such a situation, it would be appropriate for the elders to stop this as gently and firmly as possible.

If a congregation is going to experience the freedom of the New Testament Church, there needs to be people protecting that freedom from things that would destroy it. This is one of the main roles of the elder.

In order to function properly as a protector, an elder has to be a loving person who uses tough love when necessary. In addition, an elder needs to ensure that prophecy is correctly but sensitively judged. Besides this, they must prevent people from teaching strange things. In such cases, an elder should use his authority to correct the situation, preventing people from getting hurt needlessly.

Elders do need to be careful to not judge too quickly during a church meeting unless there is an obvious problem. People can be too hasty and stop the Holy Spirit's flow. Some discernment comes through knowing the people that come to the gatherings. In certain situations, allowing things to continue is good, because through the outcome, people's hearts are revealed. In fact, leaders often know what to do from understanding those they lead and how they have acted before.

It is good, however, for elders to inform people in the group that they will allow certain things to continue and help them understand why. Since Scripture speaks of preparing saints for ministry (Ephesians 4), it is also helpful for others to understand that growth is a process and every situation is an opportunity to learn.

For example: during a prophetic time, or free-sharing, it is good to allow a person to speak first, and then assess what they say afterwards. Sometimes what a person is sharing might be great, but it comes out a little rough at first. If a leader stops this too soon, the group misses an

Chapter 16: The Elder's Function

opportunity to hear from that individual. At the same time, if the person is allowed to continue, the whole group may receive a great blessing as a result. This will aid in allowing the Holy Spirit to have free reign in the meetings.

An elder or overseer needs to listen to God about whether or not to continue in the direction a meeting is taking. On occasion, in one of my previous church plants, I have felt uncomfortable about the direction we have taken, but I did not always make it stop. Even though I felt differently at first, in the end, I realized that God was giving the group a choice about what to do in our time together.

Other times, when I have allowed things to continue, it made everyone else feel uncomfortable. Sometimes asking the core group for input helps a leader to make good assessments of situations. It is even more important to listen to the Lord. In conclusion, God often teaches through mistakes.

Elders, Apostles, Controversy, and Important Decisions

Acts 15:2 (WEB) Therefore when Paul and Barnabas had no small discord and discussion with them, they appointed Paul and Barnabas, and some others of them, to go up to Jerusalem to the apostles and elders about this question.

In Biblical times, elders worked with the original apostles to clarify Church doctrine. Elders at that time were leaders from various ministry giftings who were mature in the Lord and were raised up by apostles. Even today, when a church has controversy, apostles and elders should resolve the problem.

Acts 15 gives an example of this in Scripture. This question of church doctrine was in regard to whether or not non-Jewish believers needed to follow circumcision and the Law of Moses. Paul and Barnabas went to the apostles and elders for their opinion. The apostles and elders decided with input from the church.

Church: What Was God Thinking?

Acts 15:22 (WEB) Then it seemed good to the apostles and the elders, with the whole assembly, to choose men out of their company, and send them to Antioch with Paul and Barnabas: Judas called Barsabbas, and Silas, chief men among the brothers.

After they made the decision regarding circumcision and the Law of Moses, apostles and elders also picked messengers to represent them in communicating this to those new believers. Being a part of the decision-making process is one of the essential functions of an elder.

Respect for Elders, Overseers, and Leaders

The respect the Church had for their overseers and their devotion to prayer and the Holy Spirit's guidance allowed everyone to be in unity. The intimacy that members of the New Testament Church had with God produced respect for their leaders without it being demanded of them. This allowed the Church to agree on one of the most controversial questions faced by the early Church. Close fellowship with God produces esteem for leaders that helps the Church to face difficult issues.

1 Timothy 5:17 (WEB) Let the elders who rule well be counted worthy of double honor, especially those who labor in the word and in teaching.

Matthew 6:1 (WEB) "Be careful that you don't do your charitable giving before men, to be seen by them, or else you have no reward from your Father who is in heaven.

God wants everyone to have the right attitude toward their leadership. Paul said that believers must give elders double honor. They are meant to be esteemed but not idolized. However, no one should demand this. Elders must not be motivated by wanting to look good, or to be seen as perfect. Leaders are not God's superstars; they are Jesus' servants called to minister to others. If they want more than this, if they are seeking people's honor and respect, they are not ready for a position of authority. Most people naturally look up to servant-leaders.

Chapter 16: The Elder's Function

Philippians 3:20 (WEB) For our citizenship is in heaven, from where we also wait for a Savior, the Lord Jesus Christ;

So what should a minister do if he is not appreciated? First, he must try to discover if he has hurt others and work towards reconciliation. It is of utmost importance for ministers to ensure their hearts are in the right place. At the same time, he should know that it is not always his problem.

Sometimes Christians make inappropriate demands towards their leaders. Such individuals must adjust their expectations according to the Scriptural standard for leadership. Everyone needs to understand that when people choose to follow Jesus, they become citizens of Heaven and should learn to live by the Bible's standard.

It is not always a leader's fault when people have issues with him. One sign of Christian maturity is the ability to talk to people in a spirit of humility regarding relational issues. Many times this helps others to feel safe. There are times when a leader can do nothing to work out his differences with others. Sometimes the only thing to do is rely on God and pray for the people involved. Other times, as a leader is open to correction, he will find problems in his own life through this. Through this God uses others' input to change his life. Regardless, if handled correctly, personal conflict is a great opportunity for all those involved to grow.

Submission to authority is vital to the church. I feel that I need to stress this again. Regardless of personal issues, people should still obey Scripture and submit to their leaders. Open leadership is not permission for a free-for-all. In addition, even followers that do not share the same beliefs as their church leaders still must respect and listen to their church's leadership.

If they feel they cannot, they need to examine their own hearts, and ask God for grace to deal with the situation. If, after much prayer and effort, they do not think working things out with their leaders is doable, they possibly need to find a church that is a better fit, and seek out leaders that are more compatible, but those leaders should also be obeyed. I will say again, though, that this change should only be made as a last resort.

As a leader, if people cannot respect me, I would rather they go to another congregation where they can receive from their leaders and grow. I have seen people in churches that make each other miserable trying to stay together unnecessarily. If things cannot be worked out, there is no point in mutual torture.

Some people feel they face the same issues with their leaders every time they move to a new congregation. These individuals need to examine their own hearts and expectations to make sure that this is not their personal problem. There is no ideal church, even though God is at work to perfect His Church (Ephesians 5:27). Even planting one's own church, with one's own spiritual DNA, still does not result in a perfect church.

In summary, the role of elders and overseers in the church is vital. They help maintain appropriate order and freedom, resolve crises, and work together with apostles and prophets to impart spiritual gifts. They provide discernment, correction, and love when needed. Elders are invaluable to the Body of Christ. I will talk more about overseers, or bishops, in the following chapter.

Chapter 17: Bishops or Overseers

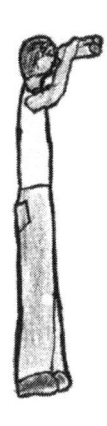

Acts 1:20 (KJV) For it is written in the book of Psalms, "Let his habitation be desolate, and let no man dwell therein: and his bishoprick let another take."

Titus 1:7-9 (WEB) For the overseer must be blameless, as God's steward; not self-pleasing, not easily angered, not given to wine, not violent, not greedy for dishonest gain; (8) but given to hospitality, a lover of good, sober minded, fair, holy, self-controlled; (9) holding to the faithful word which is according to the teaching, that he may be able to exhort in the sound doctrine, and to convict those who contradict him.

Titus 1:7-9 (KJV) For a bishop must be blameless, as the steward of God; not self-willed, not soon angry, not given to wine, no striker, not given to filthy lucre; (8) But a lover of hospitality, a lover of good men, sober, just, holy, temperate; (9) Holding fast the faithful word as he hath been taught, that he may be able by sound doctrine both to exhort and to convince the gainsayers.

Church: What Was God Thinking?

Description of an Overseer

The Greek word for "overseer" is ἐπίσκοπος *episkopos.*
Strong's definition G1985 (pronounced: *ep-is'-kop-os*)
From G1909 and G4649 (in the sense of G1983); a superintendent, that is, Christian officer in general charge of a (or the) church (literally or figuratively): - bishop, overseer.

In Titus 1:7, Paul talks about overseers (sometimes called bishops). They are apostles that watch over a church, a network of congregations, an area, or people group. In Acts 1:20, when Matthias took Judas' place, even though Judas was an apostle, the Greek word *episkopos* (overseer or bishop) was used for his office. At that time, this was the apostles' role. Overseers are a part of the Church, not to control, but to make sure that the Church is operating as it should. At times, he will supervise a group of churches.

An overseer is supposed to be a father in Christ. He must not be arrogant or quick-tempered, so that he will not destroy others' lives and push them away from God. This could block them from experiencing Christ's love. Besides this, he cannot be an alcoholic. This is important because, by turning to alcohol he would be looking outside of God for fulfillment instead of being continually filled with the Holy Spirit and relying on God for his emotional needs.

An overseer cannot be violent, because it is a sign of a serious problem. If a leader has this problem, he either does not have God's love in him or he needs intensive inner healing, deliverance, and in some cases, therapy. In addition, greed is not acceptable for him, as this would be an idol of money in his life. Jesus must be first in an overseer's life so he can lovingly care for the Body of Christ.

In addition to the characteristics he should not have, there are some qualities he must have. First of all, Titus 1:8 says he needs to be hospitable. He has to be able to make people feel comfortable and loved in most any situation. This is vital because a leader who is unapproachable has little impact on others' lives.

Chapter 17: Bishops or Overseers

The second necessary quality of an overseer is love of goodness. The King James Version translates it "lover of good men," implying that overseers should love people of virtue (Titus 1:8). There is nothing better than spending time with individuals who have a deep relationship with God and delight in Godliness. A leader who loves what God loves refreshes others.

Thirdly, leaders need a high degree of self-control, which is a fruit of the Spirit. Such a person does not find his identity from the world or his flesh, instead the Holy Spirit shows him who he is, so he can more easily overcome sins of the flesh. His life is upright and wholly set apart to God. He is disciplined, so neither his bodily desires nor circumstances rule over him. These are all qualities every overseer has to possess.

Finally, an overseer must hold firm to the truth of God's Word. He should never add to or change it for his personal benefit. He must also have the ability to instruct others with sound doctrine, refuting anyone who contradicts it, preventing people from teaching unbiblical doctrines or twisting the truth. In this way, the overseer protects the Church's Biblical foundations.

Chapter 18: The Full-Time Minister

The modern concept of pastor has influenced the Church dramatically. However, a pastor leading the church needs to fit in with Biblical New Testament Church practice. My purpose in talking about this is not to put down full-time ministers. Many have a deep desire to follow Jesus and give their whole lives to serving people. Despite having a legitimate calling to be in ministry full-time, many Christian workers are experiencing pain and hardship because they are not moving in their true calling and spiritual gifts. Traditional ideas can get in the way of God's purpose for the Church. Many traditions have influenced the role of the full-time minister. For this reason, I feel it is necessary to discuss the full-time Christian worker separately from the spiritual gift of pastor.

Ministers That Do Everything

The Biblical concept of pastor is much different from the modern idea of pastor. In the Church today, people often see him as the "head guy" who does all the teaching, visitation, administration, etc. Besides all this, he must do anything else that he cannot get his congregation's help in doing. Too often he does almost everything. Many pastors struggle to get someone to even teach Sunday School. Many people also think of the pastor as the teacher. This is significantly different from the spiritual gift of pastor.

The modern traditional church often defines the pastor as the person who makes many of the decisions. In other words, he is the one in control. Many times, the person in the position of pastor might not even be gifted as a pastor. The result is that the church becomes lopsided because one man is the only person using his gift, while everyone else is more or less a spectator, following the leader's plan. If a church allows the gifts of only one or a few persons to operate, there is much the gathering is missing. There is far more to the Church than just one person and his gift.

If full-time ministers want to have a New Testament Church, they need to try to get as many people involved as possible. They must aim to build a team of overseers that has all the giftings of the five-fold ministry (Ephesians 4:11-13). The more their congregation works as a team, the more likely they will not experience burnout from attempting to do the entire ministry alone.

They should not even try to be everything to everyone they lead. They cannot be the teacher, visionary, administrator, overseer, comforter and function in all of the five-fold ministry offices, especially for a long period of time. No one should be shocked when the full-time minister who strives to do everything himself burns out as a result. No single individual is meant to be the full expression of the Body of Christ.

Some ministers are very gifted and seem able to do everything, and enjoy their work. However, they were not created to do this. It is not God's will for anyone to do all the work.

Sometimes leaders do not have any choice because of others' expectations towards them. For many, tradition is all they know. They have been taught certain customs and church formats that say the full-time minister needs to do everything. As a result of a few pastors'

Chapter 18: The Full-Time Minister

successes at building large churches, other ministers continue to try to grow their churches without equipping their members. This is not God's will.

Those who are able to do everything are probably potential apostles in disguise. If so, they need to function according to God's design. I will explain more about that in the chapter on apostles. When apostles realize their calling and move in it, the whole Church can enter into a new level of health and growth.

Certain Christians have been believers for ten or even twenty years and still have not received healing or training for ministry. As a result, they are more easily hurt by other people who are also very broken. In such cases, the full-time minister might not know how to use his pastoral gift and so needs some training, or he may not even have the spiritual gift of pastor.

The full-time minister might be an evangelist, concerned with helping lost people become saved. He could be a teacher who only wants to teach. He might be a prophet who prefers hosting prophetic meetings, or he may be an apostle who enjoys using his many gifts. This could result in the majority of a congregation remaining emotionally broken and immature.

Ministers That Follow Man-Made Traditions

Mark 7:13 (WEB) making void the word of God by your tradition, which you have handed down. You do many things like this."

Colossians 2:8 (WEB) Be careful that you don't let anyone rob you through his philosophy and vain deceit, after the tradition of men, after the elements of the world, and not after Christ.

Christians must take care to avoid doing what Jesus talked about in Mark 7:13, rejecting God's instructions in favor of man-made traditions. Many Bible verses tell Christians to be careful about this. Those that adhere to certain customs harmful to the Body of Christ should reevaluate their thinking and, at least, stop expecting others to follow those traditions. God's Word is more important than human customs.

James 2:1-4 (WEB) My brothers, don't hold the faith of our Lord Jesus Christ of glory with partiality. (2) For if a man with a gold ring, in fine clothing, comes into your synagogue, and a poor man in filthy clothing also comes in; (3) and you pay special attention to him who wears the fine clothing, and say, "Sit here in a good place;" and you tell the poor man, "Stand there," or "Sit by my footstool;" (4) haven't you shown partiality among yourselves, and become judges with evil thoughts?

As a church, it is essential that leaders do not emphasize traditions that are not in the Bible. Some of these hurt the Church and its members. Ideas such as "dress your best for God" for the church meeting on Sunday are human customs. To make distinctions because of how well individuals dress is spoken against in James 2:1-4. This is just one example of the unbiblical concepts that have affected many of today's churches.

When traditions get in the way of what God has in mind, the Church must drop them. For example if God called a person to work with the poor, it would hinder their ministry if they required every man to show up in a suit. It is possible that the people may not be able to afford nice clothes. Even if they could, this might hinder their attitude towards worship if they were simply not comfortable wearing suits and ties. In this way, traditions can even get in the way of people coming to God.

If leaders are hindering what God wants to do, or is nullifying God's commands, I pray that the Lord will help them to deal with this. I pray that they listen as He speaks truth into their hearts, so that they cannot do anything else but follow Him. This will bring much needed change to the Church.

What a Minister Should Be Doing

Some full-time ministers protest that if they release their people, they will lose their respect and others will try to usurp their authority.

Chapter 18: The Full-Time Minister

When ministers use their gifts rightly, however, they are more likely to win the respect of the people in their churches. As such, they should not be afraid of losing their positions. This is especially true if leaders are available to their people, and take responsibility to prepare them for ministry.

I believe that individuals provided opportunities to minister are more likely to stay and bless others in return. As a result, fewer people will feel the need to change churches often in an effort to find something that should be in every Christian community. When gifts are used appropriately, people gain a sense of belonging and the congregation becomes healthy and strong.

Full-time Christian workers need to view ministry as more than a job. They should be careful to be available and accessible to serve people and strengthen them, helping them develop strong discernment so that they can differentiate truth from deceit. If a minister views his work as simply a profession, he may need healing, or he might be operating in the wrong gift. God intends ministry to be much more than an occupation.

Matthew 6:10 (WEB) Let your Kingdom come. Let your will be done, as in heaven, so on earth.

God has created each person with unique gifts and callings to function and to serve according to His master plan, working with different types of people. God gives each one of His children vision so that they can reach different people groups, helping to fulfill His plan, so that all things will become on earth as they are in Heaven (Matthew 6:10). When believers work together, they should function like a symphony of gifts doing God's work.

A Minister's Authority

Matthew 20:25-28 (WEB) But Jesus summoned them, and said, "You know that the rulers of the nations lord it over them, and their great ones exercise authority over them. (26) It shall not be so among you, but whoever desires to become great among you shall be your servant.

(27) Whoever desires to be first among you shall be your bondservant, (28) even as the Son of Man came not to be served, but to serve, and to give his life as a ransom for many."

Many leaders seem to feel that unless they are authoritative no one will recognize them as leaders and because of this, they are afraid to allow their congregations to function as the Body of Christ. No person should be this kind of leader. In fact, by controlling the church; it is as though the minister is trying to take Jesus' place. In such cases, the Lord might let that person burn out or He may deal with that person in other ways. Sometimes, church members miss God's plan for their lives because full-time Christian workers get in the way. Ministers should remember the example of Christ -- that they are meant to be servants.

1 Corinthians 14:26 (KJV) How is it then, brethren? When ye come together, every one of you hath a psalm, hath a doctrine, hath a tongue, hath a revelation, hath an interpretation. Let all things be done unto edifying.

God Is Going to Change the Church

Ezekiel 34:12, 15-16 (WEB) (12) As a shepherd seeks out his flock in the day that he is among his sheep that are scattered abroad, so will I seek out my sheep; and I will deliver them out of all places where they have been scattered in the cloudy and dark day ... (15) I myself will be the shepherd of my sheep, and I will cause them to lie down, says the Lord Yahweh. (16) I will seek that which was lost, and will bring back that which was driven away, and will bind up that which was broken, and will strengthen that which was sick: but the fat and the strong I will destroy; I will feed them in justice.

God is raising up people who want to return to the Biblical format for Church. Ezekiel 34 says that the Lord Himself will seek and take care of His own flock. Today, God desires to raise up leaders who have His heart. Many are leaving the large traditional churches and starting new ones. God is raising up leaders from everyday, common people.

Chapter 18: The Full-Time Minister

Many of these individuals could not have done what they are doing now in the churches they went to before.

Some of these new churches are established with the Biblical pattern for the Church given in the Scripture. Most of these Christian communities are small and they often meet in homes or other gathering places where people can all use their gifts. It is not hard to find books or internet sites on cell churches, micro-churches, market place churches, house churches, and so forth. I believe that this explosion of new formats is part of a move of God to bring believers back to New Testament principles and reach more people in local communities and throughout the world.

God is working, but people need to be careful not to repeat history by doing the same thing over again without leaving room for believers to use the ministry gifts and other gifts of the Spirit. Why start something new and make the same mistakes?

I also believe that people do not have to leave large churches in order to function in their gifts as long as leaders adjust the format of their churches so that they can function like the New Testament Church. One good thing about having a church building with many meeting rooms is that it provides a perfect equipping center, which allows for training and a place for believers to practice using their gifts. The secret is not to be limited by the church building, but to use it as a tool to further believers' growth.

1 Corinthians 4:2 (KJV) Moreover it is required in stewards, that a man be found faithful.

In summary, full-time ministers are a necessary part of the Church. However, Christian workers need to recognize their gifts and calling, and begin functioning in those gifts. Ministers have to help their people find healing and grow to maturity. They need to set aside human traditions, and allow God's Church to function God's way. In this way, full-time ministers contribute to the health of their congregations.

Chapter 19: Apostles in the Early Church

Foundations

Ephesians 2:19-20 (WEB) So then you are no longer strangers and foreigners, but you are fellow citizens with the saints, and of the household of God, (20) being built on the foundation of the apostles and prophets, Christ Jesus himself being the chief cornerstone;

The ministry gifting of apostle is an essential gift in the Body of Christ. Ephesians 2:19-20 says that the Church is built upon the foundation of the ministry of the apostles and the prophets, Jesus being the cornerstone. As such, it is no surprise that there is so much spiritual warfare over those with callings to be apostles and prophets.

It saddens me that until recently the Church has largely viewed the ministry of the apostle or prophet as no longer needed or necessary. In many traditional churches, if someone said he felt called to be an apostle or prophet, he would not be accepted. Without exceptional proof that this person moves maturely in his gift, people might even think he was delusional.

2 Peter 1:10-11 (WEB) Therefore, brothers, be more diligent to make your calling and election sure. For if you do these things, you will never stumble. (11) For thus you will be richly supplied with the entrance into the eternal Kingdom of our Lord and Savior, Jesus Christ.

Church: What Was God Thinking?

I have heard people say that anyone who admits that they feel called as an apostle or prophet has problems with pride. Why is it arrogant to know your gift? Paul often opened his letters with the phrase, "Paul, called to be an apostle …" He knew his calling. He even instructed others to make their calling sure. This is essential for every Christian. It is imperative that potential apostles and prophets be recognized and affirmed in the Body, and that they be equipped to grow in their spiritual gifts and ministry. Such people have unique importance in the Church.

Why the Church Needs Apostles

There are strengths apostles have that the church cannot do without. Apostles are able to look at even the most broken people, often with the prophet's help, and see who they are destined to become in the Lord. They can then coach these people, bringing out their potential as future equippers and leaders. Of equal importance is their ability to evaluate the spiritual foundation of the Church to see if it is in good shape. Without these spiritual builders, the Church would be left in great disrepair.

In this age, God is restoring the ministry of apostles. They teach with substance, sharing the truth in love, resulting in life transformation. They serve the meat of the Word, not just the milk. Sometimes this makes people uncomfortable because they have not accepted truth and need change. If people are not changing, the apostle prays to receive revelation on what is blocking growth. Apostolic ministry is essential to the Body of Christ.

New Testament apostles function with God-given authority. What I mean is they have supernatural ability to accomplish what He says they will do. People gain this authority through faithfulness in the small things. As individuals are diligent to do what the Lord tells them to do, He will give them more responsibility. He will also increase their power, ability, speed, efficiency, and impact in the things they accomplish (Luke 16:10). Obedience is the key to authority.

Chapter 19: Apostles in the Early Church

Apostles have some basic responsibilities. First, as leaders, apostles must have an intimate relationship with the Lord and the ability to help others be close to Him, too. Apostles need to hear His voice and know how to bring others into their destinies. They should not make decisions based on what they think, but from knowing and having God's heart. These are all part of the apostle's job description.

What Apostles Looked Like in the Bible

1 Corinthians 12:4-6 (WEB) Now there are various kinds of gifts, but the same Spirit. (5) There are various kinds of service, and the same Lord. (6) There are various kinds of workings, but the same God, who works all things in all.

1 Corinthians 12:11 (WEB) But the one and the same Spirit works all of these, distributing to each one separately as he desires.

The apostolic gifting is perhaps the most mysterious of all the offices, but Scripture gives us some glimpses of their ministry. Like most gifts, the outward expression of the apostolic is different with different people.

Acts 5:15-16 (WEB) They even carried out the sick into the streets, and laid them on cots and mattresses, so that as Peter came by, at the least his shadow might overshadow some of them. (16) Multitudes also came together from the cities around Jerusalem, bringing sick people, and those who were tormented by unclean spirits: and they were all healed.

To understand apostolic ministry, all Christians have to do is look at the early apostles. Peter, for example, walked by people and the Holy Spirit used his shadow to heal them! Many had an anointing for healing, but not identical to this. It does not work to put the apostolic gift, or any other gift, into a box. People cannot say there is only one expression of this gift. Even so, there are some basic characteristics that all apostles can have.

Church: What Was God Thinking?

Acts 2:37 (WEB) Now when they heard this, they were cut to the heart, and said to Peter and the rest of the apostles, "Brothers, what shall we do?"

Acts 2:41 (WEB) Then those who gladly received his word were baptized. There were added that day about three thousand souls.

There were twelve apostles in Jerusalem, all of them witnesses of Christ's resurrection. Scripture shows them moving in many different gifts. At first, they did the work of evangelists, bringing people to repentance through their preaching. They brought three thousand people to Christ at one time. After this, they continued to help these new believers grow and become effective ministers in the Body of Christ.

Acts 6:4 But we will continue steadfastly in prayer and in the ministry of the word."

Acts 6:4 speaks of the apostles' devotion to teaching and prayer. It is likely that the number of people that believed was a result of the time that they spent with God and obeyed Him. Acts 2:47 shows us the fruit of the apostle's work:

Acts 2:47 (WEB) praising God, and having favor with all the people. The Lord added to the assembly day by day those who were being saved.

The apostle's role is essential for rapid multiplication of mature believers in the church. For some apostles, this is their ministry focus. An apostle's part in that growth is to prepare the Christians under his authority so that as new people receive salvation, there will be others ready to equip these new believers. Church growth is not as effective without them.

Acts 2:42 (WEB) They continued steadfastly in the apostle's teaching and fellowship, in the breaking of bread, and prayer.

Ephesians 4:11-13 (WEB) He gave some to be apostles; and some, prophets; and some, evangelists; and some, shepherds [pastors] and

Chapter 19: Apostles in the Early Church

teachers; (12) for the perfecting of the saints, to the work of serving, to the building up of the body of Christ; (13) until we all attain to the unity of the faith, and of the knowledge of the Son of God, to a full grown man, to the measure of the stature of the fullness of Christ;

Mature apostles usually use many gifts. It is often difficult to discern what spiritual gift they do not have. It is true, however, that an apostle might not use the other gifts with the level of authority that someone in the office of that particular gift would. This ability to move in the various gifts empowers apostles to equip others with different callings, and that should be their desire, to facilitate the establishment of all the gifts and ministries in the Church.

2 Timothy 2:2 (WEB) The things which you have heard from me among many witnesses, commit the same to faithful men, who will be able to teach others also.

When a person becomes a mature believer, it is time for him to equip others. This is modeled in the New Testament. The twelve apostles trained others because that is what apostles do (Ephesians 4:11-13). In the book of Acts, Paul raised up churches and then sent other people who had matured in the Lord to strengthen them further. Then the apostles or apostolic teams would leave the group so that the people they raised up could continue to coach the new believers in ministry.

Romans 1:11-12 (WEB) For I long to see you, that I may impart to you some spiritual gift, to the end that you may be established; (12) that is, that I with you may be encouraged in you, each of us by the other's faith, both yours and mine.

An apostle has the anointing of passing abilities on to others. Romans 1:11-12 says that Paul longed to impart gifts to people in the Church. He wanted it to be a complete Body. Even today, apostles play a significant role in the Church's ability to function in all the gifts.

An apostle is able to encourage believers to stir up their spiritual gifts. When first receiving a confirming word from an apostle or prophet regarding a gift, many people lack confidence or feel unsure about how to begin using it. Sometimes individuals simply need to be reminded to pursue God for insight into how to move forward.

Acts 15:36 (WEB) After some days Paul said to Barnabas, "Let's return now and visit our brothers in every city in which we proclaimed the word of the Lord, to see how they are doing."

Philippians 2:19-23 (WEB) But I hope in the Lord Jesus to send Timothy to you soon, that I also may be cheered up when I know how you are doing. (20) For I have no one else like-minded, who will truly care about you. (21) For they all seek their own, not the things of Jesus Christ. (22) But you know the proof of him, that, as a child serves a father, so he served with me in furtherance of the Good News. (23) Therefore I hope to send him at once, as soon as I see how it will go with me.

Some modern-day apostles are meant to be like Paul, with a travelling ministry. Careful study of Scripture shows that Paul did not simply abandon those in his new works to figure out the Christian life by themselves. He sent leaders to help the believing communities become established, he wrote letters addressing problems in the churches, and he sometimes visited them to see how they were.

Some apostles thrive on establishing new works. These apostles, like Paul, begin a ministry, then move on to start another ministry. At the same time, they continue to oversee their previous work. The New Testament makes it clear that Paul cooperated with others to establish new churches. In the course of his life, Paul traveled with Barnabas, Silas, and many others. He also sent people to strengthen the churches. For example: in chapter two of the letter to the Philippians, Paul mentioned that he was sending Timothy and Epaphroditus to Philippi to assist the church (Philippians 2:19; 25-28).

1 Corinthians 1:11 (WEB) For it has been reported to me concerning you, my brothers, by those who are from Chloe's household, that there are contentions among you.

Chapter 19: Apostles in the Early Church

1 Corinthians 1:11 mentions members of Chloe's household who had contact with Paul, informing him about what was happening. There is no clear indication of who Chloe was, but she sent messages to Paul about the church in Corinth. This shows that he had a network of people to help him know what was going on in the churches he planted. In this way, Paul could continue helping the believers in various places.

When one thinks about how much Paul traveled, in an age without phones, computers or internet access, his ability to continue in communication with believers in different places is astounding. Different Scriptures show that various people sent him messages; Paul clearly had a network of believers in regular correspondence with him, otherwise they would not have known where to find him.

It is necessary to note that as Paul oversaw the churches he started, he did not control their every decision. His main objective was to facilitate their growth and to prevent them from going into error.

1 Thessalonians 3:2 (WEB) and sent Timothy, our brother and God's servant in the Good News of Christ, to establish you, and to comfort you concerning your faith;

It is common to find an apostle doing missionary work, and he often works in a team. Those he works with are not necessarily apostles, but they have been called to work with one. An apostolic team is a group of people with different gifts that help start new works. Paul is a good example of someone who worked with teams for evangelism, church planting, and equipping. He did not leave the church to figure everything out by itself. A close look at Paul's epistles shows that he sent people to different churches to train believers, including Timothy and Apollos.

Philippians 2:19 (WEB) But I hope in the Lord Jesus to send Timothy to you soon, that I also may be cheered up when I know how you are doing.

Church: What Was God Thinking?

First, Paul went into the synagogues in a new place to preach to the Jews and then to the Gentiles. He often drew crowds, and no matter how angry they became, he kept on preaching the Gospel. There were times that the persecution was so great he had to flee. Then, Paul would direct different members of his apostolic team to go back to those cities to continue training the believers there.

Other apostles, unlike Paul, stayed in the same location to oversee the church like the twelve apostles that Jesus left in Jerusalem. In the modern world, apostles often use e-mail, telephone and video conferencing to continue their work. Video conferencing allows apostles to see their ministry partners, even from a great distance. My ministry team has benefitted from this technology both receiving blessing and ministering to others. We live in amazing times with many ways to do the work of the Kingdom!

Suggested Reading: 1 Corinthians 4:15-17

Each apostle has different strengths in their ministries and giftings. For example, looking at Paul's life, it is clear that he was strong in evangelism.

Acts 14:6-7 (KJV) They were ware of it, and fled unto Lystra and Derbe, cities of Lycaonia, and unto the region that lieth round about: (7) And there they preached the gospel.

Acts 5:15 (WEB) They even carried out the sick into the streets, and laid them on cots and mattresses, so that as Peter came by, at the least his shadow might overshadow some of them.

The apostles in the Bible moved in the gifts of evangelism (Acts 2:14–41), healing (Acts 3:11), teaching (Acts 2:42), and the ability to pray for people to receive the Holy Spirit (Acts 8:17). All the apostles that I have met moved in many, perhaps all of the ministry gifts. Some of them had the same gift but a different expression of it. It is very easy to make a formula by saying that each gift has to operate in one specific way. However, God delights in diversity.

Chapter 19: Apostles in the Early Church

Since individuals have different strengths, it is important that an assortment of people with different gifts be involved in the equipping process. By alternating apostles and those with other gifts, the church is given a much richer heart-knowledge of God. In this way, believers can be trained and equipped, facilitating their unique strengths, to grow into their gifts and callings.

Acts 15:6 (WEB) The apostles and the elders were gathered together to see about this matter.

2 John 1:1 (WEB) The elder, to the chosen lady and her children, whom I love in truth; and not I only, but also all those who know the truth;

1 Peter 5:1 (WEB) I exhort the elders among you, as a fellow elder, and a witness of the sufferings of Christ, and who will also share in the glory that will be revealed.

Apostles are a vital part of church leadership (Acts 15:6). The apostles in Jerusalem were part of the church government in the city. They met with elders to make decisions about church matters and doctrine. Later, Peter and John said in their letters that they were also elders. I would like to assume that the other ten apostles were mature enough to be elders, but I cannot prove this. Not everyone that has an apostolic gift or any of the ministry gifts is mature in their gift or has the calling or maturity to be an elder. The point is that the Jerusalem apostles were leaders and had a significant role in the church in their cities of residence.

Apostles are an essential part of the local church. Since they are able to move in multiple gifts, possibly in all the gifts of the Spirit, they are more likely not to look at ministry through the lens of one particular ministry gift. An apostle who is walking in his calling will find it easy to see Church [*ekklesia*] as a gathering of believers who come together to use their unique gifts.

Church: What Was God Thinking?

Apostles Can Have Certain Ministry Focuses

According to tradition, Timothy was the first bishop of the church of Ephesus. The word "bishop" in the Greek is also translated overseer. It is likely that Timothy was an apostle.

2 Timothy 1:6 (WEB) For this cause, I remind you that you should stir up the gift of God which is in you through the laying on of my hands.

2 Timothy 4:5 (WEB) But you be sober in all things, suffer hardship, do the work of an evangelist, and fulfill your ministry.

1 Timothy 4:13 (WEB) Until I come, pay attention to reading, to exhortation, and to teaching.

2 Timothy 4:2 (WEB) preach the word; be urgent in season and out of season; reprove, rebuke, and exhort, with all patience and teaching.

Although Paul told Timothy to do the work of an evangelist, I do not believe this was his primary gift. Since Paul in 1 Timothy 3 gave Timothy a list of the requirements for overseers, it is likely that this was one of his ministry roles. He was also a preacher and a teacher of the Bible which at that time was the Old Testament. Part of the reason I believe that Timothy was an apostle is because the content of Paul's letters to Timothy are not instructions to an evangelist, rather they are more typical of the instructions that would be given to an apostle.

Also, a number of Paul's epistles make it clear that Timothy was his co-worker and have instructions for Timothy to go to different places to help the churches. (There are many Scriptures about this, including: Acts 19:22; Romans 16:21; 1 Corinthians 4:17, 16:10; 2 Corinthians 1:19; Philippians 2:19-23; 1 Thessalonians 3:2-6). Paul refers to Timothy as his son. In keeping with the ancient custom, a son was usually trained in his father's occupation. This makes it likely that while Timothy traveled extensively with Paul he received hands-on training to do the work of an apostle, just like the first apostles received their apostolic equipping while traveling with Jesus. Timothy is an example of an apostle who also used the gift of evangelism.

Chapter 19: Apostles in the Early Church

Paul commanded Timothy to use the gift of evangelism (2 Timothy 4:2-5). It is obvious that Timothy moved in many gifts and needed to put more emphasis on evangelism. This does not mean that everyone has the ministry gift of evangelism or should do an evangelist's work. Some leaders read this and encourage all of their people to become evangelists. Although all believers are called to the joy of sharing the Good News to some extent, leaders must never make people minister with gifts they do not have.[7] Paul was not telling Timothy to use a gift he did not have, rather to move in a gift that he was not using at least to the extent that he should.

In summary, apostles are builders who begin new ministries and strengthen those already in existence. The early apostles give a clear picture of what their role in the Church is meant to be. So what do apostles look like today? Do they still have an important function in the modern Church?

---

[7] Not everyone is called to be an evangelist. At the same time, according to the leading of the Holy Spirit, all believers have a part in the joyful responsibility to share the Good News, testifying of what God has done in their lives (Matthew 10:32-33; Mark 16:15-20; Revelation 12:10-11).

Chapter 20: Apostles in the Modern Church

Acts 8:5-25, especially Acts 8:14-17 (WEB) Now when the apostles who were at Jerusalem heard that Samaria had received the word of God, they sent Peter and John to them, (15) who, when they had come down, prayed for them, that they might receive the Holy Spirit; (16) for as yet he had fallen on none of them. They had only been baptized in the name of Christ Jesus. (17) Then they laid their hands on them, and they received the Holy Spirit.

Apostles have the ability to bring the move of the Holy Spirit to a new area. In the book of Acts, apostles were the first to bring the Holy Spirit to the Samaritans (Acts 8:5-25) and the Gentiles (Acts 10:21-11:18). In many places, the Church has little experience in the power of the Spirit. God wants to raise up apostles to bring signs, wonders and miracles to areas that are not experiencing His power, regardless of whether or not that area already has churches.

Some say that the apostles' role today is only through missions, that God has no place for them in the local church. However, as my ministry team has prayed prophetically with different people, the Lord has shown us that there are many called to be apostles. I believe that God also has a use for apostolic ministry in the local church today.

Apostles are needed in both local and overseas churches. Leaders can discover what position believers should have in the Church by listening to God and to those called into this type of ministry. Local churches greatly need apostles and prophets to impart spiritual gifts. The Body of Christ cannot do without those who look around and see what new ministries should be started in a particular region.

Church: What Was God Thinking?

James 2:1-6 (WEB) My brothers, don't hold the faith of our Lord Jesus Christ of glory with partiality. (2) For if a man with a gold ring, in fine clothing, comes into your synagogue, and a poor man in filthy clothing also comes in; (3) and you pay special attention to him who wears the fine clothing, and say, "Sit here in a good place;" and you tell the poor man, "Stand there," or "Sit by my footstool;" (4) haven't you shown partiality among yourselves, and become judges with evil thoughts? (5) Listen, my beloved brothers. Didn't God choose those who are poor in this world to be rich in faith, and heirs of the Kingdom which he promised to those who love him? (6) But you have dishonored the poor man. Don't the rich oppress you, and personally drag you before the courts?

James 2:9-10 (WEB) But if you show partiality, you commit sin, being convicted by the law as transgressors. (10) For whoever keeps the whole law, and yet stumbles in one point, he has become guilty of all.

A mature apostle wants everyone equipped for ministry (Ephesians 4:11-16). Many congregations focus on one or two people groups. Often, it seems they spend the most time and energy on the middle and upper classes. In contrast, the mature apostle has a burden for everyone in the city, for their physical as well as spiritual needs.

Apostles are an essential part of the local church. Since they are able to move in multiple gifts, possibly in all the gifts of the Spirit, they are more likely not to look at ministry through the lens of one particular ministry gift. An apostle who is walking in his calling will find it easy to see Church [*ekklesia*] as a gathering of believers who come together to use their unique gifts.

1 Corinthians 4:15 (WEB) For though you have ten thousand tutors in Christ, yet not many fathers. For in Christ Jesus, I became your father through the Good News.

Apostles are necessary, not only to protect the open, interactive format of the gathering (1 Corinthians 14:26), but also to raise up individuals from all the giftings in the Church. Paul said he was a "father in Christ" (1 Corinthians 4:15). The community of believers needs fathers who are wholeheartedly committed to healing the Body, helping believers grow instead of being more interested in their own

Chapter 20: Apostles in the Modern Church

needs or in following their personal vision. This is how the Church accomplishes God's heart for their geographical region (see Ezekiel 34).

Even when a community of Christians lacks mature apostles, this does not mean that they cannot think like apostles. Leaders without this ministry gift may not function as well in this area as an apostle would, but they can still try to move closer to apostolic thinking.

An apostle in charge of a congregation will pass on the mindset of equipping and releasing believers into the DNA of the church. Without someone mature in the apostolic gift, leaders may have to work extra hard to avoid focusing too much on any one particular ministry gift. Even so at least the church would be moving towards God's intention for community life.

Philippians 2:19-20 (WEB) But I hope in the Lord Jesus to send Timothy to you soon, that I also may be cheered up when I know how you are doing. (20) For I have no one else like-minded, who will truly care about you.

The ability to look after others' interests was a trait Paul praised in Timothy. Modern leaders need to learn from his example, and deal with any area of their hearts that would tempt them to lead for their own benefit. Instead they must realize that God's purpose for the Church is for every believer to come together to be used by God, to be built up in Christ, to fall in love with Jesus, and to love one another.

Hebrews 6:1-2 (WEB) Therefore leaving the teaching of the first principles of Christ, let us press on to perfection -- not laying again a foundation of repentance from dead works, of faith toward God, (2) of the teaching of baptisms, of laying on of hands, of resurrection of the dead, and of eternal judgment.

Paul examined the Church and told them what problems they had. We need apostles who look at its foundations, whether congregationally or worldwide, and identify areas that need repair. People often look at the modern traditional church and think that since it was established so long ago, it never has to change. In fact, there is much to be done to bring the Church back to its Biblical roots and its true calling.

John 15:1-6 (WEB) "I am the true vine, and my Father is the farmer. (2) Every branch in me that doesn't bear fruit, he takes away. Every branch that bears fruit, he prunes, that it may bear more fruit. (3) You are already pruned clean because of the word which I have spoken to you. (4) Remain in me, and I in you. As the branch can't bear fruit by itself, unless it remains in the vine, so neither can you, unless you remain in me. (5) I am the vine. You are the branches. He who remains in me, and I in him, the same bears much fruit, for apart from me you can do nothing. (6) If a man doesn't remain in me, he is thrown out as a branch, and is withered; and they gather them, throw them into the fire, and they are burned.

God created the mature apostle, working alongside the prophet, to motivate the Church to be active, keeping up with what the Lord is doing. If congregations do not keep up with what God is doing, members stagnate, resulting in lack of life, even spiritual death, for many people in the Body. It is important to keep a heart that is open to change. In John 15:1-6, Jesus makes it clear that if people want to keep alive in the Holy Spirit, they must always be ready to follow God's direction.

Apostles Repair Spiritual Foundations

Many years ago, my wife and I purchased a one-hundred-year-old house that needed a lot of work. When we bought it, parts of the basement walls were disintegrating. Since I had experience in building and repairing houses, we decided to fix the old stone foundation ourselves. We borrowed some house jacks and raised the house one section at a time to support it while we rebuilt the foundation. It turned out that the weight of the house resting on the foundation was the only thing holding it together. As I lifted up the house, the foundation stones collapsed.

Chapter 20: Apostles in the Modern Church

As my family, friends, and I were tearing down what was left of the foundation, we discovered how miraculous it was that the house was still standing. There were large cavities in the middle of the rock where hundreds of brown recluse spiders were living. There was no longer enough mortar to hold the stones together, just a lot of sand and loose rock. It was hard work because, after killing the spiders, we had to re-lay the rock to rebuild the foundation.

The mature apostle is like an expert foundation repair man who looks at a house with a trained eye and sees things wrong that many people would not notice. He also knows how to fix those things. Some people in history served the church this way. They re-evaluated the foundations and, as a result, the whole direction of the church was changed. These reformers included Martin Luther and John Huss. The church has been strongly influenced by the repairs they made.

Many moves of God have been released through such reformers. Unfortunately the awakenings tend to last for a short period of time, after which things evolve into a stiff, traditional format. One of the apostle's callings is to repair the foundations of the church and to keep it from becoming institutionalized.

Ephesians 2:20 (WEB) being built on the foundation of the apostles and prophets, Christ Jesus himself being the chief cornerstone;

The apostles' work is most effective in partnership with prophets. Since the apostle likes moving in the Holy Spirit, he is drawn to the prophetic people in the Church. Cooperation with prophets helps him more clearly know the direction that God wants him to take. Once he knows this, he has the ability to put together a plan to get the church moving in the right direction.

1 Corinthians 14:1 (WEB) Follow after love, and earnestly desire spiritual gifts, but especially that you may prophesy.

2 Peter 1:21 (WEB) For no prophecy ever came by the will of man: but holy men of God spoke, being moved by the Holy Spirit.

Church: What Was God Thinking?

In 1 Corinthians 14:1, Paul says that we should earnestly desire the spiritual gifts, especially prophecy. When people prophesy, they speak God's heart. Apostles need to hear the voice of the Lord to know where the problems are in spiritual foundations. God always wants Christians to be close to His heart. After God gives His people vision for ministry, many times they need someone to encourage them to walk in it. This is a perfect job for the mature apostle who is skilled in his work and is also a "father in Christ."

2 Corinthians 12:12 (WEB) Truly the signs of an apostle were worked among you in all patience, in signs and wonders and mighty works.

One of the marks of an apostle is moving in signs and wonders and mighty works. If you are not moving in these but you feel that you are called to be an apostle, it is possible that you are not yet fully using your gift. The basis for this is to grow in your relationship with the Lord, understanding that He wants to work through you to bless those who need to know Him.

There are several obstacles that hinder a person moving in signs and wonders. Sin is one of these. Others include deficiency in any or all of the following characteristics: devotion to God in prayer and worship, passionate love for the Trinity (Father, Son, and Holy Spirit), hunger for the Bible, and faith that signs and wonders are real for today. A potential apostle must deal with these issues to begin moving in his calling.

Many Christians do not believe that God will move through them because they prayed a few times for signs and wonders and nothing happened. For those with an apostolic calling confirmed through prophets, be encouraged to spend time in God's presence, persisting in prayer for signs and wonders. Your perseverance will reap a reward that will bless many.

A person who is weak in prayer, or allows unbelief to enter when they do not see immediate results in ministry should not be surprised if they are not experiencing signs and wonders (James 1:2-12). A deep, consistent prayer life is especially important for an apostle. A lifestyle

Chapter 20: Apostles in the Modern Church

of prayer brings change to his own life and to others through his ministry as well.

2 Corinthians 10:18 (WEB) For it isn't he who commends himself who is approved, but whom the Lord commends.

How can a person know if he is called to be an apostle? Someone cannot just decide to be one on his own. 2 Corinthians 10 says that it is the person the Lord commends who is an apostle. I have been around people who decided that they are apostles and I know in my spirit that they are not. People must make clearly confirm whether the Lord is calling them to this ministry.

For those of you who feel you are called to be an apostle, you should pray that the Lord will bring true prophets into your life to verify that (1 Corinthians 14:29; 2 Corinthians 13:1). Once your calling is confirmed, pray that the Lord will lead you to the right place to grow in that high calling.

Can a woman be an apostle? Why not? There is not one verse that says they cannot be apostles. Women can be a part of all the ministry callings. Since many people believe apostolic ministry is a man's job, I asked a friend in Mexico who has planted over two hundred churches whether women could do church planting. He told me that some of the best church planters were women because in his experience they were more likely to release people into their gifts and they also tended to be less controlling.

2 Corinthians 3:16-18 (WEB) But whenever one turns to the Lord, the veil is taken away. (17) Now the Lord is the Spirit and where the Spirit of the Lord is, there is liberty. (18) But we all, with unveiled face beholding as in a mirror the glory of the Lord, are transformed into the same image from glory to glory, even as from the Lord, the Spirit.

So how does a person mature as an apostle? It is crucial to live for God wholeheartedly, spending hours a day connecting with God and enjoying Him. Another way to grow as an apostle is to be equipped by a mature apostle. As a young apostle matures, in time, others will be drawn to him to receive training from him as well.

2 Peter 1:3-8 (WEB) seeing that his divine power has granted to us all things that pertain to life and godliness, through the knowledge of him who called us by his own glory and virtue; (4) by which he has granted to us his precious and exceedingly great promises; that through these you may become partakers of the divine nature, having escaped from the corruption that is in the world by lust. (5) Yes, and for this very cause adding on your part all diligence, in your faith supply moral excellence; and in moral excellence, knowledge; (6) and in knowledge, self-control; and in self-control patience; and in patience godliness; (7) and in godliness brotherly affection; and in brotherly affection, love. (8) For if these things are yours and abound, they make you to be not idle nor unfruitful to the knowledge of our Lord Jesus Christ.

Apostles need to take the time to work on their character. Those called to be apostles must be students of the Bible, lovers of God and good friends of the Holy Spirit. They have to know how to lay healthy and strong spiritual foundations that are solidly based in the truth. They should also make certain their relationship with the Lord is healthy and solid. Faithfulness and integrity are crucial to being an apostle.

2 Corinthians 10:8 (WEB) For though I should boast somewhat abundantly concerning our authority, (which the Lord gave for building you up, and not for casting you down) I will not be disappointed,

Godly authority is meant for strengthening others, not for power or honor. Sometimes people want the title of apostle (or any other ministry title) because they feel that it gives them greater authority or recognition in the way others view them. Sometimes that person's gift is apostolic but either they are still immature or lacking healing. A mature apostle does not feel a need to be idolized, rather he is interested in building others up so that they can all do the works of Jesus.

Chapter 20: Apostles in the Modern Church

If a person's main interest in being an apostle is to be in authority or so that they can become an important leader, they have missed the heart of God. The purpose of the apostolic gift is to edify people and build the Kingdom of God. The Lord does not give this gift to make anyone look good. He does not give it so the recipient can impress many with how spiritual he appears. He gives this gift so that people can see Him for who He is, head of His Church. The apostle's goal is to lay down his life so that others can become the best they can be in Jesus. This is the purpose of the apostolic gift.

Ephesians 4:15-16 (WEB) but speaking truth in love, we may grow up in all things into him, who is the head, Christ; (16) from whom all the body, being fitted and knit together through that which every joint supplies, according to the working in measure of each individual part, makes the body increase to the building up of itself in love.

2 Corinthians 10:13-16 (WEB) But we will not boast beyond proper limits, but within the boundaries with which God appointed to us, which reach even to you. (14) For we don't stretch ourselves too much, as though we didn't reach to you. For we came even as far as to you with the Good News of Christ, (15) not boasting beyond proper limits in other men's labors, but having hope that as your faith grows, we will be abundantly enlarged by you in our sphere of influence, (16) so as to preach the Good News even to the parts beyond you, not to boast in what someone else has already done.

Immature apostles can do some strange things. Some young apostles walk into churches and tell them they are in authority over that church. Such people could be mistaken about their gifts, or may be potential apostles who are not yet mature. Paul implies in Scripture that his apostolic authority was only to be used in churches he had established himself, so as not to get in the way of someone else's work (Romans 15:17-21). He seemed to feel that to do so would be overstepping his bounds. The only exception to this is when a church invites an apostle to assist in repairing their spiritual foundations. Even then, he needs to remain cautious and respectful. In general, an apostle should not take over another person's work.

Church: What Was God Thinking?

From looking at Paul's example (in Corinth, Galatia, Ephesus, Philippi, and so on), it is apparent that after an apostle has planted and established a church, his position changes to an apostolic overseer, giving encouragement and correction as needed (2 Corinthians 2:9). It is necessary to note that when the apostles of the early Church wrote letters to churches, these letters were primarily written to encourage them for what was being done right and to give them constructive criticism. Paul's purpose was not to control the church, but to assist everyone's growth, walking in love towards one another and in faithfulness to God. This shows the attitude present day apostles should maintain towards the works God leads them to establish.

Apostles have different functions. If the apostle is called to stay with the work that he has begun, like the apostles in Jerusalem, he will play a different role. He might be part of the church government and oversee it. If he is an apostle that was raised up in the local congregation, he could supervise small groups, begin new ministries within it, or start new works outside the church. Not all apostles function the same way.

One of the most significant roles of an apostle is to bring correction to the Church. In recent years, many books have been published discussing changes that need to be made in the Church. Some of these books are apostolic, giving correction to the Church. However, each person needs to search Scripture to make sure these messages are in line with the Bible.

Possible Apostolic Weaknesses

As with any spiritual gift, there can be weaknesses and abuse with the ministry gift of apostle. When people seek God in their lives, they will use the gifts best. When they try to use the gifts without the Holy Spirit's anointing, it is like trying to run a car without gas. They may be able to go downhill for awhile but sooner or later, when they need to go up a hill, they discover that they do not have what it takes. Everyone needs to learn how to use spiritual gifts in submission to God.

Chapter 20: Apostles in the Modern Church

At some point, God might call an apostle to leave the people he has raised up and the work he has started. An apostle may not wish to do this. He might not know how to step back and let others function independently. If God has called him to go elsewhere and he does not get out of the way, he risks destroying what he has already begun.

Another possible apostolic mistake is the other extreme of getting bored too easily and leaving a work with little support or oversight, just letting the people struggle through it independently, problems and all. They may still grow, but God has purposed them to have "fathers in Christ" who are available to give input and help them mature.

One way to illustrate this is to think in terms of a work situation. How many people have had bosses that would leave them with little supervision before they knew what they were doing? When trying something for the first time, the results could be disastrous. In the end, the employer, the employee, and the client would all be very frustrated.

I realize that apostles are not running a business. At the same time, they do know more about living for God and church function than a group of new believers. Because of this, apostles should ensure their people have received enough knowledge, input, and training before leaving them to carry on alone.

There are always exceptions. In some places that are closed to the Gospel, the only way to plant a church is by starting a work and then going away so as not to attract unwanted attention. If the church planter does not leave quickly enough, this could endanger the church. Ideally, it is best to have a team in place, perhaps of national believers, to provide oversight. This team could even supervise church planting teams in the region. The church planter or someone he designates might also need to take short return visits to see how everyone is doing.

One difficulty some apostles face is being misunderstood by the Church. Some people mistakenly think that apostles are undependable since they often want to move on to new works. Others think the apostle is proud or always showing off because he is gifted and enjoys using his gifts. This can be uncomfortable for the apostle.

Church: What Was God Thinking?

Apostles can also run into difficulties in the traditional church. In such churches, they may feel dissatisfied, if they are not allowed to minister. They could be labeled as troublemakers since the vision they see goes beyond what is already happening. On the other extreme, because of their multi-giftedness, they might be overworked or forced into the wrong type of ministry, resulting in burnout. These can all present challenges to apostles.

In summary, mature apostles are leaders in the Church. Some establish new foundations or repair old ones. They fulfill a need in the Body of Christ for pioneering, for new ministry, and for refreshing the Body. God is restoring this ministry to the Church.

Chapter 21: The Test of a True Apostle

Revelation 2:2 (WEB) "I know your works, and your toil and perseverance, and that you can't tolerate evil men, and have tested those who call themselves apostles, and they are not, and found them false.

The Greek word for "false" is ψευδής *pseudēs.*
Strong's definition G5571 (pronounced: *psyoo-dace'*)
From G5574; untrue, that is, erroneous, deceitful, wicked: - false, liar.

God has a plan to raise up apostles, but, at the same time, there is a demonic plan to raise up false apostles. We are in an age when God is awakening the apostolic gift and raising up apostles throughout the world. With more true apostles emerging, it is likely that there will also be an increase in the number of counterfeit apostles trying to deceive people. In this chapter, I intend to discuss criteria and guidelines for differentiating true and false apostles.

In the book of Revelation, the Lord speaks to the church in Ephesus, commending them for testing apostles to see if they were false. The eleventh and twelfth chapters of 2 Corinthians discuss some of the differences between real and counterfeit apostles. This passage of Scripture also talks about what is not appropriate for an apostle. In order to test an apostle, it is necessary to know what true and false apostles look like.

Church: What Was God Thinking?

Recognizing a False Apostle

What is a false apostle? There are several different types. I would like to list a few examples:

Some false apostles try to make everyone believe that they are apostles when they are not. Such people might not even believe in Jesus.

Others have a different gift but tell everyone that they are apostles. In this case, they could be confused, or they may desire the gift so much that they are deceived into thinking they already have it.

Some false apostles have the calling and the title but are not functioning as apostles. Such people would rather have the glory of the title than have to do the work.

People who claim to be apostles, but take over someone else's work without permission are sometimes false apostles. This can also happen, however, with immature apostles or apostles in error.

Finally, false apostles can be sincere Christians who have just missed their calling. Some people are false apostles because they want to be something that they are not. This opens them up to satan's attack and they will likely burnout from the pressure. Knowing one's calling prevents many problems.

The Holy Spirit's Help in Discerning a False Apostle

John 14:26 (WEB) But the Counselor, the Holy Spirit, whom the Father will send in my name, he will teach you all things, and will remind you of all that I said to you.

Scripture is the first and most important testing ground for apostles. This testing must be done by those who have developed discernment through diligent study of Scripture and intimacy with the Holy Spirit, by being continually being filled with Him. This is the only way to make sure that people are not judged using the wrong criteria.

Chapter 21: The Test of a True Apostle

Acts 17:11 (WEB) Now these were more noble than those in Thessalonica, in that they received the word with all readiness of the mind, examining the Scriptures daily to see whether these things were so.

Christians need to know and understand Scripture so they can thoroughly investigate what they have been taught to make sure that it is really from God. As a young Christian, the pastor of the church I attended always told the congregation to study the Bible and check it out for themselves and not simply take his word for it. Believers do need to listen to others, but at the same time they should examine Scripture to make sure that what others say has Biblical foundations. Checking things out with the Bible is vital to the Christian walk.

It is necessary to make certain that leaders are not deceiving people. At the same time, followers need to make sure that they are not following false apostles so that they will not be led astray. The enemy desires to stop the work of the Kingdom as much as possible, and will use false apostles as a means for that. All Christians must be careful and discerning.

Discernment Versus Judgment

Believers do need to be careful about judging different ministries for mistakes that they have made. Judging is different from having discernment about a problem in the Church. For example, if someone thinks that a particular ministry is not a work of God and could never be one because of mistakes that have been made, they are judging that ministry. When people judge others in this way, they are agreeing with satan's accusations and, as a result are entering into a spirit of witchcraft. (Agreeing with satan in accusation is rebellion against God which is as the sin of witchcraft. Revelation 12:10; 1 Samuel 15:23).[8] In

---

[8] For more information on accusation and the spirit of witchcraft, I recommend the following books: *Overcoming Witchcraft* by Rick Joyner and *The Final Quest* by Rick Joyner.

contrast, discernment is knowing that something is wrong, but also knowing that those problems can be changed, although such transformation might require an act of God.

True moves of God have been destroyed in the past by attacks from satan and from people who judge the entire thing as wrong because of one issue. Another way God's work is derailed is when leaders fall. Often this occurs because they have not dealt with their weaknesses and hurts. Although this happens, it does not mean God will never use such ministers again. Preferably, a minister should receive healing to help prevent falling before entering ministry, or at least during ministry. However, many people ignore the warning signs that signal trouble. On the other hand, recovered fallen ministers could come back and still have strong ministries if the Body of Christ would allow them. If others are constantly criticizing them, this may hinder the work of God in their lives.

Issues a False Apostle May Have

Control issues can be a sign of a false apostle. Such people feel that if they are an apostle, they have authority to control churches and people under the guise of leadership. In 2 Corinthians, a group of people calling themselves apostles were trying to take over churches that Paul had established. When people truly have an apostolic calling, they are willing to lay down their lives for Jesus and for the Church. God requires them to set aside any selfish ambition. This is as true for the apostle as it is for any other leader in the Church. It is essential to deal with control issues.

There are some things that a mature apostle should never do. A mature apostle must never try to take over another man's work. He is satisfied in his role as a spiritual repair man, fire starter, vision igniter, ministry starter, or overseer. A mature apostle has dealt with any control issues he has.

Chapter 21: The Test of a True Apostle

2 Corinthians 11:5 (WEB) For I reckon that I am not at all behind the very best apostles.

Here is another way to recognize false apostles. In Corinth, there was a group of people who tried to take over the work Paul had begun. They acted like they thought they were "super apostles." They taught false doctrine to the church. At the same time, they were putting Paul down as though he was inferior to them. Such pride is a warning sign of a false apostle.

2 Corinthians 11:13-14 (WEB) For such men are false apostles, deceitful workers, masquerading as Christ's apostles. (14) And no wonder, for even Satan masquerades as an angel of light.

In 2 Corinthians 11:13-14, Paul had some pretty strong words about false apostles. He said that even satan masquerades as an angel of light. One key issue was that these "false apostles" tried to take over someone else's work. This same problem is a risk in the present day Church. Leaders, if someone comes to your church, says he is an apostle, and wants to take over your church, do not give him any authority unless you are sure this is from the heart of God.

Contrast: True, Mature Apostles

Proverbs 18:16 (WEB) A man's gift makes room for him, and brings him before great men.

Mature apostles show evidence of their authority. If a person is called to be an apostle, the fruit that eventually comes out of his work will prove it. I do not simply mean that person will succeed. Sometimes true apostles fail in what they try to do for various reasons. In such cases, other possible fruit will be that he will learn from his work, or discover a different ministry focus. An apostle will not have to force his way into churches, they will come to him, wanting to benefit from the wisdom he has. If he fails in his work, then he must seek God for the reasons.

God may teach him through the experience. He might want to show the apostle different areas where he could do better, or things he was doing wrong. It is also possible that He is removing some dross from the apostle's life, dealing with issues that should not be there.

It is good to know what God is teaching in such circumstances. If an apostle is not yet confirmed in his gift, this would also be a good time to seek God to find out whether or not he is truly an apostle. On the other hand, because everyone is human, mistakes and failure are always a possibility. The point is to learn from the situation. This is part of maturing in life in God. Therefore, failure can be a sign of several things: it may mean that the apostle is being tested, is in training, doing the wrong thing, or in some cases, that he is mistaken regarding his gift. Just because someone does not succeed in every ministry situation, this does not necessarily mean he is a false apostle.

Matthew 16:23 (WEB) But he turned, and said to Peter, "Get behind me, Satan! You are a stumbling block to me, for you are not setting your mind on the things of God, but on the things of men."

Believers do need to have grace for Christians that make mistakes. A person can make serious mistakes and still be a true apostle. In Matthew 16:23, even Peter was rebuked for not having God's heart. Jesus said that what Peter said came from satan. Someone can be sincere and still not be teaching what is from the heart of God.

Apostolic Head Pastor Pushing for Everyone to be the Same

I have had certain leaders, "head pastors," that were likely apostles but they did not realize it. These leaders were very gifted and seemed like they could do anything in the church. They thought that everyone should move in any of the gifts that were needed at any given time. One church burned out over ninety-five percent of its workers because they were putting people in the wrong positions. In most cases, their giftings did not fit the demands of the roles they were asked to fill.

Chapter 21: The Test of a True Apostle

Years later, another church that my family regularly attended made one of my daughters a small group leader. She led three small groups in six years. After the third one, she did not want to even attend another small group. She burned out after leading each one. She took some time to pray and process her experience, and some time later received prophetic words from people who did not know her confirming she was not called to function as a small group leader. We came to the conclusion that the next time we started a church, as much as possible we would avoid putting people into roles outside of their gifting.

True Apostles Lead Believers to Depend on Christ

One of the things that true apostles do is work at creating a church where people focus on loving Jesus and each other. When Paul and his team started churches that is what they did. They taught the new believers how to have a sincere and pure devotion to Christ so they could be connected to the power source. Love should be the primary goal for every Christian. Jesus said if people love God with all their hearts and love their neighbor they have fulfilled all the commandments. No matter how gifted people are, if they do not have love, they run the risk of destroying each other rather than strengthening one another.

2 Corinthians 11:2-3 (WEB) For I am jealous over you with a godly jealousy. For I married you to one husband, that I might present you as a pure virgin to Christ. (3) But I am afraid that somehow, as the serpent deceived Eve in his craftiness, so your minds might be corrupted from the simplicity that is in Christ.

Apostles and other leaders must motivate others to sincere and pure devotion to Christ. If they are not, they could be unintentionally guiding people away from Christ, and run the risk of becoming false apostles. In addition, if a leader is not directing people to devotion to Christ, the question needs to be asked: where are these ministers leading? There is a risk that they are bringing people into relational dependence. Leaders need to be careful to avoid this trap.

2 Corinthians 11:4 (WEB) For if he who comes preaches another Jesus, whom we did not preach, or if you receive a different spirit, which you did not receive, or a different "good news", which you did not accept, you put up with that well enough.

False apostles deceive people and teach doctrine from satan or from their flesh. The enemy often tries to mimic the move of the Holy Spirit. Knowing Scripture helps prevent the influence of such hypocrisy and insincerity. When false apostles teach, they can pass on deceiving spirits. It is vital for believers to know the truth and be solidly grounded in the Bible.

People need to be discerning because not everyone in church is there for the right reason. Certain people are trying to deceive others. They know in their hearts that they are not apostles, or sometimes not even believers. They have ulterior motives for being in the church. Some are involved in witchcraft and want to destroy God's work. Insincere individuals could be in church because they love other things such as: gold, glory, or people's attention. Certain so-called "pastors" have even sexually abused their own church members. True believers need to be continually filled with the Holy Spirit so they will not be deceived.

In writing about this, I do not intend to make anyone fearful of the Holy Spirit or the gifts. Most of all, I believe that God gives gifts because He wants the best for His children and for believers to use what He has given. They are power tools for building the Church. He does not want anyone to be frightened of learning how to use them. When power tools are used to build a house, it will be finished much more quickly. When believers use the gifts of the Holy Spirit, they are using God's power tools for building the Kingdom of God.

One time, when I was working as a carpenter, I put up a section of fence but did not have a power outlet for my power saw. Using a hand saw, it took me half a day to cut the wood and put up the fence. If I had electricity, I could have done the work in an hour and a half. The

Chapter 21: The Test of a True Apostle

Lord showed me that it is the same way when a person tries to build the Kingdom of God without the gifts of the Spirit. The job might get done, but it would take a long time to do the same work that would have taken a short period of time if the gifts of the Holy Spirit had been used appropriately.

When believers become skilled in using "power tools," they build the Church efficiently. If the Church is built using "hand tools" because ministers are frightened of the power tools, they could spend a lifetime accomplishing little. When master carpenters do their work with power tools, they get the work done many times faster than if they use hand tools.

In reading the Bible, it is obvious that effectiveness through God's power is His intention for the Church. Life is already so short. Each person needs to plug into the Holy Spirit or else they will not function to their full potential.

1 Corinthians 4:1-2 (WEB) So let a man think of us as Christ's servants, and stewards of God's mysteries. (2) Here, moreover, it is required of stewards, that they be found faithful.

Those called to be apostles must pray continually to stay faithful and true (1 Corinthians 4:1-2). However, they should not live in fear that they are not following Jesus, unless of course, they really are not. On the other hand, those who cause others to stumble and destroy lives instead of bringing healing and wholeness have reason to be fearful. They need to cry out to the Lord for mercy, grace, and strength to repent (Romans 2:4).

Matthew 7:7-11 (WEB) "Ask, and it will be given you. Seek, and you will find. Knock, and it will be opened for you. (8) For everyone who asks receives. He who seeks finds. To him who knocks it will be opened. (9) Or who is there among you, who, if his son asks him for bread, will give him a stone? (10) Or if he asks for a fish, who will give him a serpent? (11) If you then, being evil, know how to give good gifts to your children, how much more will your Father who is in heaven give good things to those who ask him!

Church: What Was God Thinking?

Luke's version of this Scripture is slightly different.

Luke 11:13 (WEB) If you then, being evil, know how to give good gifts to your children, how much more will your heavenly Father give the *Holy Spirit* to those who ask him?" [emphasis added]

It is encouraging that in Luke 11:13 Jesus says if believers ask Him for the Holy Spirit, then that is what He will give them. The Amplified version of the Bible emphasizes continually asking God. In Matthew 7:7-11, Jesus said their Heavenly Father desires to give them, His children, good things when they ask Him. Their greatest protection is in continually asking God to fill them with His Holy Spirit, to lead them into all truth (John 16:13) and to seek to obey Him in everything (John 14:15-21).

In summary, there is a clear difference between a true apostle and a false apostle. False apostles can be recognized by such factors as their fruit, motives, and teachings. A false apostle ministers out of the flesh, destroys the Body, or tries to take over another's work. In contrast, a true apostle ministers out of a deep relationship with God, builds the Church, and respects others' work. These are just some ways to discern the sincerity of those claiming to be apostles. Being able to differentiate between a true and false apostle is a necessary safeguard for the Church.

Chapter 22: The Role of Prophets in the Church

Ephesians 2:19-20 (WEB) So then you are no longer strangers and foreigners, but you are fellow citizens with the saints, and of the household of God, (20) being built on the foundation of the apostles and prophets, Christ Jesus himself being the chief cornerstone;

Prophets are a vital part of the Body of Christ. Together with apostles, they help lay the foundation of the Church. Since people know that a prophet's words will happen, churches everywhere want them to visit. Many appreciate prophets when they speak into their lives and tell them what God's destiny is for them. I have had them speak into my life and ignite God's fire into my heart, soul, and spirit. They can have a positive impact on the Church.

The Prophet's Function in the Body of Christ

For the Body of Christ to be in step with what God is doing, it is good to have proven prophets in positions of authority. They should be on the leadership team of the local church. They could even be involved in ministering to leaders of countries, because some politicians consult with prophets. Regardless of where they are called to serve, God designed prophets to make a difference in the world.

Church: What Was God Thinking?

Prophets help people discover what is preventing them from reaching their potential. Many of these prophets are also gifted at hearing God about blockages to healing. Often when my ministry team has prayed with others, God has given us words that help bring breakthrough. This can change people for the rest of their lives.

Part of the prophet's calling is to demonstrate the prophetic gift and equip others to use it. They are able to help individuals learn how to hear from God and the authority to release the prophetic anointing on a group of people. As a result, people that previously could not prophesy may start seeing visions and sensing God's will. After this impartation, these people will often be able to continue moving in the gift of prophecy at least to some degree. Because of this, prophets are essential in training other prophets and in teaching believers in how to move in the prophetic.

Prophets function in many different ways. Some move in inner healing. Others are good at recognizing people's spiritual gifts. Some are good at knowing what is needed in church gatherings or direction of the church. Each of these functions is necessary for the Body of Christ.

Luke 2:36-37 (WEB) There was one Anna, a prophetess, the daughter of Phanuel, of the tribe of Asher (she was of a great age, having lived with a husband seven years from her virginity, (37) and she had been a widow for about eighty-four years), who didn't depart from the temple, worshipping with fastings and petitions night and day.

Prophets were made to connect with God. Many dream of spending hours in His presence. Such people are likely to be accused of being too heavenly-minded. In fact, they were made this way, so that they can become blessings to believers, impacting many. The prophetess Anna spent her life in prayer and fasting, and as a result was privileged to become one of the few who first recognized Jesus as Messiah. There were many other prophets like her throughout history, who made communion with God their life focus.

Chapter 22: The Role of Prophets in the Church

Colossians 3:1-3 (WEB) If then you were raised together with Christ, seek the things that are above, where Christ is, seated on the right hand of God. (2) Set your mind on the things that are above, not on the things that are on the earth. (3) For you died, and your life is hidden with Christ in God.

Prophets have a unique bond with God. Moses said in Numbers 11:29 that he longed for all the Lord's people to be prophets. In saying this, I believe Moses was expressing God's heart for His people. Although all believers are meant to connect with God and hear His voice clearly, prophets seem to have an exceptional connection with God. Their life focus is meant to be enjoying time with Him. Some think of nothing else. These are key characteristics of a prophet.

1 Corinthians 14:1-4 (WEB) Follow after love, and earnestly desire spiritual gifts, but especially that you may prophesy. (2) For he who speaks in another language [tongue] speaks not to men, but to God; for no one understands; but in the Spirit he speaks mysteries. (3) But he who prophesies speaks to men for their edification, exhortation, and consolation. (4) He who speaks in another language [tongue] edifies himself, but he who prophesies edifies the assembly.

1 Corinthians 14 tells us that prophecy is an important spiritual gift to be used in church gatherings. It should not be a surprise, then, that there has been so much warfare over those with a prophetic calling. I have talked to many people with this anointing who feel hurt because there is no room for their gift in the Body. It seems this situation is more common among prophets than those with other gifts. I believe one reason for this is that the enemy does not like God's purposes to be accomplished in the Church.

Scripturally, the gift of prophecy is at least as important as teaching in church gatherings. Of course, the other gifts are necessary, but Paul particularly stresses this one. The Church needs to make room for this foundational gift.

Combinations of Gifts

1 Corinthians 12:4-11 (WEB) Now there are various kinds of gifts, but the same Spirit. (5) There are various kinds of service, and the same Lord. (6) There are various kinds of workings, but the same God, who works all things in all. (7) But to each one is given the manifestation of the Spirit for the profit of all. (8) For to one is given through the Spirit the word of wisdom, and to another the word of knowledge, according to the same Spirit; (9) to another faith, by the same Spirit; and to another gifts of healings, by the same Spirit; (10) and to another workings of miracles; and to another prophecy; and to another discerning of spirits; to another different kinds of languages [tongues]; and to another the interpretation of languages. (11) But the one and the same Spirit works all of these, distributing to each one separately as he desires.

One thing that I have not mentioned before is that people can have different blends of ministry gifts. There are many possible combinations and expressions. The prophet is no exception. For example, prophetic pastors bring healing to others quickly because they listen to God while they pray. This is a dynamic mix. These individuals have the strength of the prophetic anointing along with the gentleness of a pastor.

Since the Holy Spirit gives to each person unique expressions of the spiritual gifts as He pleases, in the Kingdom of God there are bound to be a wide variety of spiritual gift and ministry combinations. God is truly a creative God who loves diversity.

For example, some individuals have both the pastor and prophet gifting, although usually one will be stronger than the other. A prophetic pastor is somewhat different from a prophet with a pastoral focus. Both of these gift blends can be effective in inner healing ministry, but the results will vary according to their anointings. Some prophets are amazing when praying for emotional healing. They are able to hear God about what needs to be done in someone's life and bring healing much faster than a pastor who does not move in the prophetic. In contrast, an inner-healing prophet does not always have the gentleness of a pastor, so pastoral support is still needed. Although

Chapter 22: The Role of Prophets in the Church

gifts seem to be similar, God has so many ways to gift and use His people. I will discuss more about the prophet in the following chapters.

Diagram 3: The Pastor-Prophet Combination

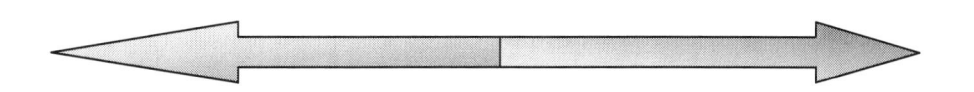

Pastoral:	God's heart	Prophetic:
Emphasize healing	Healing truths	Emphasize truth
Soft and comforting	Balanced expression	Direct/Blunt
	Soft/Direct as needed	

Chapter 23: Old Testament and New Testament Prophets

Old Testament Prophets

Deuteronomy 18:18-22 (WEB) I will raise them up a prophet from among their brothers, like you; and I will put my words in his mouth, and he shall speak to them all that I shall command him. (19) It shall happen, that whoever will not listen to my words which he shall speak in my name, I will require it of him. (20) But the prophet, who shall speak a word presumptuously in my name, which I have not commanded him to speak, or who shall speak in the name of other gods, that same prophet shall die." (21) If you say in your heart, "How shall we know the word which Yahweh has not spoken?" (22) when a prophet speaks in the name of Yahweh, if the thing doesn't follow, nor happen, that is the thing which Yahweh has not spoken: the prophet has spoken it presumptuously, you shall not be afraid of him.

2 Peter 1:20-21 (WEB) knowing this first, that no prophecy of Scripture is of private interpretation. (21) For no prophecy ever came by the will of man: but holy men of God spoke, being moved by the Holy Spirit.

There are some differences and similarities between prophets operating under the Old Covenant and modern day prophets, specifically concerning their function and role. The Old Testament prophets, moving in obedience to God's command, spoke with His inspiration to give direction for God's people, Israel.

Church: What Was God Thinking?

Many Old Testament prophets declared God's judgment on government leaders who did not follow Him. I have heard certain prophets still operating in an Old Testament model. Some New Testament prophets are called to this type of ministry but I believe that, at present, most are to be more like King David. Much of what David wrote in the Psalms was for encouragement and instruction on following God.

In the Old Testament, only certain people received the filling of the Holy Spirit. Many of these people became prophets or moved in the prophetic for a period of time. In the New Testament, all believers have the Spirit and the ability to hear God's voice, and so can walk in the prophetic. Therefore, the New Testament prophet should not only use the gift of prophecy, but also equip the Body of Christ in the prophetic. This is one reason for the change in a prophet's role under the New Covenant.

1 Corinthians 14:3 (WEB) But he who prophesies speaks to men for their edification, exhortation, and consolation.

I have been told that the test of a mature New Testament prophet is whether or not his words come true. However, prophets do not bear the primary responsibility for the fulfillment of many prophetic words. So often, believers get a prophetic word and do nothing. There is a saying, "It is hard to steer a parked car." When believers receive prophetic ministry, they need to seek God about what to do to activate the prophecies they received. Then they will see more fulfillment of the words that they are given.

The gift of prophecy is also used in exhortation. An exhortation is "an earnest request" or a message that urges someone to action (*Oxford Advanced Learner's Dictionary of Current English*, Fourth Edition, 1994). Many times, the gift of prophecy is used to encourage people to do what God is already telling them to do. Some people are passive and at times need a push to do what God asks. When a prophet learns to be sensitive about how best to reach those receiving his ministry, prophetic exhortation is an amazing application of the prophetic gift.

Chapter 23: Old Testament and New Testament Prophets

The gift of prophecy can also bring comfort to others. Some prophets have a special gift of receiving and sharing the right word for those in pain or distress. There is nothing more encouraging than receiving comfort straight from the heart of God.

The Old Testament Standard for Prophets

Deuteronomy 13:1-4 (WEB) If there arise in the midst of you a prophet, or a dreamer of dreams, and he give you a sign or a wonder, (2) and the sign or the wonder come to pass, of which he spoke to you, saying, "Let us go after other gods" (which you have not known) "and let us serve them; (3) you shall not listen to the words of that prophet, or to that dreamer of dreams: for Yahweh your God proves you, to know whether you love Yahweh your God with all your heart and with all your soul. (4) You shall walk after Yahweh your God, and fear him, and keep his commandments, and obey his voice, and you shall serve him, and cling to him.

One Old Testament standard to judge a prophet was regarding his accuracy: did his predictions come true? Sometimes this was difficult to discern, since Old Testament prophets often gave words meant for the distant future. Some of those prophetic words are just now coming to pass, thousands of years later.

In Deuteronomy, Moses gives another key regarding judging the prophet. Deuteronomy 13:1-3 speaks of someone who has a prophecy, but when it is fulfilled tries to persuade others to walk away from God. In this case, even though the word came true, others could easily discern that he was not a true prophet of the Lord.

Deuteronomy 18:20-22 (WEB) But the prophet, who shall speak a word presumptuously in my name, which I have not commanded him to speak, or who shall speak in the name of other gods, that same prophet shall die." (21) If you say in your heart, "How shall we know the word which Yahweh has not spoken?" (22) when a prophet speaks in the name of Yahweh, if the thing doesn't follow, nor happen, that is the thing which Yahweh has not spoken: the prophet has spoken it presumptuously, you shall not be afraid of him.

Church: What Was God Thinking?

The Old Testament standard for prophets was extremely high. Although Deuteronomy 18 says that if a prophet makes a mistake, they must die, or at the very least, be considered a false prophet, the context clarifies this. The death sentence was given to anyone deliberately misleading God's people by deceptively speaking in God's name, or leading others into rebellion against God.

Since Christians are under the New Covenant, the law of love and grace, they should not reject people when they make mistakes while using the gift of prophecy. Rather when prophetic words are given that are clearly contrary to Scripture, they need to be dealt with in love and grace, gently but firmly.

New Testament prophets speak for edification and consolation. I believe, the sign of a mature prophet is whether or not he is strengthening the Church. If he is not doing this, then he is not a mature New Testament prophet.

2 Corinthians 3:6 (WEB) who also made us sufficient as servants of a new covenant; not of the letter, but of the Spirit. For the letter kills, but the Spirit gives life.

Grace is one of the most significant changes between the Old and New Covenants. Grace is mentioned in the New Testament one hundred twenty-two times. Some legalistic believers in the early Church were trying to take freedoms away from Christians because they did not understand grace. Grace is mentioned often in Scripture because God wants believers to pay attention to it, think about it, try to understand it and live it.

Grace and love are vital for Christians to remember when other believers are learning to use the prophetic. The most difficult stage to deal with may be when a person begins hearing God well much of the time.

Some individuals who get to this place of accuracy in the prophetic do not like correction. The Church does need to have grace for such people, but also for themselves. Grace means undeserved favor. Having grace for people means to speak the truth in love, while

Chapter 23: Old Testament and New Testament Prophets

at the same time realizing that each person sees things differently and anyone can make mistakes (Ephesians 4:15; 1 Corinthians 10:12-13). They should keep in mind that even if someone is known worldwide as a prophet, he or she still needs to be accountable and open to correction. In addition, Christians must have special grace for those who think they know what God is saying but have not matured in the way they present those words. Without grace and love, people will have a difficult time growing in any of the gifts.

1 Corinthians 13:9 (WEB) For we know in part, and we prophesy in part;

1 Corinthians 13:9 says believers only get small glimpses of what God wants to say. When the Lord speaks to someone, it often goes through their own mental processing before they put it into words. Because of this, three prophets who receive the same word, will share it in different ways. It is good to have grace for each one because God uses people and knows their worldview when He speaks to them.

The School of Prophets

1 Samuel 19:20 (WEB) Saul sent messengers to take David: and when they saw the company of the prophets prophesying, and Samuel standing as head over them, the Spirit of God came on the messengers of Saul, and they also prophesied.

1 Samuel 10:10-11 (WEB) When they came there to the hill, behold, a band of prophets met him; and the Spirit of God came mightily on him, and he prophesied among them. (11) It happened, when all who knew him before saw that, behold, he prophesied with the prophets, then the people said one to another, "What is this that has come to the son of Kish? Is Saul also among the prophets?"

In my opinion, Old Testament prophets had the chance to learn prophecy. In 1 Samuel 10:11, the Amplified Bible indicates that even in the Old Testament there was a school of prophets where young prophets have opportunities to learn from mature prophets how to use their gifts. If people went to a school to learn how to prophesy, I am sure they would not be stoned for making a mistake. If someone opened a school and stoned his students for mistakes, there would not be anyone left alive in the end, and no one would be willing to go there. Even in the Old Testament, I believe there was grace for the prophet-in-training.

Sometimes, a prophet's anointing enables others who do not have this ministry gift to move in it when they are with him. Saul and Saul's messengers encountered a group of prophets (1 Samuel 10:5-6, 10-12, Amplified Version). When Saul was with the school of the prophets, he prophesied, even though that was not something he could normally do. Some people call this "splash-over anointing." For a person whose heart is open to God, unlike Saul, this type of experience can be a great help in learning to recognize God's voice. In this way, prophets help others to hear God more clearly.

The Church can learn from the Old Testament school of prophets. More people could move in this gift and possibly even into the office of prophet if churches provided classes or gatherings to equip those interested. Small group meetings also give an excellent opportunity for each person to practice prophesying.

Much can be done to train prophets. If a leader knows of some in his group already gifted in this way, he might let them start releasing their anointings. Such people can give prophetic words and then they can spend time as a group listening for God's voice. Even if there is not a confirmed prophet in the meeting, it is necessary to have someone present who has the gift of discernment and knows the Bible to check that what is shared is consistent with Scripture. Many would find such a gathering helpful in growing in the prophetic.

The goal is to find the heart of God, so everyone must take care not to correct others over simple differences in opinion. If most of the group hears the same thing, it is wise to pay attention; the Lord could be trying to reveal something new or significant. God gives confirmation to more than one person at a time. Of course, no one should accept anything that goes against the Bible. I will say more on discerning prophetic words in the later chapters.

Chapter 23: Old Testament and New Testament Prophets

Sometimes, God uses people's feelings to help them recognize whether or not a word is from Him. However, there are times when someone gives a word that just does not feel right. People do need to be careful about using only feelings as a test of prophecy, because other factors besides discernment can affect this. I will talk more about that in the chapters on the prophetic.

Chapter 24: Issues and Weaknesses of Prophets

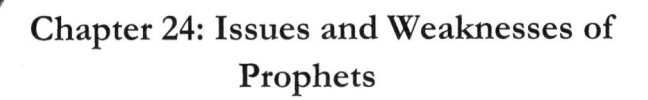

Factors That Can Influence Effective Use of the Prophetic Gift

There are some factors that affect a person being able to use the gift of prophecy effectively. One is being too analytical. There have been times that my ministry team has prayed with such people to move in the gift of prophecy. When they see a picture or hear from God they doubt it right away. They start rationalizing what He spoke to them and think that it is coming from within themselves. In this way, being overly analytical can prevent them from hearing the Lord accurately.

Another factor that hinders someone from using the gift of prophecy effectively is severe wounding or spiritual baggage. God often speaks through emotions and intuition. People that have had trauma in their lives or have been into occult practices will have so much hurt that they shut down their feelings and their experiences act like a filter, twisting what they hear.

There will likely be seasons when prophets need to step back and receive healing for different hurts in their lives. It is important that their hearts remain in the right place so their prophetic words will be more precise. Prophets need to deal with issues that hinder their ability to hear God clearly.

The Holy Spirit Can Speak Through Anyone

1 Corinthians 14:1 (WEB) Follow after love, and earnestly desire spiritual gifts, but especially that you may prophesy.

The Holy Spirit can move through new believers in the same way as more mature Christians. Some time ago, my ministry team was invited to minister at a camp. A young lady who was a new believer was also there. We felt the Lord saying that she was called to be a prophet. Soon after that, she came to one of our gatherings and prophesied over everyone in the meeting. Although she did not know anyone there, her words for people in our group were accurate. She had only been a Christian for three months. God can do awesome things even through those who are young in the Lord.

The Holy Spirit does not only give gifts to the mature. Do not underestimate what God can do through new believers. Accuracy in the gift of prophecy is not necessarily connected to one's maturity as a believer, and is not a sign that one's life is completely in order. God gives spiritual gifts out of His grace, not based on maturity as a Christian. Accuracy comes from the Holy Spirit.

Discerning The Difference Between a False and True Prophet

1 John 4:1 (WEB) Beloved, don't believe every spirit, but test the spirits, whether they are of God, because many false prophets have gone out into the world.

Jesus wants His children to look at the long-term fruit. Often, people make simple mistakes and others write them off as false prophets. This is insufficient criteria for making this judgment.

Chapter 24: Issues and Weaknesses of Prophets

One way to recognize a true prophet is through outside confirmation. Prophets can usually recognize other prophets. They will generally be acknowledged by a group of people, and even by a group of churches. Mature prophets have a good track record moving in their gift. Prophetic accuracy and recognition from others are two ways to identify a prophet.

One way to identify a false prophet is by their ungodly motivations. Some people call themselves prophets, but their goal is deception. I do not understand people like this. Some want to put on a show to make money. Others want the "glory" of having followers. Regardless of the motive, satan has twisted their minds and their hearts. The sad thing is that if they submitted to Jesus they would have a far more satisfying life and ministry. They could have become a true prophet that many respected. Unless they repent, these individuals will miss out on what life would be like following God's calling.

2 Peter 1:20-21 (WEB) knowing this first, that no prophecy of Scripture is of private interpretation. (21) For no prophecy ever came by the will of man: but holy men of God spoke, being moved by the Holy Spirit.

For believers and churches who desire to move in the prophetic, I cannot stress enough the importance of spending time connecting with God and knowing the Bible. Christians should not limit their study to doctrines that they like. Rather they need to look at the whole Bible in context. Becoming familiar with Scripture and spending time with God will help them develop discernment so that they will be less likely to fall into error.

Spiritual Issues of Which Prophets Need to be Aware

Isaiah 55:8-11 (WEB) "For my thoughts are not your thoughts, neither are your ways my ways," says Yahweh. (9) "For as the heavens are higher than the earth, so are my ways higher than your ways, and my thoughts than your thoughts. (10) For as the rain comes down and the snow from the sky, and doesn't return there, but waters the earth, and makes it bring forth and bud, and gives seed to the sower and bread to

the eater; (11) so shall my word be that goes forth out of my mouth: it shall not return to me void, but it shall accomplish that which I please, and it shall prosper in the thing I sent it to do.

Prophets need to be careful to keep a Godly attitude. They must have the heart of the Father, wanting to love and bless the Body of Christ. If this is not their main desire in ministry, they can enter into the spirit of witchcraft (1 Samuel 15:22-23). What I mean by this is, if they are judgmental, controlling, have unforgiveness, or harbor bitterness towards others, then they will no longer be able to express God's heart and are no longer prophesying.

This sin opens an entrance in their lives that allows the enemy opportunity to take a measure of control of what is in their hearts. This will show in what comes out of their mouths. Satan is the accuser, and when prophets speak out of a spirit of human judgment, condemnation or accusation, they are agreeing with the enemy, not God.

As a prophet matures, satan looks for footholds to destroy him so that his reputation and the words God speaks through him will be discredited. Believers need to be diligent to maintain purity in their hearts and lives so that God will get the glory for the good works they do (2 Corinthians 10:3-5).

Revelation 2:20 (WEB) But I have this against you, that you tolerate your woman, Jezebel, who calls herself a prophetess. She teaches and seduces my servants to commit sexual immorality, and to eat things sacrificed to idols.

In addition to the spirit of witchcraft, prophets must also avoid the Jezebel spirit. Jezebel, historically, was a woman who reigned with her husband, Ahab, as queen of Israel. Besides her involvement in idolatry and the fertility cults, she was also the controlling factor in many decisions her husband made. Revelation 2:20-23 declares God's judgment against Jezebel.

It is possible that at one time Jezebel may have been powerful in the gift of prophecy. In Revelation 2, it says she claims to be a prophetess. She will receive judgment because she is not following the

Chapter 24: Issues and Weaknesses of Prophets

Lord (Please note that the Jezebel spirit can operate through a man or a woman, despite being named after a woman).

Prophets need to keep their hearts clean before God. They must avoid moving in the spirit of Jezebel. What I mean is that they should be careful not to affirm the actions of others who are in spiritual compromise. In addition, they must never use the prophetic to control or manipulate others or take over another's work.

In saying this, I do not intend to frighten anyone, or influence them to avoid the prophetic. On the other hand, prophets need to be especially careful to be accountable to others by confessing sin and remaining open to teaching and correction. These are good precautionary actions to protect against destruction from the enemy.

Weaknesses of an Immature Prophet

Those with the prophetic gift do tend toward certain weaknesses. Before I talk about this, it should be said that it is possible that not all of these weaknesses will manifest in every prophet or in every church community that allows the use of the prophetic gift.

Also, I do want to say that in writing this list my intention is not to demean or stereotype. If people understand the prophetic personality and associated weaknesses, they can more easily have grace for the maturing prophet, trusting God to transform His people with His love (1 Corinthians 13).

The following should be helpful in understanding some immature or wounded prophets. This list comes from personal observations, and comments from leaders and prophets that I know.

I feel it is necessary for leaders to recognize the expression that immaturity and brokenness might take in prophetic people. In this way, leaders can have compassion on them, help them grow, find healing, and not sideline them, by putting them "on the shelf" (1 Thessalonians 5:14).

Church: What Was God Thinking?

In addition, for prophets, being aware of potential pitfalls will help them try to avoid these issues. I hope the reader keeps these things in mind as I discuss some of the prophet's possible weaknesses.

1 Corinthians 14:1 (WEB) Follow after love, and earnestly desire spiritual gifts, but especially that you may prophesy.

Some prophets focus too much on their own gift. When the church gathers, such people want the whole time to be used as a prophetic meeting. This issue is related to how a person's gift influences their worldview. There is nothing wrong with seeing the world through a prophetic lens; this is part of the way that God made people. It is also true that Scripture says prophecy is an important gift to be used in the gathering. At the same time, prophets must keep in mind that there needs to be a balance, so all the gifts can operate and everyone can grow in using their spiritual gifts.

Proverbs 16:18 (WEB) Pride goes before destruction, and a haughty spirit before a fall.

1 Corinthians 10:12-13 (WEB) Therefore let him who thinks he stands be careful that he doesn't fall. (13) No temptation has taken you except what is common to man. God is faithful, who will not allow you to be tempted above what you are able, but will with the temptation also make the way of escape, that you may be able to endure it.

Immature prophets sometimes have a tendency towards pride, feeling that they know what God wants better than others. They might also think that most prophetic words they have are accurate. If a prophet becomes proud, thinking his anointing is so strong that he cannot make a mistake, and will no longer receive correction, he needs to be careful because he could be about to fall (1 Corinthians 10:12-13). Prophets have to be exceptionally humble.

When a prophet moves powerfully in his gift, others often put him on a pedestal, viewing him as some sort of superstar or spiritual giant. In such cases, the prophet must be especially careful to guard his heart against pride (Proverbs 4:23; 16:18).

Chapter 24: Issues and Weaknesses of Prophets

Immature prophets can misuse their gift for glory. People need to be careful not to use prophecy to make themselves look good. Anyone who wants others to notice him because he is such a great prophet has his heart in the wrong place. In that case, the Lord may eventually let him fall.

Sometimes, feelings of pride come when a prophet is moving strongly in his gift. This issue is not always from the flesh. The easiest way to discern where these emotions are coming from is for the prophet to examine his heart to see what his motivations are. If his heart is to serve the Body of Christ, the feelings of pride may only be spiritual attack. In either case, the prophet should talk with individuals he can trust, asking them for prayer, so he can be protected in his ministry.

In the case of pride, an apostle or a mature prophet may be able to help. The apostle has such a heart for others to grow in their gift, even during stages of immaturity. He can provide accountability, and encourage humility as the prophet uses his gift.

Sometimes, prophets feel that they have to perform. Another one of their weaknesses is that they might try to prophesy when God has not given them a word. One possible reason for this is because the prophet is used to having words for people. It is easy to get into performance mode.

Since people look up to them as the "men of God," they may try to keep up this image. Usually this does not last long because people quickly discover when the prophet has been trying to operate without God's anointing. He needs to be careful not to give in to human pressure to prophecy when God is not speaking.

One of my daughters, who is gifted prophetically, loves to tell a story to illustrate this. Some years ago, she was in a school and was expected to pray over others every day. She had begun to develop the reputation of hearing God accurately for those she prayed for, and was beginning to feel pressured.

During her personal prayer time, she asked God about this, "What would happen if I go to pray for others and cannot prophesy?" She felt the Lord reply, "You are not going to hear for anyone tonight, but it is going to be good." That night His word to her was fulfilled. She did not receive any prophetic words, but chose to simply speak a blessing over them. She enjoyed it thoroughly and the people she ministered to still seemed encouraged. It was a freeing experience for her to cast aside the pressure to perform as a prophet.

Sometimes, prophets go through seasons of not hearing God as much as usual. They experience days or seasons when they do not hear God as clearly. While they mature in the Lord, they learn to be honest and let people know instead of trying to pretend that they are still hearing God. This humble response helps everyone to get their focus back to where it should be, on the Lord, the Giver of all good gifts (James 1:17). Prophets are human beings, just like anyone else.

Many prophets have stories about different mistakes they have made while learning to use their gift. Even experienced prophets still get it wrong sometimes. Regardless of maturity level, prophets must be able to admit when they make mistakes or give a wrong word. For this reason, when I prophesy over others, I generally ask them if the word feels right or if they have any feedback. Regardless of response, this provides a learning opportunity and helps keep me humble. Humility is essential for prophets.

Easily hurt feelings can be a sign of an immature prophet. This sensitivity seems to be most apparent among young prophets. As they receive more healing, much of this will disappear. It is imperative that those with a prophetic calling keep their hearts pure and learn to forgive easily to prevent them from becoming bitter or judgmental.

Another weakness for some prophets is in their expression. Such people are very direct, blunt, or even gruff, in conversation with others. This could proceed from past wounding or intensity of passion for the Truth. Despite this character trait, they often have a sensitive spirit and perceive it as rejection when people react to their harsh expression. Indeed many prophets are rejected and misunderstood because of this. One of the most important things for a prophet to learn is to be gentle and to have grace for others' expression.

Chapter 24: Issues and Weaknesses of Prophets

The wounded or immature prophet is one of the most easily misunderstood persons in the Church. A prophet may take in information or perceive things in black and white, categorizing everything as right or wrong, even to an extreme. Even when people are joking, a prophet might correct them harshly, as though they are in serious sin. Some find this irritating. The reason I mention this is so that people will have more grace to deal kindly with the rough expression of some prophets.

There are several ways leaders can deal with these issues. Sometimes, teaming a prophet with others who have different gifts brings balance and softness to them. In addition, training them to gently speak the truth in love is helpful. Leaders should also provide opportunities for their prophets to receive healing, as well as educating their people regarding the strengths and weaknesses of the various gifts.

In summary, prophets are essential to the Body of Christ. They help keep the community heavenly-minded and have a strong connection with God. They also train others to hear God regardless of their gifts. They have a focus of releasing God's heart to fellow Christians, non-believers, and even some world-leaders. However, because of the power of this gift, there has been misuse and misunderstanding. The benefits of the prophetic far outweigh the risks, and I pray that God will raise up more prophets to build His Church.

Church leaders can take steps to train more prophets in their churches. One way is to have classes or workshops to equip those interested in the prophetic. This training would make it possible for more people to begin using the gift of prophecy. In addition, those gifted and called, could begin moving into the ministry office of prophet. I will discuss more about the prophetic, and ways to facilitate it further in the following chapters.

The Prophetic

1 Corinthians 14:1 (WEB) Follow after love, and earnestly desire spiritual gifts, but especially that you may prophesy.

John 10:27 (WEB) My sheep hear my voice, and I know them, and they follow me.

In the following chapters, I wish to discuss the gift of prophecy separately from the ministry office of prophet. 1 Corinthians 14:1 says this gift is very important in the Church. Jesus tells us that everyone who belongs to Him can hear His voice. As such, I would like to discuss some practical ways that Christians can learn more about how to operate in the prophetic, with the supervision of church leadership and mature prophets.

Chapter 25: The Prophetic Gathering

Prophetic Gatherings

One way Christians can begin to move in prophecy is through prophetic gatherings. I love meetings where the leader opens the gathering by everyone listening to the Spirit together. When I have been in meetings that follow this format, one of two things has usually happened. Either everyone received the same message from God, or there have been several different, yet equally important themes that God highlighted for the group.

If mature prophets attend a prophetic gathering, it is especially fun. Often, splash-over anointing will enable those who have not prophesied before to experience what it is like. Regular prophetic meetings provide opportunities for believers to grow in the prophetic.

A Large Prophetic Gathering

In large gatherings, if the leadership sets aside some time for all those present to listen to God, people have the opportunity to share prophetic words. After this they should ask God how to respond to those words in the meeting. On occasion, someone in leadership may feel God is saying something about those messages that should be expressed to the entire group.

Leaders can also set aside time where people at the large meeting receive individual prophetic words. However, this is much easier in home groups or in small gatherings. When a group is ready, anyone present could listen to God and use the gifts as God leads.

Small Prophetic Gatherings

Home groups or small gatherings are a good place to begin using the prophetic. What is great about these more intimate settings is that there is much more quality time for hearing God's voice and using spiritual gifts. Under the leadership of the Holy Spirit, believers have some amazing times in their home gathering. Those who do not belong to a home group or small fellowship can consider joining or starting one. Small meetings should provide a safe venue for the prophetic before using it in a larger context.

Informal Prophetic Gatherings

Another good time to use the prophetic is when guests visit. Many times when people come over to my family's home, we prophesy over them. It often happens that we go one hour or more per person. In Acts 21:8-9, Paul went to Philip's house. Philip had four daughters who moved in the gift of prophecy. It is Biblical to have prophetic times in private homes. It does not need to be limited to a church setting. This

Chapter 25: The Prophetic Gathering

is a good way to encourage others and to strengthen individual's ability to hear God.

There are many possible venues for practicing the prophetic, such as when shopping, eating, during recreation or work breaks. All these can be good settings for prophecy. Prayer walking is an excellent way to practice hearing God's voice. A group could also see if they all hear the same or similar things from God. Different individuals may hear different things, but those present discern the messages together.

Prophetic evangelism is an effective way to preach the Gospel. Believers who hear God's voice should pray and ask the Lord to give opportunities for them to use this gift. This can be helpful in growing in the prophetic.

Hosting Prophetic Gatherings

I want to give some instructions for leaders hosting prophetic gatherings. When holding this type of meeting, be sure to let those attending know that this is a gathering of the school of the prophets. Inform them that the purpose of the meeting is for learning how to hear from God. Let them know that mistakes happen. This is not a big deal as long as everyone learns from those mistakes.

Make sure that there are believers present who are solid in the Bible. Such individuals can deal with any prophetic messages that conflict with Scripture gently and immediately. Each person needs to listen to what the Holy Spirit is saying both for themselves and for one another. Having discernment, knowing the Scriptures and looking at Biblical truths in context are all essential when testing prophecy.

In hosting prophetic gatherings, there is one area that a leader needs to be cautious. They can encourage others to join in, but should never be pushy about it. Since the prophetic is for blessing, participation must always be voluntary.

When individuals are consistently wrong, a leader should give patient and gentle instruction, waiting to see if they will mature in the prophetic. If a leader corrects them and they change, he helps them to

Church: What Was God Thinking?

grow in their gifts. On the other hand, if someone continues to struggle, there might be some deeper spiritual issues involved.

There are several possible reasons for people to not hear God's voice clearly. They may need basic discernment or some emotional healing. If they keep trying to prophesy but are still not hearing God correctly, either this person is not gifted in prophecy or there may be something getting in the way. It is good to try to discover what the issue is so that it can be resolved.

Often a prophetic gathering, or a series of prophetic gatherings, will be enough to discover potential prophets and awaken the prophetic in a Christian community. In some cases, a congregation needs more than a regular meeting to begin moving in this gift. Inviting a confirmed, mature prophet to visit can give the church a jump start.

Many prophets and apostles lay hands on people to minister to them and call forth gifts in their lives. Those who feel excited about prophecy will likely begin using this gift soon afterwards. Other times, inviting a prophet to train believers can be helpful, but it is necessary to find the right person to do this.

There are some ways a leader can know if someone is not the right person to train his group in the prophetic. If he invites someone who claims to be a prophet to his gathering, but that person has a pattern of giving inaccurate words, then this is probably not the right person to train the group.

This person could be a prophet who is not mature in his gift or there might be some spiritual issue. There are any number of possible factors. It could also be an indicator that the group is not ready for what the prophet has to say because of their level of openness or difference in theology.

Once, a prophet came to a church I was attending and many did not believe that he could be one because he heard God so much. For some reason, they felt that believers are only occasionally able to hear God's voice. There are many different reasons why people reject prophets, and not all of them are Biblical.

Chapter 25: The Prophetic Gathering

In conclusion, prophetic gatherings are a wonderful place to begin raising up prophets in a congregation. If handled correctly, this practice could bless the Church in many ways. In the next chapter, I want to talk about what to do with various types of prophetic words.

Chapter 26: Things to Understand Regarding Prophetic Ministry

Prophetic Words that Need to be Handled with Care

1 Corinthians 12:7 (WEB) But to each one is given the manifestation of the Spirit for the profit of all.

1 Corinthians 14:3 (WEB) But he who prophesies speaks to men for their edification, exhortation, and consolation.

When using the gift of prophecy, certain types of words must be handled with special care. People need to keep in mind that prophetic words are gifts given to strengthen believers, not hurt them.

Galatians 6:1 (WEB) Brothers, even if a man is caught in some fault, you who are spiritual must restore such a one in a spirit of gentleness; looking to yourself so that you also aren't tempted.

For example, when receiving a word about something very personal, it should be handled privately. This is especially true if the message is about weakness, sin, or wounds in another's life or corporately in a church community. Also, words of rebuke, or any word that if given in public might embarrass the person, must not be openly shared.

Sometimes this kind of word is given for the purpose of private intercession, other times it is for direct prayer ministry, to bring freedom in another's life. The prophet should ask the Lord for clear guidance about what to do with the message. When possible, that person's leaders should know about it, give guidance and hopefully be directly involved in any resulting ministry. Regardless, it must be handled privately and in a spirit of love.

Sometimes, if a person frequently receives words of this kind for others, he may have a prophetic gift that in time God will use for healing and deliverance. He might be an intercessory prophet or an inner-healing prophet and should receive training.

Those that are gifted in hearing personal words for others may function well as a part of an evangelistic team, using their prophetic gift for preaching the Gospel. Jesus used this type of evangelism when he met the woman at the well (John 4:5-30). He knew that she had been married five times and the person she was living with was not her husband. Christ's sensitivity in sharing with her resulted not only in her salvation, but in the salvation of many in her city!

For those called to preach the Gospel this way, I would just like to give a word of caution. It is important to respect those receiving your message. You need to be careful not to embarrass them, and personal words should be handled privately along with another member of your team. Everyone must always be treated with love and respect (John 13:34-35).

Besides personal words, those moving in prophecy also have to be careful about certain other types of messages. Predictions that involve details such as calendar dates, future spouses or pregnancy should be handled with care, especially for inexperienced prophets. This is because of the emotion attached to these subjects. Besides this, prophetic words that bring correction or direction must be given carefully and with respect. In addition, if someone knows the person

Chapter 26: Things to Understand Regarding Prophetic Ministry

that they are prophesying over, and carries emotion towards them, they need to be aware that this can affect the content of their prophetic words. Those who are new in the prophetic might do well to avoid sharing messages regarding these topics with other people. If they hear about such things, they should keep it between themselves and God and see what happens.

Confirming a Prophetic Word

God allows prophets to confirm things that people already know for a reason. When a prophet gives a word over a person, at least some of it usually will be confirmation of what that person already feels God is saying. When a new message is shared, this allows the person receiving ministry to recognize that the Lord is speaking. At times, God gives this word because He is getting ready to bring the person into something new. This is very helpful to people and allows them to know they are on the right track, especially if the prophet is a stranger to the one receiving ministry and has no way of knowing what the Lord has said to him before.

Some people automatically know if a word is for them, but others cannot tell. From my experience, when a prophet speaks new things into someone's life and that person is open to whatever God has for them, these messages will often ignite something in his spirit. This individual will feel a strong witness that it is true. With some people, however, if someone prophesies over them and they do not have a frame of reference for the prophetic word, they might reject it even if the message is accurate.

In my ministry team, we have experienced our words being rejected out of personal desires or theology. Most of the time that this has happened more than one member of the team heard God simultaneously say something, and someone shared the message without knowing that others had received the same word. Unfortunately, the one hearing the message could not accept the prophetic word because of his own mindset. In such cases, it is usually best to simply move on, not worry about it, and let God take care of it.

Regardless of how right a word seems to be, it must never be forced on anyone. For the one receiving ministry, he needs to pray about the words he receives, to know whether or not the message is from God and what the Lord wants him to do to fulfill it.

What It Means if a Word Does Not Feel Right

There are different reasons for words not feeling right even if they are accurate. If someone shares a message that is not encouragement or confirmation, the person who receives it should pray into it to see if God confirms it in his heart. The word and the person giving that word should not be instantly written off as false, simply because there is no immediate feeling about it. If the message is legitimate, and yet the recipient rejected it, he could potentially miss out on something great.

It is possible for feelings to confirm a word from the Lord. One great example in Scripture is given in Luke 24:13-32. Two of the disciples were travelling to a village named Emmaus. On the way, they met Jesus although they did not recognize Him. As He talked with them, their hearts "burned within them." Later, they realized it was Jesus and that this was why they had that feeling. As with Jesus' word, many times prophetic words will often burn in a person's heart as they are being received. Of course, this might not happen until sometime later, as that person is praying about them. At the same time, a message will sometimes not feel right at first, and yet be confirmed later.

There are several reasons why a word may not feel right. It could be that the message is for the future, the prophet is having a bad day, or they have not heard God correctly. It could also be that a person's heart is in the wrong place. Of course, it is possible that the minister is not gifted in prophecy. Just because something feels wrong does not necessarily mean that it is not of God.

If most or all of a prophetic group feels that the words being given are not true or just do not feel right, there are a few possible reasons

Chapter 26: Things to Understand Regarding Prophetic Ministry

for this too. Besides the issues listed in the last paragraph, there is also the possibility that a group cannot accept the message because of certain mindsets or theology. There are times that theology can get in the way of receiving what God is trying to say.

For example, if God were to tell someone to dance before him, yet the person receiving the word thinks dancing in worship is wrong, this would hinder him from obeying the prophetic word. One instance in the Bible of how theology and traditions can affect someone's reaction to a message from the Lord is told in the book of Acts when God used a vision of "unclean" food to command Peter to preach to Gentiles (Acts 10:9-23). God had to show him the vision three times before he accepted the message.

Sometimes issues in a person's life hinder them from having discernment. My ministry team has prayed for certain people, and received words for them about how much the Lord loves them. Sometimes they even weep when it is shared. Because of their hurts and brokenness, they could not receive the message or the love of God. Personal feelings are not always an accurate standard for judging whether or not a word is right.

It is important to take these issues into consideration when evaluating a prophetic word, so as to judge it Biblically, and not merely through a human, fleshly perspective. The help of the Holy Spirit and Scripture are essential to Christians in the area of discernment.

What To Do About Unfulfilled Prophecies

Believers should take specific action upon receiving prophetic messages. They need to press into God for these words to happen. They must fight for it in prayer to bring it to pass. They cannot just passively sit and wait for the words to fulfill themselves. One reason this is necessary is that the enemy will attempt to steal those words, and might succeed if people are not careful. Believers need to realize that they cannot be passive if they want their prophetic destiny to be fulfilled.

Church: What Was God Thinking?

Most prophecy requires action. Believers should not simply wait, thinking that if they do nothing, somehow those words will still come to pass. Sometimes, all the action necessary is to pray into God's timing. Some words spoken over me thirty years ago are just now being fulfilled. This might have happened much sooner if I had actively sought God on what to do with those messages.

No one should give up on words that could still come true. God specializes in the impossible (Luke 1:37). As Christians, when we seek His face and keep Him first in our lives, loving and obeying Him, we will be amazed at what He will accomplish. We need to take the initiative to seek and obey God so that His plan for our lives will be fulfilled.

In order to get the full blessing, listening to messages again is very important. It is good to have a device to record prophetic words. I have several recordings of prophetic ministry that I try to listen to regularly. As I do this, the things that have been spoken over me re-ignite my heart and give me hope.

Often, when I listen to these recordings, I have been surprised at how much I had forgotten almost immediately. There have also been things that were spoken over me that I did not hear or remember correctly. As I listen to those words, God will give me more understanding about what He was saying at the time. Repeatedly listening to prophetic messages can increase the blessing.

Prophecy Often Challenges Comfort Zones

Prophecy is for strengthening the Body of Christ, but this does not mean people should only say wonderful things that make others feel good about themselves. Sometimes, God will challenge His children because that is what they need to help them grow. At times, God also warns them so that they will be ready for the future. God's plans for His children are for the best, but that does not mean they will always be comfortable.

Chapter 26: Things to Understand Regarding Prophetic Ministry

John 12:24-26 (WEB) Most certainly I tell you, unless a grain of wheat falls into the earth and dies, it remains by itself alone. But if it dies, it bears much fruit. (25) He who loves his life will lose it. He who hates his life in this world will keep it to eternal life. (26) If anyone serves me, let him follow me. Where I am, there will my servant also be. If anyone serves me, the Father will honor him.

Somehow, many people have the mistaken idea that no matter what God's will is, they will feel happy about it and the process will be a comfortable one. Honestly, there are many things that bring people beyond their comfort zones (John 12:24-26).

It is living within God's will that brings true satisfaction. Although God bringing believers into their destiny will take them out of their comfort zones, it will also give them the greatest fulfillment. This is true both individually and corporately in the Body of Christ. There are many times that God uses uncomfortable situations to bring transformation.

Acts 17:6 (WEB) When they didn't find them, they dragged Jason and certain brothers before the rulers of the city, crying, "These who have turned the world upside down have come here also,"

God is on a mission to bring things back into the proper direction. God's ways are far beyond human ways. If people choose their own way instead of His plan, it could even be said that their ways are "upside-down" compared to His. Considering how prone humanity is to doing their own thing, when God moves in power to set things right, it may at times feel like He's turning things "upside-down."

From a natural point of view this might feel confusing until people begin to grasp more of His perspective. It is no wonder that the early apostles were accused of "turning the world upside-down" (Acts 17:6). The apostles were doing things God's way, and people living for themselves just did not get it.

In the same way, until individuals choose God's will for their lives, sometimes His words to them will cause confusion and struggle in their hearts. At the same time, they will love it when He makes the wrong things right.

Church: What Was God Thinking?

Dealing with Confusion over Prophetic Words

1 Corinthians 14:32-33 (WEB) The spirits of the prophets are subject to the prophets, (33) for God is not a God of confusion, but of peace. As in all the assemblies of the saints,

The Greek word for "confusion" is ἀκαταστασία *akatastasia*. Strong's definition G181 (pronounced: *ak-at-as-tah-see'-ah*) From G182; instability, that is, disorder: - commotion, confusion, tumult.

There are several reasons why individuals can experience confusion over prophecy. I wish to address a few. Sometimes this is because of disorder in meetings, other times it is because of the content of the messages.

Although it is not God's intention, there is sometimes confusion when prophecy is used. When Paul said that prophecy should not bring confusion in the gatherings of the church [*ekklesia*], this was in the context of the orderly function of the meetings. The word "confusion" in 1 Corinthians 14 also has the meaning "disorder." In this case, I believe the people using the gift of prophecy at that time were not taking turns but perhaps were all trying to speak at the same time. It was chaotic. Paul solves this in 1 Corinthians 14, by instructing people to share one at a time, so that everyone can have a more pleasant prophetic experience.

Colossians 2:8 (WEB) Be careful that you don't let anyone rob you through his philosophy and vain deceit, after the tradition of men, after the elements of the world, and not after Christ.

2 Timothy 3:1-5 (WEB) But know this, that in the last days, grievous times will come. (2) For men will be lovers of self, lovers of money, boastful, arrogant, blasphemers, disobedient to parents, unthankful, unholy, (3) without natural affection, unforgiving, slanderers, without self-control, fierce, no lovers of good, (4) traitors, headstrong, conceited, lovers of pleasure rather than lovers of God; (5) holding a form of godliness, but having denied its power. Turn away from these, also.
Matthew 15:3 (WEB) He answered them, "Why do you also disobey the commandment of God because of your tradition?

Chapter 26: Things to Understand Regarding Prophetic Ministry

Isaiah 55:9 (WEB) "For as the heavens are higher than the earth, so are my ways higher than your ways, and my thoughts than your thoughts.

Feelings of confusion can occur when a prophetic word does not seem to line up with preconceived ideas. However, this does not necessarily mean that the word is not from God. Some people in the history of the Church seemed to bring disorder because they taught from a different mindset than the traditional Church at that time. Martin Luther was one of those people. In many ways, he has had a significant impact on the modern Church.

People need to be careful about man-made customs (Matthew 15:3). Man has a way of making traditions that do not bring life and have little to do with following Christ. When the Church is getting away from the truth or believing unscriptural theology, there could be times when wisdom is needed to turn things around. God always wants to do something new and unique in His Body. If Christians formulize Church then, eventually, God Himself will have to turn the tables upside-down (John 2:15-16). Sometimes He uses prophecy to do that.

There are other reasons for confusion besides mistaken traditions. Sometimes, if someone's heart is not lined up with God's heart, that person will experience discomfort. Scripture does state that "God is not the author of confusion." If an individual has been living for himself and in the flesh, even God's will might seem to make them feel confused. This is because the flesh cannot understand the things of God (1 Corinthians 2:14). Emotions associated with this do not always mean that change is not of God.

Living in the Spirit helps believers to experience less confusion from a prophetic word. God is faithful to remove this confusion as people pursue Him. Such people will take things to God, asking Him to confirm the message and show them how to apply it to their lives. Students of the Word will look at the Bible to see what it says about personal struggles. The Holy Spirit helps them understand God's heart.

Feelings of confusion may also be a result of not living in the Spirit. Someone living in the flesh who feels led to be a businessman and serve the rich could feel confused about prophetic words

Church: What Was God Thinking?

encouraging him to minister to the poor. In this case, this feeling would not proceed from hunger for God, because the person's heart is not in line with God's will. It is imperative that believers' desires line up with God's heart. An essential part of embracing His desires is connecting with God to learn the mind of Christ, understand His Word, and love as He loves (2 Corinthians 3:17-18; 1 John 3:2-3).

On the other hand, another cause of confusion is that not all messages shared are from God. Sometimes, people hear incorrectly. If someone is uncomfortable about a word, besides waiting for confirmation and peace, the person may also need to ask God to change his own heart if the prophetic word is from the Lord. If it is not, they should just let it go. Humans make mistakes, and believers need to be aware and discerning about that.

Sometimes wrong words will be mixed with right ones. I have had some things spoken over me that I felt did not apply to me. In that case, it was only one word out of about ten given by that prophet. Even people gifted in the prophetic can hear incorrectly sometimes. On the other hand, just getting one thing wrong does not mean that the prophet was wrong about everything.

People do not always know what to do about new prophetic words that are not confirmation. If a prophet has a message for someone that that person has never heard from God before, the one receiving the word has a responsibility to pray into it, asking the Lord if it is true. If it does not conflict with Scripture and the person feels in his spirit that it is true, then he needs to war in prayer over that word. Just because a message is new it does not necessarily mean it is not true.

I want to share an experience of this that I had. Several summers ago, I received prophetic ministry from a couple that is mature in the gift of prophecy. One of them is a prophet and the other is an apostle. They did not know me or anything about me. It was exciting because most of the things they spoke over me confirmed what I already knew in my heart. Some things they said went beyond my dreams and other things both challenged me and made me uncomfortable. As I pursued

Chapter 26: Things to Understand Regarding Prophetic Ministry

God about these words, it launched a season of spiritual growth in my life. Even if a word is confusing, it can still bring so much blessing.

Certain prophetic words can be downright disturbing. That prophet had a message for me that made me angry because I did not believe it was true. She told me that I was passive in different ways. I started asking people close to me if this was true and they all confirmed it, revealing a blind spot. In the last six years, that message has had a huge impact on me. I have been learning to not be passive in many areas of my life. In the end, these prophetic words brought a lot of joy, excitement and increased vision. Even though it was uncomfortable, it brought a huge blessing, freeing me to change for the better.

After receiving a prophetic word, believers must fight for its fulfillment. The biggest spiritual warfare people experience might well be over their destiny. Many people receive a word from God and do nothing, simply waiting for it to be fulfilled. They feel that if it is God, it will just happen in His time, and that it does not require them to act.

Receiving a word from God is just the beginning. If we, as believers, expect to move into our destiny, we cannot be passive. Upon receiving a prophetic message, we should begin praying to know what steps we need to take to move in the direction of God's will in this area. We must also seek God regarding the timing of its fulfillment. In this way, we can see these words come to pass.

In conclusion, God has been restoring the prophetic to His Church. This can seem a little messy at times. However, as people grow in the Lord and learn to use these spiritual tools correctly, it will result in encouragement to many who are discouraged in the Body of Christ.

Chapter 27: The Gift of Pastor

Ephesians 4:11-12 (WEB) He gave some to be apostles; and some, prophets; and some, evangelists; and some, shepherds [pastors] and teachers; (12) for the perfecting of the saints, to the work of serving, to the building up of the Body of Christ;

John 10:14-15 (WEB) I am the good shepherd. I know my own, and I'm known by my own; (15) even as the Father knows me, and I know the Father. I lay down my life for the sheep.

The Greek word for "pastor" is ποιμήν *poimēn.*
Strong's definition G4166 (pronounced: *poy-mane'*)
Of uncertain affinity; a *shepherd* (literally or figuratively): - shepherd, pastor.

Many in the Church think they know what the ministry gift of pastor is, but modern day practice would indicate otherwise. It has not only been confused with many of the other gifts, it has even been considered more of a position than a gift. I hope in this chapter to bring greater clarity to the Biblical meaning of "pastor," and also to the important role that the pastor has in the Body of Christ.

Church: What Was God Thinking?

The Difference Between the Gift and Position of Pastor

Ephesians 4 lists pastor [*poimen*] as one of the key equipping gifts. It is a ministry gift given by God and is not necessarily referring to individuals in full-time ministry leading a church. In the rest of this section, I use the term "full-time minister" to refer to the common modern-day perception of pastor. I use pastor to refer to those with the ministry gift of pastor.

1 Corinthians 12:28 (WEB) God has set some in the assembly: first apostles, second prophets, third teachers, then miracle workers, then gifts of healings, helps, governments, and various kinds of languages [tongues].

Ephesians 4 lists the gifting of pastor. Some people say that since the translators used the conjunction, "and," that pastor and teacher are always a combined gifting. In 1 Corinthians 12:28, the gifting of teacher is mentioned, but not pastor. This shows that the gift of pastor does not always go together with the gift of teacher.

Pastors are not always good teachers and are certainly not meant to do everything. I have seen some Christians who are great at teaching but very weak at pastoral ministry. I have also met believers that are pastors and I am sure that they would not make the best teachers. Regardless, this gift has not been given for individuals to come into leadership to take over the church and quench the other gifts.

In many modern traditional churches, when people think of a pastor, they often think of a person who is in charge of everything. I do not believe that the pastor's job is to control people. No one has that perverse "gift." There are times during the discipleship and equipping process that people need pastors to help them set healthy boundaries, but this is different from control. Their ultimate goal is to help the believer stand on his own two feet and to mature as Christians in the gifting God has given him.

For example: at one time in my life I worked with drug addicts. In that ministry, when these individuals first started treatment, they

Chapter 27: The Gift of Pastor

needed space away from their home environment. This was because of their weakness towards substance abuse. The group only took them away long enough for them to become sufficiently strong and able to resist temptation.

As they became stronger, they were given more freedom. If it was clear that they could handle it, then they could keep it. If they could not, then they still needed strict boundaries. Our main goal was to bring them to the point where they could stay drug-free without others setting guidelines for them, until they could face life independently without falling back into sinful or harmful habits. In that kind of situation, this type of decision is appropriate for a leader to make.

Contrary to modern opinion, I believe the ministry gift of pastor operates primarily in the background: discipling, facilitating, and equipping people in ministry. This training should begin with young believers when receiving pastoral help to set the foundations for life and future ministry. The church needs to get back to the Biblical meaning of pastor.

In 1 Corinthians 12-14, the Bible talks about Church being a venue for using spiritual gifts. It is not the place for just one or a few people to use their gifts, and it is not a time for a full-time minister to be the only one using his gift. The purpose of the church gathering is for everyone to come together to grow in their gifts.

The Pastor's Ministry Role

Ezekiel 34:4 (WEB) You haven't strengthened the diseased, neither have you healed that which was sick, neither have you bound up that

which was broken, neither have you brought back that which was driven away, neither have you sought that which was lost; but with force and with rigor you have ruled over them.

Luke 4:18-19 (WEB) "The Spirit of the Lord is on me, because he has anointed me to preach good news to the poor. He has sent me to heal the brokenhearted, to proclaim release to the captives, recovering of sight to the blind, to deliver those who are crushed, (19) and to proclaim the acceptable year of the Lord."

These two passages of Scripture show the true calling of all pastors. God has chosen them to strengthen the weak, to heal the sick and broken-hearted and to bring back those who have wandered away because of hurt or temptation. This is the pastor's primary role in the Body.

The pastor's relationship with those receiving his ministry changes as individuals grow as Christians. Pastors are supposed to help people become mature. The Church is not like the animal world where sheep will always be sheep, rather in the Church, sheep can grow up to be shepherds. It is God's will for all believers to mature in His Kingdom. The Lord provides pastors primarily to assist believers in their early Christian walk, working along with apostles and the rest of the five-fold ministry (Ephesians 4:11-16) to help ensure that they are each equipped for the ministry to which He has called them. They are essential to others' growth in God.

Pastoral ministry is more for young believers than older Christians, except when equipping potential pastors. They aid in believers' growth in the Lord, and also help those who need to receive healing from their pasts. As people mature in the Lord and get rid of old baggage in their lives, they still will need mentoring and counsel at times. A pastor that does not allow his relationship with his sheep to change as they grow would stand in the way of them maturing in the Lord.

The main function of a person with the gift of pastor is to bring others into wholeness and help them grow, becoming the gifted individuals that God has created and called them to be. This helps Christians to move forward in their relationship with Christ and with

Chapter 27: The Gift of Pastor

those around them. Many counselors have a pastoral gift. Many believers feel comfortable and secure around such people. Others know that they can safely pour out their hearts to pastors because they will respond with wisdom in love. Believers need pastors especially while in the process of understanding God's love and care.

Those with the ministry gift of pastor are good at teaching groups of people how to deal with life's problems. They work in training and equipping people in areas such as: how to have better marriages, how to love and care for their children, how to love teenagers, how to receive emotional healing, and so forth. Much of the time, a pastor's work is in the background. Generally, this is most effective in small groups or on an individual basis. There may be exceptions to this, such as if a pastor is called to full-time equipping of other pastors, or hosting training seminars.

Pastoral insight is vital for people in the Christian community to prevent small issues from becoming big ones. A small fire is much easier to put out than a large forest fire. In the same way, pastors working in the background help to deal with problems in a young Christian's life, hopefully long before these problems turn into full-blown crises.

Pastoral ministry made a big difference in my life as a new believer. One obvious example I recall is the marriage seminar my church hosted when my wife and I were young Christians. To this day, we still apply what we learned from that seminar in our marriage. If the Church equipped and released those with the pastoral gift to focus on these kinds of ministries, many of the problems the Church deals with could be prevented.

Venues for the Pastoral Gift

The pastoral gift can function anywhere it is needed. Many pastors use their gifts in small groups or private settings. This provides a safe venue for ministering to areas of struggle or emotional pain. This gift can be used in many different places and ways.

The pastoral gift can also be used outside the Church. Pastors can minister in the workplace or with people they meet. In different jobs that I have had, there were always people that wanted pastoral advice. They would ask questions like "How can I have a marriage like yours?" or "What should I do when my children lie to me?" This provided natural opportunities for me to help others in a pastoral way.

The gifting of pastor can also be used in evangelism. I know a missionary who is an apostle with a strong pastoral anointing. He uses his gifts to plant new churches. One way he does this is by going into the homes of unbelievers and praying for entire families for healing and deliverance. God brings freedom to these families, they believe in Christ, and new churches are planted!

Another example of someone who used their pastoral gift in many different situations is a man named Jack Frost.[9] Although he has now gone to be with the Lord, I still enjoy watching videos of his teaching and healing conferences. He had a strong inner healing ministry that focused on helping others connect with God as a Father. Through his messages, many people have met God in a fresh way that has transformed their lives.

In addition, he would even use his pastoral gift when traveling. When people found out that he worked as a counselor, they would start sharing their problems with him. Many became Christians as he talked to them. He was truly versatile in using his gift.

The Pastor's Function in Ministry

The pastor is often the first influence in a Christian's walk with the Lord, laying the foundation for life change in Christ. Therefore, he is someone who not only feeds milk to spiritual infants, but also shows them where and how they can be fed. He is the one giving spiritual infants their milk and helps them grow to where they can take in their

---

[9] You can find out more about Jack Frost at his ministry website: www.shilohplace.org

Chapter 27: The Gift of Pastor

own spiritual food themselves. A pastor's role is similar in some ways to parents bringing up a baby.

1 Thessalonians 2:11-12 (WEB) As you know, we exhorted, comforted, and implored every one of you, as a father does his own children, (12) to the end that you should walk worthily of God, who calls you into his own Kingdom and glory.

1 Corinthians 4:15-16 (WEB) For though you have ten thousand tutors in Christ, yet not many fathers. For in Christ Jesus, I became your father through the Good News. (16) I beg you therefore, be imitators of me.

Pastors tend to be nurturing. People feel comfortable when they are present. Most of the time, young believers do not feel nervous around those with this gift. Pastors follow the example of Christ in their service through their close relationship with those they mentor. In many people's lives, pastors become spiritual parents.

There are exceptions to the typical pastoral personality. I am quite sure that God does not make everyone the same. Some skilled pastors have made me uncomfortable when we first met. It was not until I got to know them that this changed. One cause of discomfort for the young Christian may be the unscriptural concept that leaders might be distant, like a professional.

Different viewpoints of how a pastor should act sometimes influence people's feelings towards that pastor. Depending on the problems a person has, their pastor may not be able to have such a close relationship with them. In addition, some experience difficulty trusting pastors in certain stages of their spiritual growth, especially if they have serious issues that need healing. However, usually people will feel secure around them.

A pastor's role changes according to his sheep's maturity levels. He is to relate to them in similar ways to how Jesus related to his disciples. His function is one of spiritual parent and mentor. He is a representative of Christ in people's lives.

As young Christians mature in the Lord, the pastor's role of spiritual parenting becomes that of a mentor and facilitator. He walks

Church: What Was God Thinking?

will be identified and trained to meet this great need in the Body of Christ.

Chapter 28: The Role of the Teacher in the Modern Church

Acts 13:1 (WEB) Now in the assembly that was at Antioch there were some prophets and teachers: Barnabas, Simeon who was called Niger, Lucius of Cyrene, Manaen the foster brother of Herod the tetrarch, and Saul.

The gift of teaching is possibly the most freely functioning gift in the modern Church. People who use this gift can be seen everywhere and it is probably the best-known of the ministry gifts. Christians listen to sermons in meetings, on TV, from their own children, or spouses. They read them in book form. Teaching is important because everyone should always be growing in the knowledge of the Kingdom. In addition to the basic understanding the Church already seems to have regarding this gift, I would like to share some insights the Holy Spirit has given me about it. There is much more depth to this gift and it is more versatile than many people realize.

An individual with the ministry gift of teaching has the life-long focus of instructing others, causing God's word to come alive in their hearts. Although everyone in the five-fold ministry should be equipping people, this is the specific calling and anointing of teachers. When they are filled with the Holy Spirit, their gift brings revelation and freedom. Their teachings have the potential to bless many.

Church: What Was God Thinking?

The gift of teaching, when balanced with the other gifts, is indispensable. Without it, believers can enter into very serious error. When someone has this gift, they often have insight into the Scriptures that can help people grow as Christians, especially in their relationship with God. Even though the Bible says that the Holy Spirit will teach His children everything they need to know (John 14:26), God still gifts people so that they can give instruction in truths that many might not see when reading the Bible on their own.

I was once part of a church that, unfortunately, considered Bible study as something to be done only independently and privately. As a result, many there did not have a desire to know the Bible. Often, the level of hunger for the Word of God shows how much desire a person has for God. Many times, a gifted teacher can stir up that thirst for God and His Word.

Who Can Be a Teacher?

James 3:1 (WEB) Let not many of you be teachers, my brothers, knowing that we will receive heavier judgment.

Hebrews 5:12 (WEB) For although by this time you should be teachers, you again need to have someone teach you the rudiments of the first principles of the oracles of God. You have come to need milk, and not solid food.

2 Timothy 2:2 (WEB) The things which you have heard from me among many witnesses, commit the same to faithful men, who will be able to teach others also.

The Greek word for "faithful" is πιστός *pistos.*
Strong's definition G4103 (pronounced: *pis-tos´*)
  From G3982; objectively trustworthy; subjectively trustful: - believing, faithful, sure, true.

James said that not many should be teachers since they will go through a higher standard of judgment. I have often heard leaders who do not want other people to be involved in this ministry use this

Chapter 28: The Role of the Teacher in the Modern Church

Scripture as an excuse not to let others teach. I do not believe this verse is saying a teacher will be condemned to hell if he or she makes a mistake. Rather, in light of Hebrews 5, I feel James said this because of certain people's immaturity.

The author of Hebrews said that by a certain time, his readers should have become teachers. In saying this, the author connects the ability to instruct others with their spiritual maturity. They need the chance to learn how to use their gifts. Potential teachers in the maturing process can teach with faithful, mature teachers overseeing them. It is also vital that mature teachers practice what they preach, and take care when handling Scripture.

Leaders need to beware of holding people back without sufficient Scriptural reasons. If someone has been prophetically confirmed in the teaching gift and meets basic Biblical criteria, it would be wrong for a leader to refuse to equip and release that person. Scriptural conditions include: faithfulness to the Lord, submission to their leaders, and commitment to sound doctrine. When a prophet confirms a person's gift, this means it is for the blessing of the Church. It is inappropriate not to allow such individuals to teach. When leaders do this they force those people to bury talents that should be invested in the Kingdom of God (Matthew 25:14-30).

1 Corinthians 5:11 (WEB) But as it is, I wrote to you not to associate with anyone who is called a brother who is a sexual sinner, or covetous, or an idolater, or a slanderer, or a drunkard, or an extortioner. Don't even eat with such a person.

People do not need to be perfect before they can teach. I have seen leaders who will not let those in their church instruct others because of minor weaknesses and struggles in their lives. Faithfulness does not imply perfection. A weak person struggles with and wars against sin, but is saddened and grieved by it. A rebellious person has stopped caring about their sin, viewing it as unimportant or making excuses for it. Weakness is nowhere near as serious as rebellion. Of course if a person is in sin or rebellion, especially those mentioned in 1 Corinthians 5:11, then they should not be allowed to teach.

In addition, if someone who has been released starts teaching false doctrine and then resists correction, that person is not trustworthy to handle God's Word. Faithfulness in the Kingdom is the sincere desire to follow the Lord and the pursuit of that goal. Not permitting a sincere, committed believer to use their teaching gift is wrong. Allowing an immature teacher to use their gift under appropriate supervision can help them grow in God.

A person's age does not affect their ability to teach. I have seen grade school students and teenagers filled with the Holy Spirit proclaiming the Word with authority and power. Some years ago, a pastor in the church we attended had a "Preacher Boys Club." He trained a group of teenagers to teach. They were amazing! Since the gifts are from the Holy Spirit, age does not matter.

Teachers are not necessarily leaders. Also, teaching does not have to be done by a leader. In the Body of Christ, everyone gathers to share their spiritual gifts. However, the equipping should be done by those who are more mature, with the oversight of the church's leadership.

So, who should equip those called to be teachers? I believe that, if possible, it should be either an apostle or a mature teacher who is in the same local church. The best choice is someone confirmed as a teacher who has been walking in this gift faithfully for some time. If there is no such person available, those called into this ministry should pray that God would show them what to do. Quality equipping and mentoring is essential.

Biblical Teaching

Acts 20:9 (WEB) A certain young man named Eutychus sat in the window, weighed down with deep sleep. As Paul spoke still longer, being weighed down by his sleep, he fell down from the third story, and was taken up dead.

The Greek word for "speak" or "teach" is διαλέγομαι *dialegomai*.
Strong's definition G1256 (pronounced: *dee-al-eg'-om-ahee*)
Middle voice from G1223 and G3004; to say thoroughly, that is, discuss (in argument or exhortation): - dispute, preach (unto), reason (with),

Chapter 28: The Role of the Teacher in the Modern Church

speak.

Vine's definition *dialegomai*: Discourse: primarily denotes "to ponder, resolve in one's mind" (*dia*, "through," *lego*, "to say"); then, "to converse, dispute, discuss, discourse with;" most frequently, "to reason or dispute with." ... in Acts 20:7, 9; this the RV corrects to "discoursed," lit., "dialogue," i.e., not by way of a sermon, but by a "discourse" of a more conversational character.

So, does Scripture really define teaching as one person talking on and on until others fall asleep? I do not think so. I do not believe Eutychus fell asleep because of Paul's boring words. If anyone looks at the Greek word in this passage it is "*dialogemai*," from which people get the English word "dialogue." It means the teacher was leading a conversational discourse, a discussion. In the New Testament Church, an interactive style of teaching was sometimes used. Some of the best teaching happens as a result of each individual wholeheartedly participating. It is even more incredible if there is a group of people with this gift gathered together and following the leading of the Spirit. Each individual can add a little extra to what is being shared.

A few years ago, I went over to a friend's house where there was a group of people gathered for a prophetic meeting. These individuals came together about once a month for a time of hearing God and moving in the prophetic. At this particular meeting, one person felt that God was speaking to him about foundations. There were about five people who felt the Lord was talking to them about the same thing. It was great to feel the Holy Spirit move as each one added to the teaching. It was awesome!

I like to call this Spirit-led team teaching. When my family and I visit other churches to speak, we pray and ask God what He wants us to share. Sometimes we do this as a team, allowing equal time for each person. We each ask God what the whole family should teach, and what each of us should say individually. When we come together to compare notes, it is amazing! Even though each of us talks about the same subject, each person has a different perspective.

Uses for the Gift of Teaching

The gift of teaching can be used in the church meeting by individuals or a group of teachers taking turns and giving a little bit of insight. This can be done by planning teaching in advance, but is even better when it is spontaneously orchestrated by the Holy Spirit.

Here are some tips on how the gift of teaching can be used. It is necessary to note that this gift is not limited to larger gatherings. It is also be effective in home groups or house church meetings. Some of the best times to use the gifts are in small groups.

In churches that use larger meetings for teaching, the home setting should be for other gifts. On the other hand, home groups with mostly young believers who require additional teaching can alternate between doing this one week and then learning how to move in other spiritual gifts the next. If the small group setting is used for teaching, people can also make it short so that there will be a weekly time to use other gifts as well. This will help allow room for all the gifts to be used.

In addition, the teaching gift can be used effectively in one-on-one or small group discipleship. In this case, this gift functions much like the pastoral gifting and is very effective with new believers. Please note that this is different from the pastoral gifting, since pastors have a strong focus on emotional healing and spiritual growth, whereas a teacher focuses more on establishing doctrinal foundations.

The gift of teaching can be used in many different settings, including outside the church. No one should feel surprised if God uses a teacher in ways they had never considered. God cares for all aspects of His children's lives and is not at all limited in how He chooses to work.

For example: God can use the gift of teaching even in evangelism. I have taught in computer and English clubs, and even how to fix cars, all for outreach! I know a man that teaches others how to run

Chapter 28: The Role of the Teacher in the Modern Church

businesses. Those called to be teachers can look for many different opportunities to teach according to people's interests and use share the Gospel. God is not limited by stereotypes regarding a gift's use. Teaching is very versatile.

People with the gift of teaching may also have other ministry gifts. The following examples are common gift combinations involving this gift. A prophetic-teacher focuses on using prophetic words for teaching. A teacher-evangelist can use teaching to preach the Gospel. A pastoral-teacher uses his gift for healing and deliverance addressing individual's spiritual strongholds. These are all different ways that the gift of teaching can be used.

As with all the gifts, there are inherent strengths and weaknesses that teachers have. In the following chapter, I will discuss this issue further.

Chapter 29: Issues Related to the Teacher

Some leaders are frightened of releasing people who want to teach, especially if these individuals have not been to seminary. There are several reasons for this fear, including the issues related to equipping teachers in the local church. Many have recognized some of these problems, but what I share here goes beyond that. In fact, a few of these have to do with the full-time minister being the main person to use this gift. In order to equip teachers, leaders need to understand weaknesses they might have. Everyone also must learn to discern false teaching. As such, I feel it is necessary to take a look at these issues.

False Teaching

2 Peter 2:1 (WEB) But false prophets also arose among the people, as false teachers will also be among you, who will secretly bring in destructive heresies, denying even the Master who bought them, bringing on themselves swift destruction.

2 Timothy 3:16-17 (WEB) Every Scripture is God-breathed and profitable for teaching, for reproof, for correction, and for instruction in righteousness, (17) that the man of God may be complete, thoroughly equipped for every good work.

Church: What Was God Thinking?

John 14:26 (WEB) But the Counselor, the Holy Spirit, whom the Father will send in my name, he will teach you all things, and will remind you of all that I said to you.

1 Corinthians 2:14 (WEB) Now the natural man doesn't receive the things of God's Spirit, for they are foolishness to him, and he can't know them, because they are spiritually discerned.

Matthew 22:29 (WEB) But Jesus answered them, "You are mistaken, not knowing the Scriptures, nor the power of God.

Interpreting Scripture without the Holy Spirit's help can create false doctrine and false teachers. In 2 Peter 2:1, Peter gives a warning about this. If teachers are always trying to figure out what the Bible says without connecting with God through the Holy Spirit, it is possible that they will teach false doctrines. This is an easy and common mistake to make.

Believers have the indwelling Holy Spirit to guide them and many are privileged to have the Bible in their everyday language. Even so, there are also many who try to interpret Scripture from their own fleshly understanding. The Bible says that believers need the leading of the Spirit of God to understand His Word (1 Corinthians 2:14). John 14:26 says that the Holy Ghost will teach His people. Although God does use people who are not spirit-filled to proclaim truth, the Holy Spirit's help is vital to accurately interpret the Word of God.

John 16:13 (WEB) However when he, the Spirit of truth, has come, he will guide you into all truth, for he will not speak from himself; but whatever he hears, he will speak. He will declare to you things that are coming.

Without the Holy Spirit's help in understanding God's word, teachers risk repeating history and believing false doctrine. Jesus promised that the Holy Spirit will lead believers into all truth (John 16:13). Sadly, some doctrines sound wonderful and actually damage the Body of Christ. In the centuries before Martin Luther, a number of significant Bible teachings had become distorted and were destroying the Church. Among other questionable teachings, the Church taught

Chapter 29: Issues Related to the Teacher

about indulgences as Gospel truth, although it was not even in Scripture. At that time, only the most educated people could read the Biblical languages.

Martin Luther was one of the few people of that time who had studied university. He read God's Word and began to realize that the Church was teaching false doctrines. He also felt strongly about the Church at that time being opposed to translating the Bible from Hebrew and Greek into any local languages. He spoke up about these problems in hopes of reforming the Church and, eventually, became one of the first to translate the Bible into his people's native language. The rest is history.

Accountability

Ephesians 4:13-15 (WEB) until we all attain to the unity of the faith, and of the knowledge of the Son of God, to a full grown man, to the measure of the stature of the fullness of Christ; (14) that we may no longer be children, tossed back and forth and carried about with every wind of doctrine, by the trickery of men, in craftiness, after the wiles of error; (15) but speaking truth in love, we may grow up in all things into him, who is the head, Christ;

If anyone believes the Bible is saying something that is different from what the Church as a whole is teaching, it is necessary to humbly and thoroughly check it out before teaching that new doctrine. This means thoroughly searching the Scriptures and looking at all sides of any question to understand what the Bible is saying.

Proverbs 11:14 (KJV) Where no counsel is, the people fall: but in the multitude of counselors there is safety.

Ephesians 5:21 (KJV) Submitting yourselves one to another in the fear of God.

At times, individuals feel God is showing them truths He wants them to share, and they are not aware of Scriptures that contradict their new teaching. As a safeguard, this should be shared with more mature individuals who can confirm whether God is speaking (Proverbs 11:14). All Christians, including Teachers need to be accountable to their brothers and sisters in the Body of Christ (Ephesians 5:21).

In the past, some widely accepted teachings in the church were wrong. Popularity is not proof of truth. Centuries ago nearly all Christians wrongly believed that the Bible taught the earth was flat. In addition, for hundreds of years nearly everyone believed the gift of tongues was only for the early church.[10] Many people still believe this doctrine to this day.

I received the gift of tongues when I was about a month old in the Lord. Years later, I worked for a group that reached out to the poor and many of them were drug addicts in Hong Kong. My wife and I served with a team that prayed in tongues for these drug addicts, in shifts, round the clock for ten days. Men addicted to heroin for decades would be delivered of their addiction without withdrawal symptoms. By working with this ministry, I saw miracles just like those that happened in the early Church. A proof of the doctrine that the gift of tongues is real and for today is in the fruit of this ministry. Truth will always prove itself through its fruit.

Not everyone that wants to teach is ready. Some people have the desire without the maturity. Others are able to teach when they are still young in the Lord. Some may need to deepen their knowledge of Scripture. Teachers also need to receive healing, as a lack of healing can cause distortion in their hearing God's voice and interpreting His Word.

2 Timothy 2:15 (WEB) Give diligence to present yourself approved by God, a workman who doesn't need to be ashamed, properly handling the Word of Truth.

---

[10] There are those who argue that the gifts of the Holy Spirit were only for the early Church since they claim that the "perfect" in 1 Corinthians 13:10 is the Christian Bible. However this will be fulfilled when Jesus returns, since He is the only perfect one (Hebrews 4:15, 9:28) and He will return in glory (Matthew 25:31; John 14:2-3; Hebrews 10:35-37). Therefore, the gifts of the Holy Spirit continue to be for believers today.

Chapter 29: Issues Related to the Teacher

Teachers must spend much time with the Lord and studying the Bible. Teachers need to thoroughly understand Scripture. They should never stop being students of God's Word, taking time daily to read and study as much as possible (2 Timothy 2:15). All of this is essential for the potential teacher.

2 Timothy 4:3 (WEB) For the time will come when they will not listen to the sound doctrine, but, having itching ears, will heap up for themselves teachers after their own lusts;

Hebrews 4:12 (WEB) For the word of God is living, and active, and sharper than any two-edged sword, and piercing even to the dividing of soul and spirit, of both joints and marrow, and is able to discern the thoughts and intentions of the heart.

In the world today, there are thousands of different churches that believe they have the truth, but many people do not want to hear it. At the same time, many others are open to God and upon hearing the truth will repent. 2 Timothy 4:3 says that there will be a season when people cannot endure sound teaching. Those who accept lies and refuse to hear the truth forfeit the abundant life that is promised in the Bible. There is an old saying, "The truth hurts." God's eternal truth brings conviction that brings repentance and a desire to follow Christ wholeheartedly (2 Corinthians 7:10). It is God's kindness and the work of the Holy Spirit to help people turn away from sin, leading them to repentance (Romans 2:4; John 16:7-14).

One good way to discern the truth of a doctrine is by looking at long-term results. Some things sound good at first, however, a long-term fruit is spiritual dryness. This is a problem. When people receive the truth in their hearts, the fruit of the Spirit (see Galatians 5) and the anointing of the Holy Ghost will be a part of their lives. They will then be able to discern the quality of fruit, as their knowledge of Scripture and relationship with Jesus grows stronger. Results of a teaching reveal so much about the truth of that teaching.

Mixed motives, half-hearted commitment, and a divided heart cause people to distort what God is saying and doing in their lives

Church: What Was God Thinking?

(James 1:8). When believers operate in any ministry gifting, their focus needs to be on Jesus. This is especially important for teachers, because they release God's Word to others. They must be prepared to sacrifice for Jesus and be willing to give up everything to follow Him (Luke 9:23-25).

A friend of mine was a missionary in Mexico. He spent more than half his life living in the back of a truck, establishing and serving churches in Mexico. Miracles were normal to him. Focusing on Jesus enabled him to raise up many churches. He was an example of what wholehearted service looks like.

Possible Weaknesses of Teachers

As with all the gifts, there are some inherent weaknesses the teacher may have. Believers need to understand each other's strengths and weaknesses to help one another grow, recognizing everyone's role in the Body in order to have grace for each other.

One weakness a teacher can have is trying to make everyone else teachers or students. He may subconsciously feel that instruction is so important that he does not want the other gifts to operate.

This type of person cannot wait for worship and other things to be finished so he can preach his great sermon. It is not bad for a person to be excited about using his gifts, but he must make sure that everyone else has the opportunity to use their gifts as well. It is sad when the main leader of a congregation is a talented teacher, and the whole church ends up favoring teaching and centered on "head" knowledge to the exclusion of most of the other spiritual gifts.

If the teacher is doing his job, he will make room for other gifts. He will not dominate a meeting. Sometimes, his teaching may take up much of the gathering, but this should not be the usual practice.

An immature teacher might rely on his knowledge and spend more time in study than he spends in his relationship with God. Typically, if a person is not spending time in the presence of God and yet he is preaching God's Word, the result is people becoming bored and sleepy.

Chapter 29: Issues Related to the Teacher

Many believers would be ashamed to admit feeling this way about the sermon in their church. Religious communities do not often accept expression of such an emotion about a church service. Regardless of how brilliant a person's gift is, without the anointing of the Holy Spirit, there is less practical impact on people's lives.

Of course, there are rare occasions where a teacher spends little time in the presence of God, and yet people enjoy hearing him speak. There are those few who seem to have God's grace regardless and can preach effectively even with a dry heart. This teacher may have a natural talent for instruction in addition to the spiritual gift of teaching. I always wonder how much more incredible such people would be if they were connecting with God.

The teacher can make the mistake of thinking that he is a pastor or even an apostle. This is often due to the misconception that the pastor, the teacher, and the apostle are the same. Sometimes, people have a gift combination of pastor and teacher, but those that do not may waste a significant amount of time trying to be something they are not. This could result in church members becoming uneasy around the teacher, sometimes to the point of avoiding, or not wanting to be close to him. It is more likely that others, specifically pastors and apostles, are called to fill this pastoral gap.

Some immature teachers get excited about certain doctrines and only preach those doctrines. I have heard people teach on different subjects and list only the verses that they find acceptable. There may be many other passages of Scripture that contradict their point, but they ignore those since they find it uncomfortable to face the truth. The problem is that, without looking at the whole Bible, it is possible to twist God's Word to say anything they might want. It is very likely that such a person is not ready to deal with his own insecurities.

If a person does this, it does not mean that he does not have the teaching gift; it simply means that he needs more healing and maturity before becoming truly ready to teach. A mature teacher uses verses within their Biblical context. He also looks at what the whole Bible says about a subject.

Church: What Was God Thinking?

2 Timothy 4:3 (WEB) For the time will come when they will not listen to the sound doctrine, but, having itching ears, will heap up for themselves teachers after their own lusts;

Another weakness that some teachers have is saying only what people want to hear. Teachers must speak the truth no matter how others feel about it. This does not mean being insensitive to anyone's feelings, but rather being aware of how best to communicate the truth in a Godly and loving way. Teachers need to hear from the Holy Spirit about how much to challenge believers at any given time, however, they should never quit proclaiming truth in order to make people comfortable.

Galatians 1:10 (WEB) For am I now seeking the favor of men, or of God? Or am I striving to please men? For if I were still pleasing men, I wouldn't be a servant of Christ.

If a teacher is doing his job, he will not be worried about what other people think of him. His main concern will be what God thinks of him. As a result, when he speaks the Truth, it will challenge others and could make them uncomfortable. There is no way around this fact. The Father has not called His children to live in the "comfort zone" or to be "politically correct." Teaching should not be influenced by what the world is thinking or by what others are saying. Since Christians are called to speak the truth in love, teachers must never compromise the Scriptures. If people are going to grow, they need to be challenged by teachers who proclaim truth from the Bible (Galatians 1:10).

In summary, the teaching gift is very important to stir up people's hunger for God and lay foundations of truth for believers. Teaching stirs Christians to explore the depths of the mystery and beauty in Scripture. It is essential that it is done with the empowering of the Holy Spirit and considering Biblical context. Also there needs to be a balance among the gifts, that all the gifts be used. Finally, potential teachers must be trained and allowed to minister as they show themselves faithful. These are key components to healthy Christian community.

Chapter 30: The Evangelist

Ephesians 4:11-12 (WEB) He gave some to be apostles; and some, prophets; and some, evangelists; and some, shepherds [pastors] and teachers; (12) for the perfecting of the saints, to the work of serving, to the building up of the Body of Christ;

Acts 21:8 (WEB) On the next day, we, who were Paul's companions, departed, and came to Caesarea. We entered into the house of Philip the evangelist, who was one of the seven, and stayed with him.

The Greek word for "evangelist" is εὐαγγελιστής *euaggelistēs*.
Strong's definition G2099 (pronounced: *yoo-ang-ghel-is-tace´*)
From G2097; a preacher of the gospel: - evangelist.

The role of evangelists in the Church is a significant one. Without them there would be fewer new believers, less people to equip them, and there would be stagnation in the Body. Besides sharing the Good News themselves, evangelists help each believer to remember who they were without Jesus and that there are others out there who still need Him. They also encourage everyone in the joy of sharing their faith.

Church: What Was God Thinking?

All are called to preach the Gospel. This does not mean that it is meant to be on as wide of a scale as evangelists. Ephesians 6 says that the shoes of the Gospel of peace are a part of every believer's spiritual armor. The difference between these people and the evangelist is that some individuals primarily share their faith within their own circle of friends, family, and acquaintances. I believe this is important for many reasons.

One reason in particular is the accountability that results from sharing the Good News. When people know that someone is a believer, they generally hold them to a higher standard and look to them as an example of how Christians should act, especially when facing common struggles. It is not about saying the right words, but rather becoming a living witness of a transformed life and representing the love of the Father. However, this does not mean that believers are supposed to preach to everyone in sight. All are called to proclaim the Gospel, but this is the life and ministry focus of the evangelist. They are meant to use this gift themselves and train everyone in the Body how to preach as well.

Fortunately, the Church gives evangelists a great deal of freedom in using this gift. Perhaps the bigger issue in modern days is how the Gospel is preached. I wish to share some insights God has given me regarding evangelists and evangelism.

Acts 16:5 (WEB) So the assemblies were strengthened in the faith, and increased in number daily.

Evangelists are essential in the Body of Christ. In the book of Acts, the Church was added to daily. If a Christian community is healthy, it will not only grow by having evangelists, but when new people are continually coming in, they influence others with their fresh love and excitement for God. This helps prevent church members from becoming like the older brother in the story of the prodigal son (Luke 15:24–32), where people cannot accept new believers because they are not as mature as the older believers. The evangelist also helps the

Chapter 30: The Evangelist

church have an outward focus whereas the other gifts are mainly helping those already in the Body of Christ.

Evangelists are easy to recognize. It seems that wherever they go, they preach the Gospel to someone. They usually have excellent results. On the other hand, the evangelistic gifting is not only for evangelism, it is also for equipping.

Billy Graham is a good example of an evangelist. He is well known and people come to the Lord everywhere he goes. Through many years of his ministry, wherever he has gone, his team conducts training so that local believers will be better equipped for continued outreach and follow-up of new believers. However, not everyone is a big crowd evangelist like Billy Graham.

A friend of mine in Hong Kong also has the gift of evangelism. He is a "people magnet." He seems to be able to make friends anywhere. After people become friends with him, they often want to go to church with him. In his case, his gift is used on a more personal level. He may never lead big crusades, but he is effective in bringing people to the Lord, one by one. These are just a couple examples of the many different types of evangelists.

Another type of evangelist is the street preacher. A few years ago, I went to a conference with my wife and one of my daughters. During one of the breaks some of my daughter's new friends went out to preach the Gospel. Soon one of the girls was preaching to strangers in the street and within a few minutes had three new people saved and filled with the Holy Spirit. These individuals were from very anti-Christian backgrounds, but she had no trouble reaching them at all! Evangelists come in many forms.

One easy way to recognize an evangelist is their passion for the lost. Many times, when they talk about the Bible it seems that they only see Scriptures about preaching the Gospel, as though their whole perspective is about people needing to get saved.

When people are talking about other topics in the Bible, they may seem bored, or as if they feel others are missing the point. It is not that they do not love the Word of God, it is just that their passion is to share the Gospel and bring many people to meet Jesus (John 1:40-42).

Many evangelists think that the Good News is the main point of all ministry.

Acts 21:8 (WEB) On the next day, we, who were Paul's companions, departed, and came to Caesarea. We entered into the house of Philip the evangelist, who was one of the seven, and stayed with him.

Acts 8:5-7 (WEB) Philip went down to the city of Samaria, and proclaimed to them the Christ. (6) The multitudes listened with one accord to the things that were spoken by Philip, when they heard and saw the signs which he did. (7) For unclean spirits came out of many of those who had them. They came out, crying with a loud voice. Many who had been paralyzed and lame were healed.

Philip is a great example of an evangelist. He went to Samaria, preached the Gospel with signs and wonders, and multitudes came to Christ. People cannot easily deny that Jesus is real after experiencing healing, deliverance, or some other miracle. Philip blessed many in his day, by allowing God's power to flow through him, using his gift to glorify God.

Biblical Ways to Share the Gospel

It is essential that evangelists preach and equip others to share the Good News in a Biblical way. In order to do that, I want to look at several Scriptural evangelism methods.

Luke 10:1 (WEB) Now after these things, the Lord also appointed seventy others, and sent them two by two ahead of him into every city and place, where he was about to come.

Perhaps one of the first methods recorded in Scripture is when Jesus sent out seventy-two people to tell other communities about the Kingdom of Heaven (Luke 10). Jesus instructed the disciples to look for the person of peace in a community. When they found this person,

Chapter 30: The Evangelist

they were to live with him and his family and preach the Kingdom from his house. I believe that often the disciples found not just a single man of peace, but a family of peace.

In Luke 10, the disciples were instructed to not only proclaim the Kingdom, but also to heal the sick and cast out demons. This is such an amazing way to preach the Good News! When the Gospel is demonstrated to people with the power of God, they become disciples, not just converts. Those equipping new believers have a much easier job when those who come to know Christ do so through the Spirit of God touching their lives. As a result, leaders do not have to work as hard to help them be passionate about following God (Mark 16:15-18).

1 Corinthians 2:4 (WEB) My speech and my preaching were not in persuasive words of human wisdom, but in demonstration of the Spirit and of power,

Believers need to return to demonstrating the power of the Spirit when they evangelize. Many Christians like to use things that they have learned from others and human wisdom to share the Good News. In contrast, Paul said that he preached the Gospel with the demonstration of the Spirit and power.

Christians often use tools such as four steps to know Jesus, "scaring people out of eternal damnation," and encouraging them to pray a prayer of decision in order to "buy fire insurance" to "get out of hell free." Individuals either feel pressured into believing in Jesus or respond to momentary emotion, but then nothing changes. People that encounter God's power are more likely to keep walking with Him.

Recently, some evangelists and prophets have been using the gift of prophecy to preach the Gospel. They hear God for unbelievers, sharing messages from Him about things they could not possibly know. Sometimes, the Lord will even give them personal information such as the address where that person lives.

In John 4:7–42, Jesus met a woman at Jacob's well. He then used the gift of prophecy, sharing personal information, proving to her that He was the Christ. He talked about her love life, how she had been married five times but was now living with a man that was not her husband. He did this privately and with such sensitivity and compassion that He won her heart.

She realized Jesus was a prophet, went back to her city, and told everyone about Jesus and that He miraculously knew her past. Because Jesus used the gift of prophecy, many people believed in Him. When this type of word is given, many times unbelievers will make a decision to follow Jesus.

My ministry team has experienced the impact prophetic evangelism can have on others. One night, our fellowship felt that the Lord was leading us to go out to preach to some young people hanging out in the park. We saw a group of two guys and two girls and sensed that the Lord wanted us to share the Gospel with them.

When we started talking to them about Jesus, the guys got up and walked away. We were able to pray with the girls and we received some prophetic words for them. Soon, they were crying because they could feel the love of God. When it was over, they definitely knew what it was like to be touched by the Holy Spirit. This is one form of preaching with God's power.

Others use the gift of healing to bring people to the Lord. They pray for the sick and their pain and illnesses are cured. Sometimes blind eyes are opened, lame people walk and deaf people hear. Such miracles open doors and open hearts for people to believe in Jesus.

Sometimes, the power of God simply touches a person and his life is changed. As I mentioned in the first chapter, when I came to the Lord it was because some Christians prayed with me and the power of God fell on me. Although I did not understand at that time what happened, I left knowing God was real.

Venues for the Gift of Evangelism

There are different places and ways to preach the Gospel. The gift of evangelism can be used in large gatherings, especially when people know there are unbelievers in the meeting. This is a great opportunity

Chapter 30: The Evangelist

for an evangelist to share the Good News. He may do it from the platform or in a separate meeting, such as a visitor's meeting. Both are excellent venues for preaching the Gospel.

If unbelievers come regularly, however, it might be better to use a small group setting, so the long-term believers do not suffer from lack of depth. Another possibility is to occasionally use the large meetings to preach the Gospel so that members of a congregation can see the gift of evangelism in action. The important thing is that you find some way to share the Good News with visitors, without sacrificing the use of other gifts and the spiritual depth of the gathering.

The gift of evangelism can be used during a home group or house church meeting. The Gospel can also be preached in a more relaxed way during meal times, refreshments, and prayer. Sometimes the Holy Spirit will touch the unbeliever during prayer. This happened to my wife and I, and God used it to change our lives forever. Christians should not limit God; He is creative in helping people encounter Him.

The evangelistic gift can function in many ways. It can operate in the church, but it is usually used outside the regular meeting. The evangelist has the God-given ability to sense who is ready to hear the Good News. Some use the gifts of healing, miracles, prophecy, word of knowledge, word of wisdom, and signs and wonders. Regardless of how his gift operates, the evangelist has the specific ability to bring the love of Christ to people who may otherwise never experience it.

Weaknesses of the Evangelist

One of evangelists' key weaknesses is that they may not necessarily be the best person to oversee a congregation. Some immature evangelists feel the other callings are less important. Such people have limited vision to disciple or pastor others, so this area of their ministry is weak. If this is the case, their teaching becomes one-dimensional.

In a minister's position, an evangelist may be able to grow a big church, but there could be some issues. Every congregation needs an equipping team that functions in all the gifts of the five-fold ministry,

Church: What Was God Thinking?

and has strong Biblical teaching and discipleship available for all. Without this, people may leave as quickly as they come because of lack of spiritual depth in the community.

Overemphasis on evangelism causes neglect of a congregation's spiritual growth. In such a situation, often those that do stay have the gift of evangelism or feel guilty because they have difficulty sharing the Good News or are not as passionate about it. They may not realize that there are other giftings in the Body of Christ and might feel there is something wrong with them if they have other gifts. Such a church may become a social club.

Another possibility is that of the evangelist who is functioning as the "head pastor" spending most of his time trying to motivate those who do not share the same gift to focus on evangelism. Others who might be potential evangelists preach the Gospel without growing into some level of maturity. I have heard some who actually say that if everyone goes out to share the Good News as their primary ministry, spiritual growth will come automatically. The result of this belief is often a community of frustrated believers who are not strong in their faith. One way to balance this is for such a minister to have a fully-functioning five-fold ministry team working with him. The Church will function most effectively having a holistic focus where all the gifts work together in ministry.

An evangelist can grow a large congregation, but it may reach a small fraction of its potential in quantity and quality without ministers with other gifts working alongside him. He might have a church of ten thousand, but it is possible with five-fold ministry leadership and an Ephesians 4 style equipping team, he could have had thousands of churches reaching that number of people or more! I cannot over-emphasize the power of team ministry, the importance of the right people being in leadership, and bringing believers into maturity.

Another weakness of some evangelists is that they are often more comfortable doing than being. Some enjoy time with people so much that they neglect their relationship with God. When an evangelist does not spend enough time with the Lord, he may try to use gimmicks to

Chapter 30: The Evangelist

attract people to church instead of using God's power through signs and wonders. Many big-name evangelists spend hours a day communicating with God in prayer and that is the reason why they have had such an impact.

If people believe in Christ without experiencing the power of God, this limits their spiritual growth and they could become lukewarm. Evangelists must to learn good time management, making time to connect with God before they try to help others connect with Him. This is like the airline stewardess demonstrating the proper use of the oxygen mask -- make sure yours is in place before trying to assist others.

In summary, the gift of evangelism is a very important and versatile gift. It can operate in almost any setting. The evangelist helps keep the church fresh and free from stagnation. When he preaches the Biblical way, through the power of God, this lays a solid foundation for new believers to become strong disciples. When functioning correctly, it is an amazing gift!

Chapter 31: Other Spiritual Gifts

In previous chapters, I discussed the equipping or ministry gifts in detail. In fact, these are not the only gifts mentioned in Scripture. There are three other passages of Scripture that list spiritual gifts, specifically 1 Corinthians 12:7-10, 27-31, and Romans 12:6-8. In this chapter, I want to talk about other types of gifts including manifestational gifts, function gifts, and faith gifts.

Manifestational Gifts

The manifestational gifts in 1 Corinthians 12 are different from the equipping gifts in Ephesians 4. Equipping gifts are available to everyone and given for the individual's lifetime use. Manifestational gifts operate in the Presence of the Holy Spirit. They are given for what the Lord wants to do at a certain time and to any believer when God chooses to use them in that way. The Lord gives these gifts to any believer at certain times and for specific purposes. This is not related to that person's five-fold ministry gift.

Church: What Was God Thinking?

1 Corinthians 12:4-7 (WEB) Now there are various kinds of gifts, but the same Spirit. (5) There are various kinds of service, and the same Lord. (6) There are various kinds of workings, but the same God, who works all things in all. (7) But to each one is given the manifestation of the Spirit for the profit of all.

Gifts function in many ways with different expressions. The most important thing is that they are used for the others' benefit. Believers must be very careful not to limit God.

Words of Wisdom and Knowledge

1 Corinthians 12:8a (WEB) For to one is given through the Spirit the word of wisdom ...

Like most spiritual gifts, words of wisdom and knowledge both involve hearing God's voice. When someone listens to others share about a problem or situation and receives wisdom for them through the Holy Spirit, this is a word of wisdom. Often such words touch and encourage them. Sometimes when God gives a word of wisdom for others, they may feel challenged or uncomfortable. Individuals' responses might be related to issues in their relationship with God, their degree of brokenness or the expression of the one sharing the word. Regardless most people will be greatly encouraged upon hearing this type of message.

1 Corinthians 12:8b ... and to another the word of knowledge, according to the same Spirit;

Words of knowledge are similar to words of wisdom. Words of knowledge are communications from God revealing previously unknown information. Some reasons that the Lord gives words of knowledge are to: share with the individual, intercede, or train in hearing God's voice. This supernatural information can be about anything. God has even given me words of knowledge about Bible questions or other people. This happens most often when I listen to

Chapter 31: Other Spiritual Gifts

God in prayer for someone regularly. I used to experience such training when praying for the minister who taught in my church. Many times the Lord told me what he was going to teach the next Sunday and confirmed it during the service.

The Gift of Faith

1 Corinthians 12:9a (WEB) to another faith, by the same Spirit...

Have you ever been around someone that always seems to have faith, and whatever they believe for often happens? This person probably has the manifestational gift of faith. All true Christians have a degree of faith, but for some, their faith is exceptionally strong because they have this gift. Those with the gift of faith often tell others that if they simply believed, they would experience God more. Although this could be true, such people might not understand that they have so much faith because they have the gift.

Luke 17:5 (WEB) The apostles said to the Lord, "Increase our faith."

All believers can ask the Lord to give and increase the gift of faith in them like the apostles. At times in my life, God has given me greater faith when I asked Him. Although the answer was not always immediate, sooner or later, God answered my request. The Father gives good gifts to His children.

Most times that I have been given the gift of faith, I was in difficult situations, and God asked me to trust Him for something I needed. I am a faith missionary. What that means is I never raised enough support to live on, instead I trust God to provide what I need when I need it. There have been times when I was low on money and faith. I would think about finding extra work to help make life more comfortable and the Lord would speak to me and tell me "No!" During such times, I asked God to increase my faith. In the end, He has always provided and He has used these situations to strengthen my faith at the same time. God is so faithful!

Church: What Was God Thinking?

Sometimes when the Lord speaks to me directly or through someone else, I have a firm trust that what He said will happen. This trust is the gift of faith. One time I was walking home with my family. I had forty Hong Kong dollars, that's about five U.S. dollars, in my wallet and about one hundred Hong Kong dollars (about twelve US dollars) in the bank. The Holy Spirit spoke to me and told me to give all the money in my wallet to a beggar on the street. At the time, I only had enough to feed my family one more day, so I really did not want to give it to the beggar. I thought it could not be God. I kept walking but God kept telling me to go back and give him my money. After several blocks, I was persuaded that it was the Lord speaking to me and that I needed to go back. So I did, giving him all I had. The next day, He provided the money we needed. It is because of times like this that my family in Hong Kong has learned how faithful God truly is.

Gifts of Healing

1 Corinthians 12:9b (WEB) … and to another gifts of healings, by the same Spirit;

Gifts of healing are another type of manifestational gift. Although the most recognized type of healing gift is the God-given ability to release healing to others, another less recognized expression of this gift is the touch that the Holy Spirit gives to a sick person so they can get well. The healing gifts have many manifestations that any believer can pray for and experience.

Healing is not always instantaneous. Persistence is the key to regularly seeing others healed. In my ministry, this sometimes happens instantly. More often, it takes long-term, persistent prayer to begin seeing some change. When fighting something caused by the enemy, there will be warfare involved. Regardless, physical healing should be more common among Christians and believers should persist in prayer until it is accomplished.

Sometimes healing is partial and gradual. For example, one young man that my family has ministered to is developmentally challenged.

Chapter 31: Other Spiritual Gifts

Over some years, my ministry team has regularly prayed for him about this. Each time he has become a little bit smarter. I believe that if he continues pursuing God he will become completely normal. This will come as we continue praying for him to receive the gift of healing. Partial healing is a promise of complete healing as long as believers persist in prayer.

Other times, we have seen God quickly heal people. Some time ago, a woman asked us to pray for her son. He had blisters all over his body and medicine was not helping. After five minutes of prayer, the blisters began to disappear. Even the spots left by the blisters were gone by the next morning. In this case, God healed only after praying together one time.

The Gift of Miracles

1 Corinthians 12:10a (WEB) and to another workings of miracles ...

The next gift mentioned is the gift of miracles. Some people with this gift hear from the Lord about what He wants to do and are involved in the process of releasing it. Others always seem to experience miracles. When they need something, it is provided for them in ways many do not experience. This is such an amazing gift!

1 Corinthians 12:28 (WEB) God has set some in the assembly: ... then miracle workers?

Many different people can receive the gift of miracles. I have met individuals who have experienced food being multiplied, miraculous provision, and many other miracles. I believe that, due to economic problems in the world today, Christians everywhere will experience the gift of miracles operating in the area of finances. I also believe that many healing evangelists who are able to help others receive instant healings operate in this gift as miracle workers for God. This is a versatile gift.

Church: What Was God Thinking?

This gift functions in many ways. One way is the multiplication of food. I know of a couple in Canada that have experienced this when guests have come over for dinner and they did not have enough food. When they pray that God would multiply it, He does. This is just one way this gift operates. Sometimes believers pray for someone that needs a miracle to pay their rent and they receive what they need the next day. Other times, individuals who want to go on a missions trip encounter difficulty in getting a visa, after prayer, receive official permission to go. These are just a few common examples of this gift.

I have experienced this in many different ways. For example, when I first became a Christian my wife and I needed a better car. A friend of mine offered to sell us his car at a good price but we still could not afford it. We did not feel right about borrowing money to buy the car, so we prayed that God would provide cash. One of my co-workers laughed at us and said, "If you buy a car you have to go into debt to pay for it." Soon after this, a friend of ours gave us a gift not knowing how much we needed. The amount given to us was just enough to pay for the car and registration. My co-worker became a Christian soon after that. In this case, we saw two miracles happen. The best miracle was my co-worker giving his life to the Lord.

My wife and I experienced another miracle of provision shortly after we had our first baby. We did not have insurance at the time and our baby girl was four-weeks premature. Since she had to stay in the hospital our bill was very expensive. We decided to mainly eat vegetables from our garden so that we could pay all of it. Two days after we paid our bill, a leader in our church who did not know our situation brought over a quarter of a cow. We never dreamed that we would eat steaks and brisket for the rest of the month. Our small refrigerator was not large enough to hold all the meat so we shared a lot of it with our neighbors. We told them the story of how God saw our need and provided so abundantly through our friend from church. This miracle was a great testimony of how God cares for His children.

Another time our grass needed to be mowed. I only had a little gas in the tank but I decided to mow as much as I could. It was not long

Chapter 31: Other Spiritual Gifts

before most of the front yard was mowed. I was astonished! As I was finishing the front yard a person walked by and I was able to talk to him and share the Gospel. As soon as he left, I tried to start the lawnmower back up and it would not start because it was out of gas. This was a simple, yet obvious miracle. I am sure there are many other ways that this gift operates and as the *ekklesia* is being restored the Church will see more miracles.

The Gift of Discernment

1 Corinthians 12:10 (WEB)…and to another discerning of spirits …

The gift of discernment of spirits has a variety of uses. It is a God-given gift used to identify spiritual atmospheres or to recognize the presence of angels or demons. This gift is also used to determine the source of people's words, especially teaching or prophecy, as from the flesh, the enemy, or God. Besides this, it also helps in discerning people's motives and intentions, or other spiritual activity. One example of this gift in operation is when a person sees angels next to someone and as a result knows that God is releasing healing for that person. Discernment of spirits is also useful in praying for people that have spiritual problems. Through this gift the Holy Spirit shows what the problem is and how to pray against it. It is important in the Kingdom of God.

Hebrews 5:14 (WEB) But solid food is for those who are full grown, who by reason of use have their senses exercised to discern good and evil.

Living in Hong Kong, my ministry team has often needed the gift of discernment of spirits and it has become stronger in us because of frequent use. Although there are many churches here only a small percent of the population is Christian. The majority of people believe in a mix of Buddhism and Chinese folk religions. Idol worship is common and we often sense the resulting spiritual oppression. This is particularly intense when walking by an idol, religious symbol or temple. Prayer walking, asking God how to pray while walking, is a good way to develop this gift, especially if used in an intercessory way. Discernment needs to be developed through practice.

Many times God alerts someone with this gift about another's spiritual situation during prayer. This is particularly helpful when new people are attending a church gathering. In addition, it is not uncommon that word of knowledge and discernment will work together. When my ministry team prays for people it is not unusual for us to sense how they are feeling. Often, this comes through a word of knowledge. For example, sometimes we know a person is struggling with sadness because we start feeling sad when we pray for them. Other times, we know someone has a problem with anger because of a sudden feeling of anger during prayer. This kind of sudden and unusual emotion could be God's way of alerting a person to a problem so that God can use the situation to deal with it.

In order for discernment to function accurately and appropriately, any personal issues must be dealt with as quickly as possible. Sin and hurts can reduce the ability for clear discernment. In contrast, healing from wounds of the past or forgiveness of offenses in the present brings increase to the pure flow of this gift. A person's accuracy in this gift is proportionate to how clean and whole his heart has become. Repentance, healing, and forgiveness will clear blockages to clear discernment.

People with this gift can often see angels and demons. Members of my ministry team see them sometimes. When we see angels we know that God is working, giving special assignments related to us. When we see demons, we know we need to pray more, especially if we see them in our apartment. In such a case we pray over our home, commanding any spirits that are not of God to leave. This ability allows us to know when God is working and to be aware of spiritual warfare.

On a side note, if someone senses oppression in his house he can pray as he walks through it. In Jesus' name, just command the spirits

Chapter 31: Other Spiritual Gifts

that are not of God to leave. That way the home can be spiritually clean as you live in obedience to the Lord.

When my wife and I first learned about spiritual housecleaning, it was because of problems with some of the places where we lived. Our first apartment was old and we used to wake up in the middle of the night because we both heard footsteps upstairs even though no one lived there. Because we were frightened by this, we would leave the house and get doughnuts. Each time we arrived home we found the door to the second level open. This was strange since there was no longer a staircase leading up to it. Finally, because we were unsure how to deal with the situation, we moved.

About a year later, after living in a farm house and having our first child, we moved back to the city. To our dismay, after moving into another old apartment, the sounds in the night also returned. One of our neighbors was a Christian and we told her about this problem. She then taught us about our spiritual authority and how to use it against the spirits in our house. As a result, the next time that we heard the noises, we bound them in the name of Jesus and told them to go. We never heard them again. After this, if there was anything in our house that seemed wrong, we would pray over it. Even today, we still find this practice to be very useful.

Acts 27:23 (WEB) For there stood by me this night an angel, belonging to the God whose I am and whom I serve,

Although many think discernment of spirits is limited to being aware of the demonic, discernment involves much more than this. God does give some people the gift of seeing into the spiritual world. Ability to discern angels is an exciting and helpful part of this gift. This is not limited to the "super-spiritual." I believe that all who desire to see them can ask the Lord, and in the right time, He will open their eyes. Some question what use such sight would have, but often, people can know what the Holy Spirit is doing through what they see angels doing. For example, someone might see an angel blowing on a person with sickness and know that God is getting ready to heal. This is just one of many uses for the ability to see angels.

Many amazing things have happened when angels have appeared in our church gatherings. Sometimes we have seen angels during the meeting simply standing in worship. When this happened we knew that the Lord wanted us to spend specific time in worship. Other times, we have seen angels dancing and have danced with them. Angels have even appeared with vials of oil that they poured out, releasing fragrances into the room such as frankincense and myrrh or lilies and roses. Along with the aroma, everyone received a strong sense of God's presence. This was especially powerful for those among us who could not see angels but still physically smelled the fragrance. Such signs and wonders allow God's children to feel that He is near.

Colossians 2:18-19 (WEB) Let no one rob you of your prize by a voluntary humility and worshipping of the angels, dwelling in the things which he has not seen, vainly puffed up by his fleshly mind, (19) and not holding firmly to the Head, from whom all the body, being supplied and knit together through the joints and ligaments, grows with God's growth.

I feel that I need to give a warning: People can get into the flesh about angels and focus on them more than on our Lord who sends them as His servants. Colossians 2:18-19 talks about certain people that seem spiritual but are just operating in the flesh. They were worshiping angels and having spiritual experiences that were not from God. Paul said that these things were not a result of connecting with God but that they came from a sensuous mind. No one should worship angels. Christians are only supposed to worship God. Angels are ministering spirits and not a substitute for God. In the Bible, whenever someone encountered an angel and began worshipping him the angel would stop that person. This is a sign that a spirit is from the Lord.

Some Christians seem to think that talking about angels or even seeing them implies worship. This is not true. Many New Testament believers saw angels and talked about their experiences. Of course, any spirit that appears like an angel but requests worship is in fact a demon.

Chapter 31: Other Spiritual Gifts

Angels in the Bible always told men not to worship them. Rather, when people saw them, these heavenly beings were worshiping God, bringing messages from Him, protecting the righteous, or bringing God's judgment to the rebellious. Angelic ministry was common in the early Church and believers talked about it without falling into sin.

Hebrews 13:2 (WEB) Don't forget to show hospitality to strangers, for in doing so, some have entertained angels without knowing it.

Paul said that when believers are hospitable to strangers sometimes they are ministering to angels. When I first became a Christian, I wanted to see angels. I would look for them wherever I went. Somehow I hoped God would open my eyes to see them so I would know who they were. At that time, I always picked up hitchhikers, hoping to meet an angel. Although I did meet many interesting people, I do not think I picked up any angels but then, maybe I did. Regardless, Scripture instructs His people to be kind to others; they may have the opportunity of blessing angels as a result.

The Gift of Tongues

1 Corinthians 14:13 (WEB) Therefore let him who speaks in another language [tongue] pray that he may interpret.

1 Corinthians 14:23 (WEB) If therefore the whole assembly is assembled together and all speak with other languages [tongues], and unlearned or unbelieving people come in, won't they say that you are crazy?

Like most manifestational gifts, tongues is one that most Christians can receive. It is a language often used in prayer and given to strengthen a person's spirit or to speak supernaturally to a foreigner in their language despite having never learned it before. One of the greatest benefits of the gift of tongues is that regular use strengthens the anointing and impact of the believer when moving in all his other gifts.

Church: What Was God Thinking?

Some people pray for the gift of tongues one time and then stop because nothing happens. Such individuals automatically assume that God does not want to give it to them. This is not true. God wants them to learn perseverance as they ask Him for this gift. In addition, there can be blocks that prevent believers from receiving it immediately. Issues that get in the way of Christians receiving the gift of tongues include: a sense of unworthiness, a belief that one must be mature or perfect to receive this gift, unbelief towards God, a tendency to analyze spiritual experiences, and preconceived ideas about how the gift is received.

Once I met a guy who thought that this gift could only be received by having flames of fire appear like in the book of Acts. He thought that if this did not happen when someone started speaking in tongues it meant their gift was not real. He said that he had received the gift in this way. I do not believe that it has to be that dramatic. I have seen many believers receive the gift of tongues in different ways. Some of these people were new believers with serious issues such as drug addiction. God can give His gifts to anyone He wants in any way He wants.

My oldest daughter prayed for a year before she spoke in tongues. One time a friend gave her a prophetic word that she would receive it before she went to sleep that night. Just as she was going to bed it happened. There was rejoicing in our house that night.

When I pray for them, some people hear the language in their head but think that God will force their mouths to open and make the sounds. In truth, most people have sounds come into their minds before they speak. Those who have had this happen should take a step of faith and use what they have been given. Of course, they might feel the need for confirmation. Such people can always ask others with this gift to help them with this.

When I received tongues it began through a dream. In my dream, I was speaking in tongues and when I woke up I did not stop. Later I called someone at CBN to make sure that my gift was real and they confirmed it for me.

Chapter 31: Other Spiritual Gifts

Many have received this gift and yet rarely use it. If someone prays in tongues once or twice, they might not experience many of its benefits. However, if an individual prays in tongues for at least half an hour a day he will experience significant increase in the anointing on his other spiritual gifts. This will also deepen a Christian's sense of the Holy Spirit's presence. If used regularly, this gift can be beneficial to the believer.

1 Corinthians 14:4 (WEB) He who speaks in another language [tongue] edifies himself, but he who prophesies edifies the assembly.

The gift of tongues is the only gift for building up the individual. The other gifts are for strengthening the Church. Although tongues can be used in the gathering, it is mostly for private use in prayer. Because it is for self-edification, I believe it is available to all believers. However, there are some blocks to certain individuals receiving this gift, including a need for emotional healing or correction of certain doctrinal errors.

Tongues in church gatherings can be used almost like prophecy. In such cases, an interpretation is necessary so others will know what is being said (1 Corinthians 14:27-28). Usually, if God wants a person to speak out in tongues He will give that person or someone else the interpretation. This will bring much encouragement to everyone.

1 Corinthians 14:39 (WEB) Therefore, brothers, desire earnestly to prophesy, and don't forbid speaking with other languages [tongues].

At the same time, believers are commanded not to forbid speaking in tongues. However, prophecy is more important and believers are even told to covet it. This is because prophetic words are messages from the heart of God to His children. In my experience, the Holy Spirit moves in amazing ways when people follow His leadership, including prophesying or speaking in tongues in a gathering of believers.

Church: What Was God Thinking?

1 Corinthians 12:11 (WEB) But the one and the same Spirit works all of these, distributing to each one separately as he desires.

When believers gather, it can be like a symphony where God is a conductor and His children are the instruments. Individuals desire Him to work through them and He decides what He wants to do through each one. When people submit to God with a pure heart, He will use them. Those who do not feel God wants to use them need healing in some area of their lives. Each person that comes to Him is precious in His heart, no one is excluded from being valued by Him, or used by Him in order to bless themselves and others.

I want to use my personal experience to illustrate how manifestational gifts can be used in a gathering of Christians. Years ago, I went to a meeting at a charismatic church. As I entered, I could sense that the Holy Spirit was there in a special way. I enjoyed the entire service but especially the worship because the pastor and many others were dancing. Although the minister was over sixty years old, he could dance like a young man. After a few worship songs it felt like the whole group had entered the Holy of Holies. Someone gave a message in tongues and another gave the interpretation. After this, several people gave prophetic words regarding the move of God in that congregation. Then someone else began giving words of knowledge about people that needed healing. They prayed for the sick and many recovered as a result. Afterwards, someone taught on spiritual gifts and at the end of the meeting they prayed for anyone that wanted the gift of tongues. Many that came to the service were impacted by God's power. It was a refreshing experience!

In summary, manifestational gifts add much to the church gathering and the Body of Christ. I pray that all of them become commonplace among God's children.

Chapter 31: Other Spiritual Gifts

Function Gifts

1 Corinthians 12:28 (WEB) God has set some in the assembly: first apostles, second prophets, third teachers, then miracle workers, then gifts of healings, helps, governments [administration], and various kinds of languages [tongues].

1 Corinthians 12:28 has a different list of gifts from Ephesians 4:11 and 1 Corinthians 12:7-11, with a few additional gifts mentioned. These are function gifts, describing a believer's role within the Body.

The first gift mentioned here that is not in any other list is the gift of helps. To some this may not sound very spiritual but it is a gift given by the Holy Spirit. It is also greatly needed in the Body of Christ. People with this gift want to help others with their needs; it fills them with joy. The Lord gives them special insight or awareness that helps them in how to serve others with needs. This is not limited to serving those inside the church. They might fix someone's broken-down car or wash another person's dishes. They may babysit so a couple they know can have a date night. People with the gift of helps enjoy assisting others in practical ways. They understand that God also cares about day-to-day details.

As with all gifts, there are some potential issues or weaknesses. Persons with this gift might feel that they are the only ones doing the practical work and that others do not even care about the needs they see. They may not realize that people without it might not be as excited as they are about assisting others. Of course, someone does not have to have this gift to serve others in need and people with the gift of helps may be able to encourage others to lend a hand when necessary. People with the helping gift provide practical balance to the Church and show that God cares about every aspect of people's lives.

Church: What Was God Thinking?

The Greek word for "administration" is κυβέρνησις *kubernēsis*.
Strong's definition G2941 (pronounced: *koo-ber'-nay-sis*)
From κυβερνάω *kubernaō* (of Latin origin, to steer); pilotage, that is, (figuratively) directorship (in the church): - government.

The second gift in this list not mentioned elsewhere is the gift of government or administration. Those with this gift are easy to recognize. In a governmental sense, they help give direction, as in charting a course. They have supernatural anointing and insight in managing administrative details. They like to make sure everything is organized and enjoy managing practical things. Some might view this as the result of parental training or natural ability, but I disagree. I have talked to many people who have this gift and some of them share that before they became Christians, they could not even organize the paper clips on their desk. After they were filled with the Holy Spirit, however, they had an amazing administrative ability. This is a wonderful and significant spiritual gift. Management of practical things is not the only manifestation of the administrative gift. I also believe that some people with this gift have the ability to know what the Lord wants to do next in gatherings, often when everyone else is not sure what to do. This may function through a word of knowledge God gives to someone with the gift of administration.

The administrator can also have the unique ability to know how to manage the time in a meeting. This does not mean he controls the time. Rather his function is to make room for the Holy Spirit to accomplish all that He desires in the meeting. Of course, it is possible that God will reveal more to the group than what should be accomplished in just one meeting, but this gift would be important in getting that started and charting a course for the process. As usual, leadership should have the final say in this. They should make sure that this gift is not used to control or interfere with what the Lord seems to be doing. The administration gift must always be used in submission to the leadership.

Many who have the gift of administration also have a unique ability to orchestrate practical day-to-day work, through hearing God's voice, for themselves and sometimes, to a degree, for others. The Lord

Chapter 31: Other Spiritual Gifts

might give them an information download, a word of wisdom, about how to take practical steps to fulfill some God-given plan. This gift has a variety of possible functions. It is necessary to note that some individuals who are poor administrators in the natural sense can be wonderful in a church gathering. Still others can work well in an office but not in a church meeting. This gift may surprise people in its flexibility and variety.

The spiritual gift of government or administration is not to be confused with what would seem to be a natural gift that some people have for administration. Please note that God does not give this gift to meet an unhealthy "need" to be in control or manage things. God is not a controller and none of the gifts He gives are to be used for purposes of manipulation or control.

Faith Gifts

Romans 12:4-8 (WEB) For even as we have many members in one body, and all the members don't have the same function, (5) so we, who are many, are one body in Christ, and individually members one of another. (6) Having gifts differing according to the grace that was given to us, if prophecy, let us prophesy according to the proportion of our faith; (7) or service, let us give ourselves to service; or he who teaches, to his teaching; (8) or he who exhorts, to his exhorting: he who gives, let him do it with liberality; he who rules, with diligence; he who shows mercy, with cheerfulness.

A third list of gifts is in Romans 12:4-8. I refer to these as the faith gifts because they are to be used according to the amount of faith an individual has. They are also strengthened through the increase of faith in someone's life. "According to the measure of faith" is a key phrase. For some there might be a sense of pressure or compulsion to use these gifts beyond the level of what God has asked of them. None of these gifts are to be used under such circumstances. Rather, they should operate according to God's leading and that person's level of confidence and comfort. Using these gifts appropriately can strengthen believers' faith and anointing in ministry. In other words, these gifts grow with use. The reader may notice that prophecy and teaching have been mentioned before. The fact that these gifts are listed here too emphasizes the importance of faith in the use of teaching and prophecy. Their faith affects how God directs them to use this gift.

The second gift listed is serving or ministry. A person with this gift loves to serve others and seems to sense the best way to do this. It can be expressed in natural or spiritual works of service. This type of ministry brings the love of Christ to others in a way that they can feel. Through this, people may come to know the Lord or feel God's love in a new way. A key difference between the gift of service and the gift of helps is that helps often functions according to felt needs in the natural. Service can be used to meet needs in the natural or spiritual. In addition, service is a faith gift, which means how it is used will depend on the faith of the one with the gift.

A third faith gift is encouragement. Those with this gift see people's strengths and potential and are not hesitant to compliment or encourage. They are also sensitive to what will build up or motivate others in specific situations.

Some people have this gift and are limited in their use of it because of past rejection when they tried to encourage. My ministry team especially sees this in Hong Kong culture because often positive words are not as accepted as negative ones. Many local people that we have worked with do not receive compliments or encouragement well. Because of this, those who try to be encouraging may experience criticism, rejection, and misunderstanding. In some cases, this causes them to stop blessing people in this way. In this type of situation, Christians might need to experience inner healing before they can continue using their gift. It is also possible that they should only use their gift in environments where they feel safe and comfortable.

Chapter 31: Other Spiritual Gifts

Christians everywhere must recognize that as citizens of heaven (Philippians 3:20), we are called to live according to the Biblical standard. There are times when this will go against the grain of earthly culture. We each need to be sensitive to how God wants us to live and express this in a practical way.

A fourth gift listed in Romans 12 is generosity. Those with this gift enjoy giving to others. Often people limit this to a financial sense when, in fact, their contribution could be giving of time, resources, or many other different things.

Another faith gift is leadership. God has gifted some specific people to take up leadership in specific situations or communities. This includes, but is not limited to elders, overseers, and apostles. Not everyone with this gift will lead large groups of people or be a leader all of the time. Rather, it is according to the administration of the Holy Spirit.

The final faith gift is mercy. Those with this gift tend to be full of compassion for people, typically those with physical, mental or emotional problems. They are the sort of people that can minister and reach out to those that others could not or would not be willing to help.

Although many of these gifts might seem natural, they are supernatural and a great blessing to others.

The Body is Diverse

1 Corinthians 12:29-30 (WEB) Are all apostles? Are all prophets? Are all teachers? Are all miracle workers? (30) Do all have gifts of healings? Do all speak with various languages [tongues]? Do all interpret?

After listing the gifts, Paul states that different people have different gifts. He views this as something that should be obvious. In contrast, many modern churches have made serious mistakes because they do not understand this truth. They try to make everyone small group leaders, administrative helpers, or evangelists. It is as though the leaders of such congregations seem to think that people are machines and can do anything that the ministers can do. I have even heard leaders say, "If I can do it, you can do it." This mentality has caused burn out for many.

If everyone had the same gift, things would become boring very quickly. It would be like an orchestra made entirely of violins. This is one reason why many modern churches are filled with bored members. On the other hand, if a church allows and encourages everybody to operate in their gifts the result is exciting. Each person adds a different flavor to the meeting. So, each time a new member is added to a group, even if they have the same gift as somebody else, they bring special depth as they use the same gift in different ways.

1 Corinthians 12:31 (KJV) But covet earnestly the best gifts: and yet shew I unto you a more excellent way.

Paul commands believers to covet spiritual gifts. The word "covet" here means to strongly desire. The Bible rarely commands people to desire something this intensely. Christians do need to make sure that they do not focus on the gifts more than on the Lord. If they do, they will not move in the gifts to their full potential. The only way to experience spiritual gifts in their fullness is through pursuing God as the primary goal, pressing into Him for hours each day. This is the best way to express desire for God and His gifts.

In summary, there are many spiritual gifts besides the ministry gifts that believers can have and use to bless others. The main types are manifestational, functional, and faith gifts. I have tried to give an overview of these in this chapter. There are a few particular gifts, however, that require more attention, specifically prophecy, tongues, and a related practice, singing in the Spirit. I would like to talk more about these things in the following chapter.

Chapter 32: Prophecy, Tongues, and Songs in the Spirit

1 Corinthians 14:1 (WEB) Follow after love, and earnestly desire spiritual gifts, but especially that you may prophesy.

1 Corinthians 12-14 gives a detailed and specific picture of what is important for the Church. 1 Corinthians 12 discusses the function of the Body of Christ, and some spiritual gifts. 1 Corinthians 13 emphasizes that love is the most important. Finally, 1 Corinthians 14 discusses two significant gifts: tongues and prophecy. In this chapter, I would like to take a detailed look at the instructions of 1 Corinthians 14.

Revelation 19:10 (WEB) I fell down before his feet to worship him. He said to me, "Look! Don't do it! I am a fellow bondservant with you and with your brothers who hold the testimony of Jesus. Worship God, for the testimony of Jesus is the Spirit of Prophecy."

The importance of prophecy is unquestionable; it is the communication of God's heart (Revelation 19:10). When people prophesy they are expressing God's heart, testifying about Jesus, and sharing His thoughts with His bride. It is the Bridegroom saying to the Bride, "I love you so very much!" Because of this, prophecy strengthens the spirit more than any other gift. It encourages both the

Church: What Was God Thinking?

giver and the receiver. When a person is used by God to touch another, it brings great joy. Prophetic ministry allows Christians to experience God in a very intimate way.

1 Corinthians 14:2 (WEB) For he who speaks in another language [tongue] speaks not to men, but to God; for no one understands; but in the Spirit he speaks mysteries.

Tongues is one of the most mysterious gifts that God has given the Church. When I was a young Christian, I wanted to speak in tongues all the time. I enjoyed the fact that I was speaking mysteries in the Spirit. Afterwards, I waited on God to receive the interpretation and would often receive it. I had such a great time. I used to wonder what language I was speaking and felt amazed that I was speaking a language of angels. This excited me. At that time, I did not understand Paul when he said he would rather use the gift of prophecy. As I have grown in the Lord, I understand that speaking to someone's spirit with a word of prophecy brings more refreshing than merely speaking over them in tongues.

1 Corinthians 14:3 (WEB) But he who prophesies speaks to men for their edification, exhortation, and consolation.

Prophecy gives people hope and encouragement. Recently, a woman visited my family. She was depressed and wondered how much the Lord loved her or if He even loved her at all. We began praying for her and God started speaking to her about this. He was using us in the gift of prophecy to show her what it meant to be the Bride of Christ. By the time we finished, she cried tears of joy and told us that she felt very refreshed. This is a good example of the power of prophecy.

1 Corinthians 14:4-5 (WEB) He who speaks in another language [tongue] edifies himself, but he who prophesies edifies the assembly. (5) Now I desire to have you all speak with other languages [tongues], but rather that you would prophesy. For he is greater who prophesies than he who speaks with other languages [tongues], unless he interprets, that the assembly may be built up.

Chapter 32: Prophecy, Tongues, and Songs in the Spirit

The gift of tongues is the only gift that is meant for personal edification. It is intended to build up the individual so that each person will be full of the Holy Spirit to use the other gifts. It strengthens people's sense of connection with God.

Tongues encourages on a personal level while prophecy edifies the whole Body. The more I pray in tongues before a meeting the more I sense the Spirit moving through me during the gathering. Because of this, I believe the instructions in 1 Corinthians 14 do not mean Paul was commanding everyone to stop speaking in tongues. Rather he was saying that, unless someone can interpret, prophecy is more important. This builds up the Body of Christ. Interpretation of tongues is like a prophetic word but with the added mystery of the original message being in an unknown language. Sometimes people have asked me why God would give the gift of tongues to people. I think that God created people with the ability to enjoy mystery and surprises.

Romans 8:26-27 (WEB) In the same way, the Spirit also helps our weaknesses, for we don't know how to pray as we ought. But the Spirit himself makes intercession for us with groanings which can't be uttered. (27) He who searches the hearts knows what is on the Spirit's mind, because he makes intercession for the saints according to God.

The gift of tongues is helpful when believers have things in their hearts that cannot be expressed through words. Sometimes people face situations that bring up feelings that cannot be communicated using their mother tongue, and there are no words to communicate their needs and feelings to God. Through tongues the Lord has given language to express these things. Sometimes this comes out as sighs or groans that are too deep for words and burdens are released to God by expressing the heart's cry to Him in this way. One way my ministry has experienced this is when praying with others for emotional healing. Sometimes those we are ministering to start to groan in prayer. We can tell that it is not demonic, rather it is coming from their spirit. Afterwards, they often feel that they have been freed from areas of struggle. This gift is helpful in this type of situation because it allows

Church: What Was God Thinking?

the Holy Spirit to pray through the believer in ways that would not be otherwise possible.

1 Corinthians 14:6-11 (WEB) But now, brothers, if I come to you speaking with other languages [tongues], what would I profit you, unless I speak to you either by way of revelation, or of knowledge, or of prophesying, or of teaching? (7) Even things without life, giving a voice, whether pipe or harp, if they didn't give a distinction in the sounds, how would it be known what is piped or harped? (8) For if the trumpet gave an uncertain sound, who would prepare himself for war? (9) So also you, unless you uttered by the tongue words easy to understand, how would it be known what is spoken? For you would be speaking into the air. (10) There are, it may be, so many kinds of sounds in the world, and none of them is without meaning. (11) If then I don't know the meaning of the sound, I would be to him who speaks a foreigner, and he who speaks would be a foreigner to me.

Paul says in 1 Corinthians 14:6 that it is more important to encourage and strengthen others by interpretation, revelation, knowledge, prophecy or teaching than to only speak in tongues. Living in Hong Kong has helped me understand what Paul meant. Cantonese, the dialect of Chinese spoken here, is difficult for an English speaker to learn. It was challenging for me because I have had hearing problems for much of the time my family has lived here. For a long time, I would attend meetings and only understand a few scattered words, even though I had worked very hard to learn the language. Because of this those meetings were not very rewarding or productive for me. It is the same with tongues. Without interpretation it just seems noisy and chaotic.

1 Corinthians 14:12-14 (WEB) So also you, since you are zealous for spiritual gifts, seek that you may abound to the building up of the assembly. (13) Therefore let him who speaks in another language [tongue] pray that he may interpret. (14) For if I pray in another language [tongue], my spirit prays, but my understanding is unfruitful.

Note that Paul does not say people should stop using the gift of tongues in church. He says that they must pray for the ability to interpret tongues so that everyone can be encouraged. Prayer using

Chapter 32: Prophecy, Tongues, and Songs in the Spirit

tongues and interpretation is very effective. When the believer does this, they are praying according to God's heart and will see many prayers answered as a result (1 John 5:14-15). This is what the Apostle Paul was talking about in Romans 8, when he discusses how the Holy Spirit prays through His people.

1 Corinthians 14:15 (WEB) What is it then? I will pray with the spirit, and I will pray with the understanding also. I will sing with the spirit, and I will sing with the understanding also.

Tongues can be used in more than one way. In 1 Corinthians 14:15, Paul says the same thing about singing as he does about prayer. It is enjoyable to sing in the Spirit and then sing the same song in English. I would recommend trying this. It is simple. People can start singing in tongues and wait on the Lord for an interpretation. Those who do this will be amazed at the songs that result. Often they will receive a prophetic song as the interpretation. For those gifted in prophetic song the interpretation might come immediately. For others this gift will need to be practiced often to begin receiving interpretation more quickly. Regardless, it is a delightful experience.

1 Corinthians 14:16-17 (WEB) Otherwise if you bless with the Spirit, how will he who fills the place of the unlearned say the "Amen" at your giving of thanks, seeing he doesn't know what you say? (17) For you most certainly give thanks well, but the other person is not built up.

In verse 16, Paul expresses that interpretation of tongues is also important for the gathering to be able to agree in the thanksgiving expressed. In many modern churches today I do not think that this is a common problem. People are more likely not to speak in tongues at all. Leadership controls the meeting so much that there is little room for the gifts to manifest. This is not what God intended or Paul would not have given so many instructions about using the gifts properly.

The Benefits of Praying in Tongues

1 Corinthians 14:18 (WEB) I thank my God, I speak with other languages [tongues] more than you all.

Paul obviously felt that the gift of tongues is important because he claimed to use this gift more than anyone in the Corinthian Church. He is an example for all Christians.

Using this gift can change a believer's life. Speaking in tongues is like blowing on hot coals in the heart; the fire of God increases. Some people who seldom practice this gift do not feel anything when they pray in tongues. In contrast, praying in the Spirit for an hour a day can make a big difference in how sensitive a person is towards God and hearing His voice and how much power is on them when they minister. Many will find it necessary to work up to one hour a day, starting at fifteen minutes, moving on to half an hour, then forty-five minutes, and finally an hour. I would recommend anyone try it for two or three months and see what happens. However, change is not instantaneous for everyone so no one should feel discouraged if it takes awhile.

I would like to share a few of my experiences with speaking in tongues. One of my first was when my family was young and I worked in a medical building. Because I opened up the building first thing in the morning, I had about two hours of prayer time each day. As I got the building ready, I spent most of the time praying in tongues. The longer I did this, the more I heard God and experienced His presence. One section of this building housed doctors working with the mentally ill. At times when praying for this area I sensed spiritual heaviness. When I felt this, I prayed to command the demons to leave. Soon afterwards, I heard that this group had begun working with a Christian woman to develop inner healing ministry for believers that came to them for help.

Some time later I experienced praying in tongues more extensively. This was while I was working with St. Stephen's Society in Hong Kong. I worked on a team praying with individuals to come off drugs. I wish everyone could have this experience. We spent hours praying in

Chapter 32: Prophecy, Tongues, and Songs in the Spirit

tongues over drug addicts and as a result, saw many come off heroin without any extreme withdrawal symptoms. If they refused to pray as they were coming off the drugs, they would get very sick. When they began experiencing these symptoms, if they decided to participate as people prayed with them, their discomfort would go away.

More recently, in 2003 just before the SARS epidemic hit Hong Kong, I felt that God wanted my family to begin praying around the clock. As the epidemic worsened people spent as much time as possible at home. Because of this, we had some extra time. We decided to each take six-hour prayer shifts. Much of this time I spent praying in tongues. Because of this extra prayer I felt a dramatic change during ministry. I could tell that the anointing of the Spirit was on me. When I taught the Bible people listened more closely than usual. When I prophesied over others they were touched more deeply than before. This special prayer time brought me closer to God and I experienced more of His power in my ministry than I had before. It was a good part of my life that I plan to get back to soon.

Prophecy Versus Tongues in the Gathering

1 Corinthians 14:19 (WEB) However in the assembly I would rather speak five words with my understanding, that I might instruct others also, than ten thousand words in another language [tongue].

When the Holy Spirit gives a message and a believer instructs people with it, he brings life to others (Isaiah 55:9-11). Paul wrote that he would rather speak five words in a gathering that people would understand than ten thousand words in tongues. He preferred to bring revelation, knowledge, prophecy or teaching to the church gatherings because he knew that these things ignite the Holy Spirit's fire in people's hearts.

1 Corinthians 14:20 (WEB) Brothers, don't be children in thoughts, yet in malice be babies, but in thoughts be mature.

Church: What Was God Thinking?

God desires that His people go on to maturity, not staying babies in life and thinking. In fact, Christians are commanded to mature. Just as healthy parents love their children and want them to grow up, the Father enjoys each believer in the stage they are in and yet at the same time He looks forward to them becoming mature Christians. One factor in facilitating spiritual growth is the ability to recognize which spiritual gifts are important in church gatherings.

Tongues Are a Sign for Unbelievers

1 Corinthians 14:21-22 (WEB) In the law it is written, "By men of strange languages and by the lips of strangers I will speak to this people. Not even thus will they hear me, says the Lord."* (22) Therefore other languages [tongues] are for a sign, not to those who believe, but to the unbelieving; but prophesying is for a sign, not to the unbelieving, but to those who believe.

*Isaiah 28:11

The gift of tongues is a fulfillment of an Old Testament prophecy. In 1 Corinthians 14, Paul shows that Isaiah's prophecy in Isaiah 28:11 is fulfilled in this gift. Tongues has been given as a sign sent by God to unbelievers, but the majority will not listen and cannot understand. The Amplified version of 1 Corinthians 14:22 helps clarify by saying that it is a sign for unbelievers on the point of believing. This might seem strange to some and yet is clear in this Scripture.

In chapter one, I told my salvation story. The power encounter my wife and I had that helped bring us to the point of salvation was through tongues functioning in this way. As I mentioned in chapter one, a group of people prayed for my wife and I in tongues before we became Christians. I have described how intensely I felt God's presence. What I did not share earlier was the surprising fact that my wife although not yet a believer received the interpretation of their tongues! From this point, despite all of her other doubts and hesitations, she knew without question that God was real and working in her life. This experience was an important step towards her decision

Chapter 32: Prophecy, Tongues, and Songs in the Spirit

to follow Jesus. For us the gifts of tongues and interpretation allowed us to encounter God in a unique way that eventually led to our salvation.

How Prophecy and Tongues Can Be Used in the Assembly

1 Corinthians 14:23 (WEB) If therefore the whole assembly is assembled together and all speak with other languages [tongues], and unlearned or unbelieving people come in, won't they say that you are crazy?

The gift of tongues is used differently in a group setting than when it is used privately. In 1 Corinthians 14:23, Paul instructs believers not to all speak in tongues at the same time in the gathering of the whole church in one place. If unbelievers or new Christians that have not yet learned about tongues are present they will not understand and will think Christians are insane. At the same time, if everyone knows that no unbelievers are in a meeting then praying in tongues is permissible. In one of my previous church plants praying in tongues while waiting on the Holy Spirit for direction was an important part of our meetings. Believers should pay attention to whether there are unbelievers present when they gather.

Often, if unbelievers are not close to believing in Jesus and someone speaks in tongues, they will think he is out of his mind. The first time I went to a Pentecostal church it scared me to death. People were yelling and two men were on stage preaching passionately. I left quickly and wondered if that church could actually be a church because there was so much shouting. I had grown up in much quieter churches. As a child, if I even whispered in church I would get in trouble. These traditions were a hindrance to me until I encountered God and He changed my idea of Church. So for me, until I experienced the Lord for myself 1 Corinthians 14:23 proved true.

Church: What Was God Thinking?

1 Corinthians 14:39 (WEB) Therefore, brothers, desire earnestly to prophesy, and don't forbid speaking with other languages [tongues].

At the same time, as cautioning believers about using tongues with unbelievers present Paul commands leaders not to forbid speaking in tongues during the church gathering. When people obey God as He leads them to prophesy or speak in tongues the Holy Spirit moves in amazing ways. My family has heard many testimonies of people experiencing this and we have experienced it ourselves.

1 Corinthians 14:24-25 (WEB) But if all prophesy, and someone unbelieving or unlearned comes in, he is reproved by all, and he is judged by all. (25) And thus the secrets of his heart are revealed. So he will fall down on his face and worship God, declaring that God is among you indeed.

As 1 Corinthians 14:24-25 expresses, prophecy is a great evangelistic tool. God is renewing understanding of uses for this and many are rediscovering prophecy in evangelism. It can be used not only outside the church in an evangelistic way but inside it as well. When new people come into a church meeting, believers can use this gift to share God's heart for them. This is a very effective way to help others experience the Father's love.

1 Corinthians 14:26 (WEB) What is it then, brothers? When you come together, each one of you has a psalm, has a teaching, has a revelation, has another language [tongue], has an interpretation. Let all things be done to build each other up.

In 1 Corinthians 14:26, Paul talks about true fellowship and emphasizes the purpose for it, mutual edification. When everyone contributes with a gift from the Lord, the gathering becomes an opportunity to participate in God's spiritual symphony allowing Christ to be the director. Each part of the meeting can then bring people into a deep experience of the Kingdom of God.

1 Corinthians 14:27-28 (WEB) If any man speaks in another language [tongue], let it be two, or at the most three, and in turn; and let one

Chapter 32: Prophecy, Tongues, and Songs in the Spirit

interpret. (28) But if there is no interpreter, let him keep silent in the assembly, and let him speak to himself, and to God.

There are some guidelines for giving messages in tongues in church meetings. When Paul shares about its use in Christian gatherings, he says "if any speak in a tongue." I believe he is referring to individuals speaking out in a tongue to give a message to the group that should be interpreted. In this case, he instructs the church that it should be just a few people, perhaps only two or three. When a person speaks out a message in tongues it should be because God told him to speak it out so everyone can hear him. This provides opportunity to discover those in the group who have the ability to interpret tongues.

I find the gift of tongues and interpretation very exciting. I like the mystery of this gift. In addition, I have never been in a meeting where a message in tongues has been given without another present who received an interpretation. There have also been times that I have felt someone has shared what they thought was the interpretation but was actually an independent prophecy. If this happens, the gathering needs to continue praying that the message in tongues will be interpreted.

1 Corinthians 14:29-32 (WEB) Let the prophets speak, two or three, and let the others discern. (30) But if a revelation is made to another sitting by, let the first keep silent. (31) For you all can prophesy one by one, that all may learn, and all may be exhorted. (32) The spirits of the prophets are subject to the prophets,

Paul gives additional guidelines for the church regarding prophecy. These guidelines are similar to the instructions on messages in tongues. Paul writes that only two or three should speak, one at a time. One reason for this is that people need time to process what is said. Afterwards, others can take their turn prophesying. In this way, everyone with a message can have a chance to share it.

People should take turns prophesying. In 1 Corinthians 14:30, Paul says that if a revelation is given to another in the gathering the first speaker should be silent. Sometimes, as a person is growing in the gift of prophecy he flows so comfortably in his gift that he will not let anyone else prophesy. This person needs to make room for others who have revelation as well. God wants everyone to have the opportunity to prophesy not just those that are in the office of prophet.

Here is an example of this. The prophetic team in one of my previous churches, which had about five or six individuals with a prophetic gift, would occasionally host a ministry night where others could come to receive prophetic ministry. We would take turns prophesying over two or three people often one at a time. Sometimes the anointing for prophecy was so strong that some received at least fifteen prophetic words at one time. In groups where several people function at this level of anointing, others might not have a chance to speak. It can be very frustrating when one single person is dominating the prophetic time. This is one reason that Paul instructed prophets to take turns.

Issues That Interrupt Prophetic Flow

Before concluding, I want to talk briefly about some issues that disrupt the flow of the anointing during prophetic time. During this type of ministry, no one should ask questions or in other ways verbally process what is shared. It is also not the right time to share opinions about the prophecy unless something that is said obviously contradicts Scripture. It would be best for individuals to talk to the leadership about these issues and then leave it to the leadership to address.

I have experienced disruptive verbal processing during prophetic ministry. One of my previous churches was full of young, easily excited prophets. Sometimes as I was prophesying over someone I would only get a chance to say one sentence. Because others felt the same thing they would get very excited and start talking without waiting until I was done. This is something that should wait until after the prophetic ministry has finished and it is time for feedback from the one receiving ministry and from the team.

In the same way, I have also experienced individuals coming to the prophetic gathering and judging prophetic words based on traditional

Chapter 32: Prophecy, Tongues, and Songs in the Spirit

or historical criteria. In this case, it had more to do with the development of western church culture, or past experiences of certain ministers, than Biblical discernment. A few individuals in my church were hurt over these incidents. In such a case, it would be better if anyone who feels what is said is wrong would talk to leadership after the meeting instead of during the gathering. In this way, the leadership will be able to handle the situation with sensitivity and tact so they can deal with any issues that might be related to a specific prophetic message.

1 Corinthians 14:39 (WEB) Therefore, brothers, desire earnestly to prophesy, and don't forbid speaking with other languages [tongues].

In 1 Corinthians 14:39, Paul restates that prophecy is important. He also says that we must be careful not to forbid speaking in tongues. It is easy for churches to go to an extreme and not allow tongues in church. When Paul commands to earnestly desire to prophesy, I do not believe he means that the other gifts are not important or should be neglected. He is saying that the Body is strengthened the most by the gift of prophecy.

1 Corinthians 14:40 (WEB) Let all things be done decently and in order.

Doing things decently and in order does not mean kicking the Holy Spirit out of Church. It seems that many churches take this command to an extreme and have so much human structure and tradition that they quench the Spirit's move among them. This is not how it should be. Believers are meant to experience the excitement of meeting with the Holy Spirit as their leader. As individuals begin hearing the Lord's voice more clearly they become confident in using their gifts. The Body of Christ grows strong and matures becoming more sensitive toward God and functioning under the leadership of the Holy Spirit. People then gain a sense of belonging in their congregation. As a result, they are more likely to want others to come and begin more actively preaching the Gospel.

Church: What Was God Thinking?

It takes time to get used to doing church in this way. It may feel uncomfortable at first, especially for people who are used to their traditions or have a problem with control. However, if they give themselves time to adjust, they will discover a richness and depth in Christian community that they might not have experienced before.

I want to give a few instructions for those who want to have church in this way. At the beginning of the meeting, you should pray and do whatever the Holy Spirit is directing. Be discerning, but do not worry too much about whether or not what you are feeling is from God. It is not that hearing from the Lord is unimportant, rather if you worry too much about it, you could miss Him. Make sure that most of the group feels good about what has been suggested then proceed. While following this format and seeking God's guidance you will learn to discern when it is the Spirit and when it is not. Usually the more you practice listening for God's voice, the more you will know when you have heard from Him and when you have not.

There have been several times that my ministry team has prophesied over people because we felt like we should and not because that was what the Holy Spirit was telling us to do. One time, a man that was coming to our gathering brought his son and wanted us to prophesy over him. His son did not want this ministry but he did not say so. When we started to listen to God for him it was difficult to hear. Before we were finished it was clear that he did not want prophetic ministry. It seemed to kill the atmosphere for the rest of the meeting. Sometimes we have learned when something was from the Spirit through trial and error. If there is power on it, it is often from the Lord. If it was dry, many times it was not God.

Sometimes, when asking the Holy Spirit what to do, two people will start different things at the same time. If this happens, they should just take turns. On rare occasions, two people might insist that they should go first. In such cases, leadership may need to step in and make a decision. In gatherings I have led most of the time the rest of the group will also let me know what they feel we should do at that time, helping me make a decision. In this way, everyone can participate.

Chapter 32: Prophecy, Tongues, and Songs in the Spirit

Ephesians 5:20-21 (WEB) giving thanks always concerning all things in the name of our Lord Jesus Christ, to God, even the Father; (21) subjecting yourselves one to another in the fear of Christ.

Ephesians 5:20-21 says Christians should submit to one another. During a gathering many times the Holy Spirit will use one or two persons in the group to bring direction. Sometimes just one individual will feel that the meeting should go in a certain direction. In such cases, my ministry team would listen to them. Often everyone else will either feel the same way or at the very least not have a problem with it. This is one way to submit to each other in a gathering.

Sometimes when I am leading a meeting someone else will want the group to go in a different direction from what I sensed we should go. As a servant leader, I can choose not to say anything and just submit to see if the Holy Spirit was in what they wanted to do. Usually, the Spirit blesses it. Other times we can tell that it is not what we are supposed to do. Usually the whole group will feel the same way and so we move on to something else. If only one person feels that we should change and the rest do not feel we should then we do not change what we are doing. Even the leaders can submit to others in this and so everyone can learn from the experience.

Psalms, Hymns, and Spiritual Songs

Colossians 3:16 (WEB) Let the word of Christ dwell in you richly; in all wisdom teaching and admonishing one another with psalms, hymns, and spiritual songs, singing with grace in your heart to the Lord.

Besides spiritual gifts another important component of the gathering is worship. It is also a good way to learn how to hear God's voice. A common practice in the New Testament Church was to use singing to teach and admonish each other. When I mention this some may protest that they cannot sing, but God listens to the heart. Believers need to grow in grace towards themselves and one another. Expertise is not necessary for this.

Church: What Was God Thinking?

In the New Testament Church, when believers came together they would each have a song or a psalm. They had opportunity at different times to lead out in song or with Scripture. This is best done in an attitude of seeking God about what He wants in the meeting. In gatherings today, it is still true that God loves this type of worship and participation (1 Corinthians 14:26).

Before this can be implemented in a gathering there may be some things that need to be done first. People might find it helpful to practice singing worship at home so that they feel more comfortable leading in song at church. While doing this privately some may even be surprised at how well they can sing without the pressure of others' criticism. If a small group has a hard time to sing together without accompaniment, there are some ideas that could help. Perhaps, those that have received musical training can teach the congregation how to use their voices. It is also helpful to have musicians that are able to identify and play in any key when someone leads out in song.

This requires some skill and training, but without that, even having someone who can play simple percussion in steady time on an instrument, such as a hand drum can be helpful in keeping everyone together. Some small group fellowships may even use some recorded worship music until there is someone who can help.

I believe that God created humans to be musical. Of course, some people cannot sing well even after training and practice. These people might need to receive prayer because there could be some physical, emotional, or spiritual block that prevents that person from having the fabulous voice that God wants to give them. Regardless, those that can sing should help lead the church in worship, joining in when someone who cannot sing leads out in song. In this way, at least some will be able to sing in tune and everyone can worship God.

In one of my previous churches, certain individuals who have difficulty singing on key would sometimes lead in worship by starting a song, or calling out the name of the song they have in mind. The rest of the group would make up for their lack by joining in quickly. In this way, everyone could enjoy worshipping together. Regardless of singing

Chapter 32: Prophecy, Tongues, and Songs in the Spirit

ability we were glad people felt free to take part in our group worship time.

Sometimes spiritual problems in someone's life can keep that person from singing well. One time I went to a camp with a small group from my church. One individual could not sing although she enjoyed it very much. During the camp, some spiritual issues surfaced so we prayed for her. One of the results was that she was able to sing better than before. I love it when God works miracles for His children!

Besides free participation in worship there are other times and ways that song can be used in ministering to one another. For example, my ministry team often finds it helpful when praying for individuals for emotional healing to take breaks for worship at different times, leading out in song while keeping the focus on Jesus. Other times, the Holy Spirit will give one of us a song to sing over the person receiving ministry. This can be planned in advance, but is more often spontaneous.

Prophetic song can also be particularly powerful where God gives an individual a word and instead of speaking it they express the message through song. I know of many people who have been deeply blessed through this type of ministry.

My daughters like to share one of their amazing experiences regarding tongues, prophecy, and prophetic song. Some time ago, my family visited a camp that was full of people hungry to encounter God and we made friends with many of them. On the last night my daughters and some of the young people began praying for each other and the power of the Holy Spirit hit every one of them. They spent the whole night in the presence of God together speaking Scriptures over each other, prophesying, and singing songs of freedom and blessing over one another. The presence of the Lord was so sweet and intense that they began after dinner and continued ministering to one another in this way until dawn. Although they were exhausted, to this day they talk about that night as one of the deepest, most powerful, beautiful, and encouraging experiences they have ever had.

Church: What Was God Thinking?

In conclusion, prophecy, tongues, and spiritual songs are very important elements to church gatherings and should not be neglected. Paul's instructions regarding taking turns with messages in tongues, prophecy, and participation can help believers have a rich and enjoyable experience in church. In the following chapter, I will share more about church planting and the church gathering.

Chapter 33: A Picture of the Gifts Working In Body Life

In this book, I have talked a fair amount about individual gifts, their strengths and weaknesses. Now, I would like to move on and share about how these gifts can work together in establishing a church. In addition, I feel it would be good for the reader to have a sense of how all the gifts can function in a gathering. So, come along with me and enjoy the ride!

Church Planting in Apostolic Teams

First, I want to say that the things I will share in this chapter are not limited to church planting, they can also be applied to an existing work or outreach. The insights I share can help establish a strong foundation for any church.

The Apostolic Evangelistic Team

An apostolic evangelistic team is an apostolic team with the specific focus of evangelism to bring people to the Lord and to open new church plants. Not all the members are apostles, but they work together in an apostolic way. The individuals in this team have passion for Jesus, hunger for learning, and enjoyment of ministry, spending much of their time in activity related to these things. They are often, but not always, outgoing and often have wide circles of friends. This team is especially effective in pioneering new works.

There are many ways that an apostolic evangelistic team can minister. They might pray with individuals for healing or miracles, prophesy over them, or share an anointed message, depending on the Holy Spirit's guidance. Sometimes an individual from the team receives a prophetic word that reveals the secrets of one's heart, things he has not shared with anyone, showing him that Jesus is real (1 Corinthians 14:24-25). Other times, an individual who has sickness or pain receives healing through prayer. When there is a need, the Lord might even guide the team to multiply food for a group of people. Regardless, this team brings an anointed touch from God.

Since they move in the power of the Spirit, people become curious and start asking questions. Someone then shares the Good News, and asks who wants to follow Jesus. The apostolic evangelistic team is powerful in ministry.

The apostolic evangelistic team is not interested in making "converts," their desire is to reach people who need Jesus. They are not excited about mere intellectual belief; members of the team want to know who will be serious about following God and willing to give Him every part of their lives.

The team then gathers these believers together for discipleship and equipping (Matthew 28:18-20). They understand that some people feel uncomfortable in a church building, and recognize that there are many acceptable venues for fellowship and discipleship, such as homes, parks,

Chapter 33: A Picture of the Gifts Working in Body Life

restaurants, or most any other place where people feel comfortable. The team is flexible and sensitive to others' needs.

The apostolic evangelistic team also understands the Lord's command to look for people of peace, that is, individuals who have a unique openness and hunger for God, as I discussed in my previous chapter about evangelists. After finding such people through prayer they train these individuals. They prepare them first to be members of a church plant, and as they mature, to become strong, servant leaders.

Heidi and Rolland Baker live in Mozambique Africa, doing an apostolic work. With their team, they start churches through power evangelism, with a network of over ten thousand churches having been planted through their ministry from 2001 to 2010.[11] God's power moves through them to heal the sick. As a result of these miracles, whole villages listen to the Gospel. Soon, they start a church and begin equipping local believers to become pastors. This is an amazing way to plant churches.

In summary, an apostolic evangelistic team breaks new ground, bringing people to the Lord and gathering those new believers together to become a Christian community. Let us look at a scenario of what this team can look like in action.

An Apostolic Evangelistic Team in Action

Riverside Fellowship, a house church, sent out a group of people to start a new church. The team has one apostle, four prophets, and two evangelists. They gathered on Wednesday to pray before going out to preach. One of the prophets, Emily, had a vision that they should go to a park by the subway station, where there would be a bench with three guys sitting on it. The guy in the middle would have a shoulder injury.

Since no one heard anything else, they went to the park. When they arrived, the three guys Emily had seen in her vision were there,

---

[11] www.IrisMinistries.co.uk/about-iris-- Accessed 01 August 2011

and the guy in the middle had a sore arm. They asked him if they could pray with him and when they did, his arm was instantly healed. After this miracle, the apostle, Jack, and one of the evangelists, Willie, talked to all three of them about how to become followers of Christ. Two of them believed right away, but the third was skeptical. Jack and Willie invited the two new believers to a gathering on Friday. The whole team felt thrilled and happy about what God had done.

The Apostolic Equipping Team

An apostolic equipping team is a group of believers with various gifts that work together to perform the apostolic function of equipping, preparing individuals to minister and to train others.

After the apostolic evangelistic team starts a church, the apostolic equipping team takes over the work. Sometimes people that were previously on the evangelistic team are also a part of this team, other times it is a completely different group of people. During transition, some members of the evangelistic team remain with the work since the new believers have already connected with them, but they should gradually step back to allow new relationships to form.

Once everyone becomes comfortable with members of the equipping team, everyone in the evangelistic team can gradually transition back to their primary focus of reaching the lost. This should be done with great care to make sure that people are connected with God and each other during this process and that the team does not leave too soon. When change comes too quickly, people's inclination is to return to the familiar.

In the first phase of growing a church, the leadership will do a lot of the ministry. This is only temporary because it is imperative that all believers new and old share the gifts the Lord has given them. It is very important from the beginning for new believers to learn the Bible, recognize God's voice, and grow in the gifts (1 Corinthians 14:26).

From the beginning, new Christians are encouraged to read the Bible daily, especially the New Testament. It is the handbook God has

Chapter 33: A Picture of the Gifts Working in Body Life

given us for life. Apostles and prophets listen to God to confirm the spiritual gifts of new believers. All those serious about following God should begin receiving training for their future ministry. At this time, leaders begin laying the foundation for the Christian life and minister healing to all the new believers.

At the same time, teachers begin instructing the young Christians, setting Scriptural foundations and principles to help them learn more of God's ways and how to study the Bible themselves. Prophets train everyone in hearing God's voice. Pastors help new believers renew their minds and receive freedom from their past (Romans 12:1-2; 2 Corinthians 10:3-5). In addition, evangelists provide coaching in how to win the lost. Finally, apostles teach how to move in signs and wonders and they also oversee the whole process, ensuring that everyone is equipped in all the essentials.

In essence, each leader's goal is to multiply the number of believers who can minister, even to the point of working themselves out of a job, so that they can then continue on to what else God has for them to do.

Each member of the apostolic equipping team has a dual purpose. The first is to equip the new Christians in their gifts. The second is to strengthen the church plant through all the believers using their own gifts. From the beginning, leaders need to teach on truths that will help the young believers mature as much as possible and challenge all believers to continue to grow in the Lord. People also must learn how to hear God's voice and begin using their spiritual gifts. This will maximize growth.

The apostolic equipping team is there to fulfill their God-given role, preparing believers for healthy spiritual adulthood. Some new Christians put their leaders on a pedestal until they mature and become their own person. At the same time, it is wrong for ministers to build relationships for the purpose of receiving such admiration. Relational idolatry is unhealthy and carries many serious risks for everyone involved.

Church: What Was God Thinking?

Sometimes young believers mature faster than what a leader finds comfortable. This is just part of what it means to be a leader, whether of a family, a church, or a church plant. It is essential that the apostolic equipping team, including those with a pastoral gift, helps new Christians grow as much as possible before they enter the teenage stage of the Christian life. For the Kingdom of God to spread, ministers need to raise up adults in Christ quickly. Healthy leaders help their people grow.

These are the first two steps in church planting. In time, the Christians in the community will be able to function as a Body and will be mature enough that more equippers can be raised up from the church plant. These new ministers then form more equipping teams to multiply the work, starting and growing more new church plants and ministries.

Regardless of format, size, or meeting place, each church should have gatherings where most people can use their spiritual gifts. In this way, believers can grow into maturity. The only people who should be restricted or not be released are those who mishandle their gifts and resist correction. As in such situations, the goal is repentance and restoration (James 5:20).

It is important to note that people who use their spiritual gifts well are not necessarily mature Christians in other areas. Some new believers only two months old in the Lord have come to my church and moved in the gift of prophecy as though they had been using it for years. Some Christians can work miracles, perform signs and wonders, or have strong healing ministries and still be immature in the Lord. A strong anointing is not necessarily a sign of spiritual maturity.

Sometimes people are so gifted that they become Christian superstars. Many wonder what to do with these people because their gift draws much attention from the Church, the media, and possibly the whole world. One reason this happens is that they use a gift that is not as common as it should be in the Body.

Such people are often released too quickly into a bigger ministry because their leaders equate being gifted with spiritual maturity. Often

Chapter 33: A Picture of the Gifts Working in Body Life

time proves that they did not have the maturity or the healing to handle that ministry or that type of attention. It is vital that believers with exceptionally strong anointings be fully accountable to mature leaders who can help them learn to handle their gifts and the resulting attention.

Such individuals must be good followers, listening to their leadership. If people become arrogant and refuse to obey their leaders, in some cases the Lord will allow those individuals to crash and burn. Hopefully after this, they can be restored.

God does not intend any believer to experience the pressure or isolation of being a Christian superstar. Rather, He intends gifted believers to have loving leaders who hold them accountable. He also wants these gifts to become more common so ministry can be done in teams so that no one person is the central focus.

Galatians 6:1 (WEB) Brothers, even if a man is caught in some fault, you who are spiritual must restore such a one in a spirit of gentleness; looking to yourself so that you also aren't tempted.

Many people in the world today seem to think that if a person falls, especially someone in a position of authority, that he could not have ever been a sincere Christian. Some conclude that anything the person has done or taught in his ministry must be wrong. However, Galatians 6:1 clearly states that believers who fall can be restored. Not only is this a valid ministry in the church, it is essential and must not be ignored.

I believe that it is important to realize that people can be restored. It is terrible when leaders fall and the church acts like a group of vultures finishing off the kill. The Bible says to restore people with a spirit of gentleness (Galatians 6:1), not to kick a person further down who has already fallen. Judging ministers who stumble not only makes it more difficult for them to get back up, it also brings spiritual sickness to the Body of Christ. Words are powerful and can be hurtful, causing great harm not only to the one being spoken against, but also to the entire Church.

Judgment Versus Discernment

Matthew 7:1 (KJV) Judge not, that ye be not judged.

I want to clarify again that judgment is different from discernment. Discernment says, "I see a problem." Judgment either says, "Because of this problem, that person can never be used again," or "Some or all of what they have done in ministry is invalid." Once a person judges others, they enter into the Biblical cycle of sowing and reaping, and this will come back to harm the one making the judgment.

Believers need to remember individuals in the Bible such as King David, who committed serious sin, were restored by God with the help of ministry through prophets (2 Samuel 11-12). The Church should pray about how to restore those who make serious mistakes rather than hurting them further.

Restoration is a process that needs the help of other individuals in the Body of Christ. Loving confrontation is sometimes necessary at the beginning. Once a person has shown proof of repentance, they should begin a healing process that deals with any underlying issues that were a factor in them falling in the first place. When their leadership feels that they are again ready to handle the pressures of ministry without falling into temptation, they can then continue to use their gifts in blessing others, preferably as a part of a team and with ongoing accountability.

So, if spiritual giftedness is not sign of maturity, what characteristics do show maturity? To put it briefly, maturity is a deep relationship with the Lord, a history of faithfulness to Him, love for others, purity of life, integrity, and skill to handle the anointing and use the gifts in a respectful and responsible way, the tenacity to go through difficulty without blaming God for hardship, the ability to raise others into maturity, and the desire to care for others in addition to caring for oneself. To read more about this, refer back to chapter nine, "Stages of Maturity."

Chapter 33: A Picture of the Gifts Working in Body Life

What a Gathering with all the Gifts Could Be Like

I want to give people a picture of the potentially amazing experiences believers can have when all the gifts are used in the gathering. Since I want everyone to see this, I wrote it as an ideal situation without saying anything about potential problems that might arise and issues that may need to be fixed. In my Christian life and in church planting, I have experienced many meetings this incredible. Of course, there were others that were not so amazing. This is normal. I pray that the reader gains a sense of excitement for how God intends Church to be.

Daniel, a new believer, went to church for the first time today. Although Melanie, his wife, had been going there for a few years, Daniel has always been wary of large gatherings, and the formality of a traditional church is just not his style. However, his new friend, Michael, one of the most relaxed persons he has ever met, invited him to an informal gathering of Christians in a home.

Daniel did not know what to expect, so he felt somewhat surprised when, after enjoying a wonderful home-cooked meal, Sam, the group leader, asked everyone to stand up and pray, beginning the meeting by asking God for direction. There were no unbelievers in attendance, so everyone prayed in tongues. Daniel was somewhat surprised, but Michael had prepared him for this.

During the prayer time, Stan began singing, and the whole group joined him. After this, Maria continued the worship by leading the group in another song. Although Daniel did not know any of the lyrics, he closed his eyes, relaxed and thought about Jesus, which made him feel as warm and happy as the day he became a believer.

Jennifer is a prophet who is sensitive to the Holy Spirit; she prayed to release anointing to the group. Many were touched through this, some were in tears, some were lost in God's love, many smiled or laughed for joy, and still others felt like they were in the Third Heaven. Although Daniel had heard people should close their eyes when they prayed, he could not help looking around, trying to understand what

Church: What Was God Thinking?

was happening. He too felt something, a pleasant sensation that he could not identify. And this was just the beginning of the meeting!

After worship, Michael, who is in fact an evangelist from the apostolic evangelistic team, began sharing about someone he led to Christ. Daniel knew Michael was talking about him, and was prepared for this, but he still felt a little nervous. Even so, he began to share with the group what his life had been like before and how excited and happy he now feels as a result of inviting Jesus to come into his heart. Also, he told them how thrilled he is that the Lord healed him of acid reflux when Michael prayed with him. Upon hearing this, everyone clapped their hands, and Emily led the group in a song about God's goodness and power.

Abigail, a prophetess, heard from God that He was going to continue his work by healing Melanie from arthritis. Daniel and Melanie were thrilled! She had arthritis for ten years and could hardly walk. The whole group prayed for her and she was instantly healed! Now she was getting excited!

Dylan, a gifted teacher, then shared about how to keep a healing, not allowing the enemy to steal it. He shared from Scripture that often sickness comes from judging others, or unforgiveness towards oneself or others. He also mentioned that in the Bible, everyone who came to Jesus was healed. He then taught on blocks to healing, or ways the enemy steals a healing. Jamie, another teacher, then added to Dylan's teaching by sharing practical ways to receive healing, such as persevering in prayer. Two others also shared testimonies of their healing experience.

Steve, a pastor, then shared from the Bible about emotional healing and renewing the mind (Romans 12:1-3). He taught on learning to think like a heavenly prince or princess, not an orphan, and how a person who knows who he is can more easily receive miracles from God. Daniel could have listened to him all night, and thought about asking him for prayer to learn to think and feel like a child of God.

At this point, Derek led the group in communion. Afterwards, he asked everyone to pray for each other regarding any need. During this

Chapter 33: A Picture of the Gifts Working in Body Life

time, more people received emotional and physical healing. The prophetic team joined in prophesying and encouraging everyone.

Daniel and Melanie asked Steve to pray for them and Abigail joined them. Abigail saw a vision about Daniel's childhood grief when his father died of a heart attack. Steve joined Abigail in praying for Daniel to experience God as his Heavenly Father. He felt like he was receiving a warm embrace. Just then, Steve asked Daniel if he could hug him. Daniel agreed, and when Steve hugged him, he started to cry. He felt like fifty years of pain was being lifted off of him.

Steve and Abigail also prayed for Melanie, that God would remove any thought patterns or depression that came along with her arthritis. Daniel knew something had happened because when they were done praying she looked ten years younger! For two more hours the believers ministered to each other and so many were blessed. Daniel wished he had started going to a church like this years ago. He was definitely planning to come back!

In summary, spiritual gifts are an effective tool in establishing churches, but also in the community of believers.

I hope in this chapter, the reader has been able to sense the excitement of what God intends the church experience to be.

Chapter 34: Putting It All Together

So, people are probably wondering how this all fits together. A look at the beginnings of Church will make it more clear. When the Holy Spirit came upon those in the Upper Room, one hundred and twenty people were gathered together. In other words, there were at least one hundred and twenty people in the very first church. There were possibly more than that, taking turns praying in the Upper Room.

They were all devoted to prayer, seeking God, as Jesus had commanded. While they were doing this, the Holy Spirit came and the power of God entered the Church. Soon afterwards, the apostles hosted their first evangelistic event, organized by the Holy Spirit and three thousand were saved. From the very beginning, the Church was filled with God's Spirit and power.

Next, the new believers devoted themselves to the apostles' teaching, to fellowship (group participation), to the breaking of bread and prayer (Acts 2:42). At this time, many signs and wonders were being done through the apostles. They had meetings daily in the temple, broke bread from house to house, and ate their food with gladness, praising God. As a result, they enjoyed favor with many, and the Lord added to the church daily.

Church: What Was God Thinking?

Next, the Church established its own culture. Here is a list of some of the things they did because the Holy Spirit touched their lives (Acts 2:42).

The church began moving in the gifts of the Holy Spirit, with tongues and prophecy being the first received. As the church grew, healing and other gifts also manifested.

The next gift mentioned was the gift of teaching. Initially, the apostles taught foundational Scriptural truths and equipped others in their various gifts.

The apostles moved in signs and wonders.

Everyone met daily in the temple, and broke bread from house to house, eating together gladly, with wholehearted devotion to Christ.

They praised God, enjoyed favor with all the people, and the Lord added to the church daily.

The apostles and prophets worked together to call out people's spiritual gifts (Ephesians 2:10; Romans 1:11; 1 Kings 19:13-16; 2 Timothy 1:6; 1 Timothy 4:14). They listened to the Holy Spirit to confirm each individual in their gifts. During the equipping process, the apostles would test the prophetic word to make sure that they had heard God correctly. Then, as the people matured in their gifts, the apostles would commission them to train new believers, with teachers equipping teachers, prophets coaching prophets and so forth. If church is going to become what it is meant to be, leaders must equip the people in their churches, preparing and releasing them to replicate and multiply their ministries.

As the church matured, the Lord raised up more apostles, with unique roles according to the Holy Spirit's leading. Some of these functioned in groups along with elders as decision-makers for questions that came up about Christian faith and practice (Acts 15:27-29, 21:25). Others became facilitators in different types of ministries and gatherings (Acts 6:2-4). Many began new ministries in the city, still others were sent out as missionaries (Acts 13:1-3). In addition, the Lord appointed apostles who brought encouragement and correction

Chapter 34: Putting It All Together

to the church (2 Corinthians 13:9-10). In this way, the church could grow with a healthy foundation.

1 Peter 2:5-6 (WEB) You also, as living stones, are built up as a spiritual house, to be a holy priesthood, to offer up spiritual sacrifices, acceptable to God through Jesus Christ. (6) Because it is contained in Scripture, "Behold, I lay in Zion a chief cornerstone, chosen, and precious: He who believes in him will not be disappointed."

Church today should follow the pattern of the early Church, because that is what the Bible says it is supposed to be. It was not meant to be centered around a building, an organization or a religious culture. Believers were never meant to simply attend meetings with little interaction (1 Corinthians 14:26). Peter describes the Church as living stones being built into a spiritual tabernacle (1 Peter 2:5-6).

The Church is meant to be a community of believers in various maturity levels growing together and blessing each other. I call this "multi-generational, interactive Christian community." It is multi-generational because believers should mature into spiritual parents who raise up spiritual children. These children then mature into adulthood and raise more spiritual children, all with the benefits of the wisdom and maturity of multiple generations. It is also interactive because each person can bless each other and the communities around them by using their gifts according to their God-given abilities.

In truth, a Biblical church is less complex than a church focused on following centuries of tradition. As church goes to a relatively simple format, centered on Scriptural principles, rather than merely keeping historical traditions, there is more flexibility. What I mean is that it can more effectively reach out in ways and to places it could not in the past.

The picture that I have of this is that the old mentality makes the Church like a large block of ice still in the freezer. The Biblical mentality is more like crushed ice melting on a warm day. Large blocks of ice are locked into a solid form and, although they may have some impact on their surroundings, it is limited.

Church: What Was God Thinking?

Crushed ice melts, flowing freely. As it becomes liquid, it acts much more quickly to influence its environment. In the same way, as the church equips and releases its people, they can be more flexible and effective, like the melting ice chips, having an impact in many ways that they could not before, bringing transformation. In this way, the influence of Christian community increases to reach beyond local communities and cultures, to impact unreached peoples and regions locally and around the world.

I hope through this book that the reader will be challenged and inspired to take the next step into experiencing the Biblical Christian Community that is called Church. I hope especially that leaders and full-time ministers will take a look at this and start applying some of these concepts, applying Scriptural principles to their congregations, regardless of structure and format.

I have heard that, every year, there are a large percentage of full-time ministers that feel burnt out and ready to quit. I pray that they will gain renewed vision, try to discover their gifts and implement the principles from this book in their churches.

I hope that individuals will meet together to apply these things as well. The best way to learn is to prayerfully jump in and try it, making whatever adjustments needed to make it work for your group. I realize that some people will grab hold of this and have it work well right away. Others will face some challenges. My website (listed below) does have a forum where people can ask questions and discuss issues related to this book.

May God bless the Body of Christ to become all He has called and created it to be!

For more information about Bruce's ministry or to contact him, please go to:

www.ekklesiaconstructionset.com